P9-DVZ-341

The Small Library Manager's Handbook

Medical Library Association Books

The Medical Library Association (MLA) features books that showcase the expertise of health sciences librarians for other librarians and professionals.

MLA Books are excellent resources for librarians in hospitals, medical research practice, and other settings. These volumes will provide health care professionals and patients with accurate information that can improve outcomes and save lives.

Each book in the series has been overseen editorially since conception by the Medical Library Association Books Panel, composed of MLA members with expertise spanning the breadth of health sciences librarianship.

Medical Library Association Books Panel

Barbara Gushrowski, chair
Lauren M. Young, AHIP, chair designate
Dorothy C. May
Karen McElfresh
Kristen L. Young, AHIP
Megan Curran Rosenbloom
Michel C. Atlas
Tracy Shields
Heidi Heilemann, AHIP, board liaison

About the Medical Library Association

Founded in 1898, MLA is a 501(c)(3) nonprofit, educational organization of 4,000 individual and institutional members in the health sciences information field that provides lifelong educational opportunities, supports a knowledge base of health information research, and works with a global network of partners to promote the importance of quality information for improved health to the health care community and the public.

Books in Series

The Medical Library Association Guide to Providing Consumer and Patient Health Information edited by Michele Spatz

Health Sciences Librarianship edited by M. Sandra Wood

Curriculum-Based Library Instruction: From Cultivating Faculty Relationships to Assessment edited by Amy Blevins and Megan Inman

The Small Library Manager's Handbook

Alice Graves

ROWMAN & LITTLEFIELD
Lanham • Boulder • New York • London

Published by Rowman & Littlefield
A wholly owned subsidiary of The Rowman & Littlefield Publishing Group, Inc.
4501 Forbes Boulevard, Suite 200, Lanham, Maryland 20706
www.rowman.com

16 Carlisle Street, London W1D 3 BT, United Kingdom

Copyright © 2014 by Medical Library Association

All rights reserved. No part of this book may be reproduced in any form or by any
electronic or mechanical means, including information storage and retrieval systems,
without written permission from the publisher, except by a reviewer who may quote
passages in a review.

British Library Cataloguing in Publication Information Available

Library of Congress Cataloging-in-Publication Data

The small library manager's handbook / [edited by] Alice Graves.
    pages cm. — (Medical Library Association books)
  Includes bibliographical references and index.
  ISBN 978-1-4422-3987-6 (cloth : alk. paper) — ISBN 978-1-4422-3013-2 (pbk. : alk.
paper) — ISBN 978-1-4422-3014-9 (electronic) 1. Small libraries—Administration—
Handbooks, manuals, etc. I. Graves, Alice, 1951– editor.
  Z675.S57S63 2014
  025.1—dc23

                                                                      2014026984

♾™ The paper used in this publication meets the minimum requirements of
American National Standard for Information Sciences—Permanence of Paper for
Printed Library Materials, ANSI/NISO Z39.48-1992.

Printed in the United States of America

The mission of the librarian is to improve society through facilitating knowledge creation in their communities.—R. David Lankes

For Bill and Stephen

Contents

Acknowledgments

I wish to thank everyone who helped grow an abstract idea into the book you now hold in your hands.

First and foremost, this book would simply not be possible without the support of the Medical Library Association. I am profoundly grateful to the MLA Books Panel for allowing me the opportunity to bring this book to fruition.

A collective thank you and tip of the hat (or hats) to all of the librarians who contributed to this book. They have enriched our profession by generously sharing their successes, learning experiences, and best practices with the rest of us. May their tribe increase.

Thank you to Charles Harmon, my Sherpa at Rowman & Littlefield who was always a phone call or an e-mail away to answer my questions and guide me through this process. His encouragement and generosity of spirit served as my beacon.

Thank you to R. David Lankes, a true visionary who stands at the precipice of our evolving profession and whose enthusiasm and brilliance inspires librarians and library students everywhere.

Thank you to the great Judith Siess, whose books, articles, and blog created an awareness of solo librarians working behind the scenes in small and barely visible libraries.

I wish to thank my professors and mentors in the School of Information at the University of South Florida, who taught me well and encouraged me to work harder and happier than I ever remember working. They made me realize that this is what I was born to do.

And last but not least, I thank my husband and son for their endless love and support. I could not have completed this project without them.

Introduction

Alice Graves

The Small Library Manager's Handbook is a one-stop, how-to-do-it guide to running a small library. The twenty-eight chapters that follow present the collective knowledge of librarians working in small academic, public, and special libraries. They work in hospitals, prisons, museums, colleges, courthouses, and corporations. Their libraries consist of resources ranging the entire Library of Congress and Dewey decimal classification schedules.

Small libraries, and the professionals who staff them, are frequently hidden from public view in city skyscrapers, industrial parks, museum basements, and courthouse nooks. Often their public access is limited. Small libraries and the librarians who run them may be hidden, but it is those very professionals who are responsible for keeping their libraries alive, relevant, and critical to the larger organization. The contributors to this book have emerged from the shadows to share their expertise, experiences, and best practices.

Even though librarians in small libraries are often one-man or one-woman operations, they are part of a greater organization comprised of many professionals and practitioners. Often they report to nonlibrarians who may not understand the skills and knowledge that constitute librarianship, and they must justify both the library's worth and the librarian's indispensability to that organization.

The librarian in a small library wears many hats. One might observe that the smaller the library, the more varied the role of the librarian. In addition to collection development, cataloging, and research assistance, these librarians court potential donors, master technology, write annual reports, engage in community outreach, apply for grants, and justify their very existence. They supervise volunteers, library students, and other professional librarians. In addition to the skills they learned in library school, they must develop and sharpen their administrative and organizational skills. Efficient time management is essential.

A librarian may wear the hat of a new acquisitions cataloger in the morning and don a new hat later in the day to prepare the budget, research granting agencies, or meet with the organization's board of directors.

Because they usually have limited (or no) interaction with other people working in a library, solo librarians must make a concerted effort to stay connected to their profession. This can be done in person and virtually. Technology makes it simple for even the most isolated rural librarian to connect with fellow professionals daily. The plethora of professional organizations for specialized librarians makes it possible for medical librarians, prison librarians, and museum librarians to collaborate and communicate regularly.

Some librarians seek out careers in smaller libraries; others find themselves in small libraries by chance. Together, they form an open, welcoming community of cohorts.

About This Book

This book is divided into five parts that form the basis for library management: "Administration," "Finance and Budgeting," "Cataloging and Managing the Collection," "Marketing and Outreach," and "Using Technology." Each part consists of multiple chapters addressing some aspect of the issue. You'll find that some parts have more chapters than others and that the section on "Finance and Budgeting" has the fewest, suggesting that perhaps of all the work small library managers do, they have the least control over their budgets.

The chapters themselves reflect the knowledge and best practices of each author. Part I addresses general issues in administering a small library. Diana Weaver writes that efficient day-to-day management and effective leadership are both crucial to the success of a library, and she explains how one person can do both. Jezmynne Dene writes about providing opportunities for developing each staff member's professional growth to create an efficient, stress-free workplace. Elizabeth Martin and Lynn Sheehan assert that effective time management is really about learning to efficiently manage one's workload. Deirdre D. Spencer tells us how to determine the needs and desires of library users to ensure the library is vital and relevant. Robin Shader provides useful tips for becoming involved and engaged at the community level to advance library awareness and support. Paul Glassman discusses library renovation and the need for involving library staff and users in the process. And Jeff Guerrier rejuvenates and rebuilds a library that has been neglected.

Part II deals with financial and budgeting issues. James Anthony Schnur cautions against diving headfirst into a fund-raising activity without first investing time to gather data on library influencers and possible partners to ensure best results. Sheila A. Cork sets out best practices in writing a successful grant proposal.

Part III addresses the day-to-day management of the collection. Miguel Figueroa-Pagán discusses acquisition on a low budget, including resources that can be obtained at no cost. Erica Shott writes about best practices in aligning a collection with the library's mission. Ashley Krenelka Chase discloses the steps in choosing and the ongoing management of electronic resources. Joy M. Banks discusses the world of integrated library systems and how to choose the one that best meets the needs of your library. Wanda Headley tackles best practices in developing a collection that aligns with the mission of the library, doesn't break the bank, and provides resources needed by users. Beth Dwoskin discusses various cataloging tools available and how to determine which one is the best fit for your library. Arwen Spinosa addresses the intricacies of both copy cataloging and original cataloging. Charles Ed Hill provides a primer on cataloging and tips on training nonprofessionals to assist in cataloging needs. Corinne Nyquist discusses policies and laws guiding interlibrary loan. And Sherill L. Harriger explains knowing when and what to weed and how to go about it.

Part IV of the book looks at marketing and outreach initiatives for small libraries. Lee Ann R. Benkert points out that a small library's greatest advocates may not be its users. Robin Henshaw and Valerie Enriquez stress the importance of publicizing the assets of your library. Joyce Abbott writes about providing support and services to external library users as well as members of the parent organization. Lana Brand and Raleigh McGarity write about building relationships within the organization through outreach, promotion, and marketing as critical to library survival. Lindsay Harmon gives a step-by-step approach to promoting your library within the parent organization, and finally, Mara H. Sansolo teaches us that a large part of providing reference is really outreach.

Part V gives us best practices in making optimum use of technology. Amelia Costigan discusses providing virtual reference by creating reference resources based on customer inquiries. Zach English writes about using simple technology, even if you are not a techno-wiz. Last but not least, Jill Goldstein shows us how even a novice can produce a professional-looking, easily navigable library website.

Both the author and the Medical Library Association hope that this guide to managing a small library will not only provide nuts-and-bolts guidance for day-to-day activities but also inspire in its readers creativity, a comforting sense of community, and dedication to our profession.

Part I
Administration

Chapter 1

How to Lead and Manage the Library

Diana Weaver

Overview

The workday of a librarian in a small public, academic, or special library is filled with responsibilities that can vary as widely as changing lightbulbs in the restroom to thinking about future innovation and growth. In this indeterminate landscape, the very distinct differences between being a manager and being a leader get blurred. Efficient day-to-day management and effective leadership are both crucial to the success of a library. What's the difference between the two, and how can one person do both?

John Kotter, Harvard professor and best-selling author on business management and leadership, explains how the two roles are complementary yet separate. Simply stated, he defines management as "coping with complexity," whereas leadership is about "coping with change." He describes three sets of responsibilities for leaders and managers: "deciding what needs to be done, creating networks of people and relationships that can accomplish an agenda, and then trying to ensure that those people actually do the job."[1] Leaders and managers fulfill these responsibilities in different ways.

Setting the Agenda for Managers and Leaders

Consider the responsibility of a library budget. As a library manager, I work with my funding agency to anticipate how much money can be expected from the different sources of income available to my library. From that bottom line, we create a plan for spending, or a budget. Budget lines include salary and benefits for employees, amounts to be spent on materials, and projected costs for library operations and maintenance. Then we set targets for how much we can spend per month for each budget line.

When I think about being a library manager, I think of all the things I have in common with my brother, who owns a small family business. In so many ways, his job as business owner is like my job as a library manager. We both support a payroll for our employees. We both manage inventory. We order goods and negotiate services (for example, in the library, adequate Internet access). We worry about property maintenance (including equipment and computer upgrades). We find ways to market our products and services. We struggle with bad debt (long-lost, and never-coming-back, materials checked out from the library). And we understand the crucial importance of excellent customer service. All of these need to be accounted for in our distribution of the budget.

The leader's job with a budget starts long before the money gets to the bank. It starts with a vision of the future. My current library board chairman likes to ask the question, What will success look like? A leader will be able to envision success and determine the strategies to get there.

How do you see into the future and imagine what success will look like? Here are three suggestions to help you create your vision. First, and most important, you must listen. A key advantage to being the director in a small library is the accessibility you have to your stakeholders and to your patrons, the people whose lives your library touches and enriches. Small libraries are natural places for conversations. Ideas and concerns shared across the circulation desk and in the stacks will suggest the focus for your vision of success.

The next step in creating a vision is to gather data. Learn to use the reports from your library's circulation system. Find out what people are checking out from your library. Notice what people are asking for that you don't own and have to borrow from other libraries. Another tool you can use is a short, formal survey. Distribute it in the library to your patrons, but also take some out to people in your community who don't often visit the library.

Once you gather the data, search for trends and patterns. Have more conversations with staff, patrons, and other stakeholders about what you've discovered. Data tells a story that should inform your vision.

Another idea is to start a focus group to investigate the feasibility of a new idea. A focus group should have a single goal, a select group of participants, and a defined time frame. This is the method we used at my library to explore the impact of e-readers and e-books in our community.

By late 2010, anyone observing library trends and watching advertisements from Amazon knew about e-books. In my role as a leader, I listened and had conversations with patrons. They wanted to know if they could check out e-books from the library. Several patrons expressed the concern that this would be the end of libraries. Clearly, there was a need to develop a vision and devise a strategy for how to deal with this revolution in reading and publishing.

Our first step in the strategy was to advertise that we recognized the excitement for reading generated by the new e-readers like the Nook and the Kindle and tablets like the iPad. We assured everyone we were aware of the potentiality and were positioning ourselves to meet the new demand.

Next, we tried to learn everything we could. Our library board gave us funds to purchase some of the new devices for experiment and play. I collected data. I considered the research conducted by the Pew Research Center,[2] and using their survey as a model, I asked our community, How many owned an e-reader? What kind? If not, would they consider purchase of one in the future? The results showed that this was an important topic in our community.

Toward the end of the year, we invited members of the community to explore this new phenomenon with us. We created a focus group, which we called the Digital Readers Group. I sent invitations to a select group of patrons in which I wrote, "We have purchased several digital reading devices, or e-readers, to use in exploring this revolution in reading. Now we need readers like you to try them out and give feedback on your experience."

The project had clearly defined tasks and a clearly defined time frame. The ten participants spent eight weeks exploring various e-readers. I likened it to an audition for the devices and suggested activities so they could get a feel for the experience of reading on each one. We met twice, once at the beginning of our exploration and again at the end. Our goal at the final meeting was to gather recommendations from the group about how the library could move forward with e-readers and e-books. I made sure we had food and gifts for the participants.

The number-one recommendation from the group was for the library to provide content for patrons' e-readers. Other suggestions included classes, circulation of devices preloaded with content, one-to-one tech help, and an e-reader fair. These suggestions became the strategies for implementing a new service in our library.

Finally, in order to create a vision for your library, mimic success. Take the time to visit other small libraries. What are they doing that is successful? Join the Association for Rural and Small Libraries, or the Medical Library Association, and get on their e-mail LISTSERV. LISTSERVs can be valuable resources for gaining insight and ideas. Become a member of your state's library association. Look up and follow the blog posts and webinars on Tech Soup, an organization that not only publishes success stories but also offers multiple software products to nonprofits at a discount.

Another suggestion is to follow other librarians on social media. Do you need to write a strategic plan? Ask members of your network on the LISTSERV and on social media about their strategic plan. Or pick up the phone and call someone you met at a conference. Then borrow the parts that are relevant to your library. Do you need to write an RFP or an annual report? Just ask. Librarians, on the whole, are very generous with their knowledge and their successes.

Once you've created a vision and formulated a plan for producing success, you need to get people on board. Kotter calls this persuasion "aligning people"[3] to your vision. This takes time and can often only be accomplished in small incremental steps. Fortunately, these steps can be taken during your daily business of running the library.

Tip: Make sure your agenda is realistic and not overly ambitious. A realistic goal has a greater chance of being met.

Aligning People to a Vision while Running the Library

Linda Hill defines a manager as a "generalist and agenda-setter" and as a person who "orchestrates diverse tasks."[4] The agenda set by a director in a small library will most likely include a list of procedures that must be done daily in order for the library to function. Library policies are decided by the governing body, but day-to-day procedures are the responsibility of the director.

A good manager "orchestrates diverse tasks" as efficiently as possible. To do that, a good guideline to follow is

- define the tasks needed to run the business of the library,

- create a list of job duties,

- decide reporting relationships and then delegate authority,

- communicate the plan effectively to staff and volunteers, and

- monitor implementation and give feedback.

Use whatever tools you need to make this work. Sometimes a flowchart is helpful. I use to-do lists, several of them throughout the day, rearranged as my priorities change. A manager's job as a generalist is open ended and will include the most important work in a library: unexpected and sometimes time-consuming requests from patrons.

Even if you're in a one-person library, there will be people you need to rely on to get things done. Managing staff and volunteers, or the crew that takes care of maintenance, is often the hardest part of being a library director. Hill identifies the most important qualities of a manager as "self-confidence, willingness to accept responsibility, patience, empathy, and ability to live with imperfect solutions."[5]

The best managers approach the job as teachers and mentors. Managers should avoid assuming the identity of a peer; the objective is to be respected, not necessarily liked.

To secure self-confidence, make sure you have the stable framework of simple, easy-to-understand policies. Familiarize yourself with your policies, and use them to communicate expectations to those you manage and also to your library's patrons. If you don't have personnel or code-of-conduct policies when you first start as library director, work with your governing body to get those defined and in place as soon as possible. Include policies and job descriptions for volunteers. Make sure you communicate the intent of the policies clearly and implement them consistently.

While policies give you a guidebook for those you supervise, many of the people you deal with on a daily basis will not come under your authority. "Management," says Hill, "has just as much, if not more, to do with negotiating interdependencies as it does with exercising formal authority."[6] This is especially true in small libraries. It is essential that you learn to be a good communicator and network builder.

A good communicator is adept at explanation. Lee LeFever is the founder and chief explainer at Common Craft, a website that specializes in video explanations of a multitude of difficult concepts, most dealing with technology. In his book *The Art of Explanation*, he asks, "What do great explainers have in common? In a word, it is empathy. Great explainers have the ability to picture themselves in another person's shoes and communicate from that perspective."[7] This is excellent advice for articulating organizational structure as well as a grand vision to all relevant stakeholders, including staff, volunteers, patrons, and governing officials.

But beyond explanation, how do you persuade and inspire people to join you in accomplishing your vision? First you have to establish your credibility.[8] This can take weeks and months after you've started a new job. Credibility is earned by a consistent track record and reputation for trustworthiness. In other words, do what you say you're going to do.

Volunteer your time to organizations and activities that are important in your community. You might have to convince your governing body that being out in the community is part of your job as library director. I've served as a buyer for a local CSA (community-supported agriculture), on the local tourism council, and as treasurer of the chamber of commerce and flipped pancakes for Lions Club fund-raisers.[9] Use your time volunteering and supporting others to build a strong network of relationships with people who care about your community. Discover a shared value, and figure out a way to collaborate on a project that serves your common vision.

Before you ask people to work with you on a project, consider it carefully from every angle. Take the time to build your expertise and your plan. When I asked people to participate in our e-book focus group, I spent many hours learning about the devices to minimize the group's initial frustration. I designed the project to be fun for the participants because I considered how much time I was asking them to devote. By doing this, I let them know I valued both their input and their time.

When talking to others about the library, either during informal conversations or when giving formal presentations, always be ready with some relevant facts. Use raw data sparingly, however. Instead, tell stories that resonate with your audience. A few years ago in the town where I was the library director, the local medical center had been purchased by a large conglomerate, and several townspeople had been laid off. On the morning I was to give my annual presentation to the chamber of commerce, a woman who had just lost her job at the center came into the library for help. She had worked there for over twenty years and only knew the computer skills required for her job. I helped her set up an e-mail account and suggested websites for job searches and then went to the chamber meeting. As I faced the audience of community businesspeople, I abandoned my prepared remarks and instead told the story about what had happened that morning at the library. From my vantage point at the front of the room, I could see the impact the story had on my audience. All libraries have similar tales. Collect the stories at your library and share them.

Tip: Establishing your credibility and expertise with your networks is essential to success. Become an expert in whatever goal you set out to accomplish.

Getting the Job Done—Don't Leave Culture to Chance

Accomplishing daily tasks, serving patrons, and still having time for thinking about the future doesn't happen by chance. It happens in a work environment that has a healthy and innovative culture. All work environments and work groups develop a culture, for good or bad. As both a manager and leader, you must deliberately work to build a culture of success in your library.

What is culture? It is a system of shared values and shared language resulting in congruent attitudes and behaviors. There's agreement among stakeholders about what's important, and there is excitement and intensity about the shared mission. It's a part of the day-to-day business, and it infuses discussion of the future. Managers and leaders must instill key cultural values in everything they do.[10]

The most important job of a library manager is to support and develop people, including patrons, staff, and relevant partners. As a manager, you must be clear and specific in your expectations. But don't be a slave to your policies. Your policies need to reflect your culture. Give those you manage a sense of control. Empower your staff to make exceptions, and let them know you trust their good judgment. The goal is quality customer service and a positive experience. If someone on your staff makes a decision that you may not have made but it doesn't conflict with the business of the library, remember Hill's admonition to develop the "ability to live with imperfect solutions."[11]

If you have staff or volunteers, recognize that they have lives beyond the library. They have children who get sick or elderly parents who need care. Perhaps they have their own health issues or have marriages in trouble. Be flexible with schedules. Develop a culture of caring and support for each other.

Realize that all of us have our strengths and weaknesses. Set high goals for those you manage, and provide feedback through regular evaluations. Discover the passion of others, and try to include it in some task they do for you. Remember that healthy cultures need lots of humor and celebrations of success.

Good leaders cultivate a strong culture by guiding people in a different way. Make sure you have a clear idea of your library's values, and then model appropriate behavior. People will be watching the signals you send about

- what you spend your time on,

- what you ask and what you decide not to ask,

- how you follow up,

- what you celebrate,

- if you share information rather than engage in gossip, and

- how you increase your own skills and knowledge.

The way that you align your actions with your values will mean more than your words and will determine the quality of your library's culture.

As a leader, make it a practice to involve others in your projects. You might create a special team to tackle a specific project. Nurture leadership skills in others by letting them take the lead. Include young people and people with diverse skills in your work as well. Let them know their opinions count. Help build a vibrant and creative culture by providing opportunities for others to learn and grow.

Tip: Being a flexible, empathic leader who is generous with information will yield better results.

Management Is Technique, Leadership Is You

Some of the critical management skills you will need to learn as a library direc-tor include efficient use of your time, the ability to set priorities, and the courage to be decisive. You can help yourself as a manager by scheduling time when the library is closed to finish items on your to-do list. Find some chores you can outsource, too; I would particularly recommend that you find a small account-ing firm to administer your payroll.[12] My favorite technique for management is to take regular walks around the library, noticing and adjusting things as I go.[13]

Leadership skills are learned through a process of self-development. Many of us in libraries aren't dynamic extroverts. This doesn't mean we can't be effective leaders. One of my favorite books on leadership is titled *Leading Quietly*.[14] Find a mentor whose style is similar to yours, and learn from them. Many commu-nities offer leadership classes or institutes that can be beneficial for personal growth and for building relationships in the community.

Good leaders must understand the politics in their community. Take the time to identify and observe the power players. Who gets things done? Who works well together, and who should you never seat together at a table? As Badaracco advises, "keep an eye on the insiders."[15]

Successful management calls for a slow, steady style, but leadership requires a combination of cautious observance punctuated by bursts of energy. The energy of a passionate leader with a love for his or her chosen field is infectious. It can motivate and inspire at all levels of an organization.

In a small library, there is an inherent relationship between management and leadership. It's like two different kinds of coaches on the same team. One coach stands on the sidelines and directs players for each play as the team moves down the field toward a goal. This is the manager's role. A leader is in the coach's box, high up in the stands where he or she can see the entire field and notice shifts and patterns and recommend adjustments to the overall progress. As library directors, we sometimes need to focus on one apart from the other, even though they will often blend as we work from our values toward our goals.

Tip: Find someone whose leadership style you admire, and ask them to mentor you. Chances are they will be delighted.

Notes

1. John P. Kotter, "What Leaders Really Do," *Harvard Business Review* 68, no. 3 (May–June 1990): 104.

2. Princeton Survey Research Associates International for the Pew Research Center's Internet & American Life Project, "Reading Habits Survey," Pew Internet: Pew Internet & American Life Project, January 4, 2012, http://libraries.pewinternet.org/files/2012/04/Topline_for_-e_reading_report_4_surveys.pdf.

3. Kotter, "What Leaders Really Do," 107.

4. Linda A. Hill, *Becoming a Manager: How New Managers Master the Challenges of Leadership* (Boston: Harvard Business School Press, 2003), 6.

5. Ibid., 167.

6. Ibid., 262.

7. Lee LeFever, *The Art of Explanation: Making Your Ideas, Products, and Services Easier to Understand* (Hoboken, NJ: John Wiley & Sons, 2013), 10.

8. Jay A. Conger lists four essential steps for persuasion. See his article, "The Necessary Art of Persuasion," *Harvard Business Review* 76, no. 3 (May–June 1998).

9. It's also very important to spend money locally whenever you can, even if it costs a bit more. If you support local businesses, they are much more likely to support you.

10. For more information, see Jennifer A. Chatman and Sandra Eunyoung Cha, "Leading by Leveraging Culture," *California Management Review* 45, no. 4 (Summer 2003).

11. Hill, *Becoming a Manager*, 167.

12. For more advice on time management, see Laura Vanderkam, *168 Hours: You Have More Time than You Think* (New York: Penguin Group, 2010). She titles one chapter of the book "Get Someone Else to Do the Laundry."

13. Rachel Singer Gordon, *The Accidental Library Manager* (Medford, NJ: Information Today, 2005), 269. The management theory "Managing by Walking Around" is listed along with several other theories that may be applicable in libraries.

14. Joseph L. Badaracco Jr., *Leading Quietly: An Unorthodox Guide to Doing the Right Thing* (Boston: Harvard Business School Press, 2002).

15. Ibid., 24.

Chapter 2

How to Develop Effective Staff

Jezmynne Dene

"You are not just an employee, volunteer or board member. You do not merely catalog books, organize periodicals and manage resources. You are the gateway into the mind of the idea people who come to our facilities to find or fuel a spark. It is your calling to trespass into the unknown and come back with a concrete piece someone can hold onto, turn over, and use to fuel their mind and soul."—"Anythink Staff Manifesto"

Overview

You want your staff to be wizards, geniuses, explorers. You want your staff to be the connectors between your users and their information or recreational need. You want your staff to be engaged with the library and their community. You want your staff prepared to handle any situation. You want your staff to seize opportunity and get things done. You want your staff to be effective. This level of effectiveness is where you want your entire operation to be. This is where your library provides the best service and achievement of goals and objectives. But how do we get there? How do we cultivate a team where effectiveness is a core value shared among staff? This chapter serves as a guide to developing effective staff in small libraries.

Investing in Effective Staff

Being effective is being ready for service. This is a simple goal but one that can be challenging to achieve. However, this process doesn't have to take a lot of resources, fancy team-building events, or expensive consultants. With a little bit of money and, most importantly, time, attention, and forethought, you can build an effective team for your library. Why would we bother to take the time to invest in staff development? Why is it important? What is the purpose of doing so? It comes down to the impact effective staff have on creating and maintaining a relevant and useful library, an effective library, for your users. Investing your time and attention into your staff reaps great rewards. Your staff will be more engaged, more interested in the library's users and services, and more dedicated to keeping the library relevant and useful to the community. Effective staff members are passionate, happy, and enjoy their jobs. Effective staff members support the mission of the library and transmit their happiness and passion to the lives they touch when providing library service. No other resource for your library is as important as the staff. They are the backbone of a good library that provides value to the community and stays relevant. It is a very worthy cause and one that ought to have high importance in the management structure.

Know Your Staff

Determining the strengths and weaknesses of your staff is a very important first step toward cultivating a more effective environment. Each staff member needs assessment to determine where they are skilled and where they best fit into the organization. A good manager will observe staff and interact with them to begin determining each person's place in the organization. Meet with staff members individually to discuss what they like and do not like about their work, which will add insight to this process. Establish clear channels of communication, and listen carefully to what you hear. Paraphrase back to staff the data you hear to ensure that staff and manager are on the same page. Make sure that communication channels are regular and ongoing, and strive to find the solution that works best for your individual library. Communication via regular one-on-one meetings or e-mail or a discussion board for sharing experiences and perception of work situations are some options. Ensuring that regular communication occurs will enable you, the manager, to see where people excel and where they struggle. Once these channels of communication are built, maintain them. Continue to listen and encourage honest feedback. Do not penalize staff for stating their likes and dislikes about their jobs. Remain objective to their input, and understand that each person brings value to the organization through what they do. It may be that the young clerk who does not adjust well to dealing with patrons that challenge library policy or work flow will excel in data management and cataloging. Listening to and observing your staff will help you to identify what your staff enjoys and does well. Once you have an idea of where people work best, adjust staffing schedules and duties to pair staff with tasks they'll enjoy and be successful. It might be that the gamer clerk works the desk less and does more programming with teens and the cataloger ends up with more reference shifts. A good manager will work to place staff where they fit best and are happiest. People who enjoy what they do and feel passionate about their duties will be more effective. Find out who your "subject specialists" are, both with your collections and in other areas of service, programming, and projects. Staff members who love to work with people and help them find things will enjoy their desk duties more than staff who prefer to organize materials, assign metadata, and order books. Discover what different staff members enjoy doing the most and what they do best, and try to match them to those tasks. Yes, you will assign duties to people that they don't like to do, but if they enjoy most of the aspects of their job, they'll work harder to be effective and contribute. Maslow's point on personal fulfillment or self-actualization is sound. When people feel good about what they do, they will work harder and be more effective.

Assessment and Feedback

Essential to managing and building effective staff is quality assessment and feedback. Ensure that you establish a regular review of each staff member to assess their work. In your review process, share the annual and strategic plan for the library, and ask staff what goals they'd like to set and what projects they'd like to design and execute. Set a regular review timeline; most organizations manage annual reviews of staff. At the review period, see if those goals were met and projects were completed. You may want to create a rubric similar to grading scales for staff assessment. Ask staff to self-assess against this rubric to gauge where they think they succeeded. Compare your assessment to theirs, and discuss any differences presented. As you talk about goals and objectives and point out areas to explore and grow, make sure you take the time to reflect back on everything the staff member accomplished in the previous time. Recognize the positive things they've done, the great interactions they've had, and the hard work they've achieved. Often we in libraries need to be reminded of our accomplishments, and as a manager you get the job of pointing out forgotten successes.

Rewarding Staff on a Tight Budget

All libraries live on a tight budget, and often the library staff does not make "big bucks" or get regular bonuses. We simply cannot afford such luxuries, but we can find other ways to acknowledge and reward effective behavior. One of the biggest rewards is working in a library—we're surrounded by programs, information, books, computers, techie gadgets, software, the Internet—all the toys we love. Exceptional staff ought to be encouraged to find something of interest to them and create a project for the library as a whole. Make a reward out of creating a gaming program, starting a chess club, working on the website, writing book reviews, or doing outreach with community partners. Consider allotting one or two hours a week for staff members to work on a project that makes them happy. Have staff identify tasks that they enjoy, and allow them release time from their regular duties to work on that task. Perhaps one staff member will begin to do something another staff member doesn't care to do, and the trade makes each staff member happier.

One library allocates 1 percent of the salaries and benefits line for staff awards. This small line covers the purchase of coffee, tea, and snacks to be made available. Or perhaps the awards line buys the staff pizzas as a special treat after a hectic round of summer reading or at the conclusion of a major project. This small awards line allows regular acknowledgments and special treatment of the staff and comes with a hearty "thank you" from the administration. And of course, the most important reward is thanking staff with sincerity for a job well done. When you recognize a job well done, take a few minutes and acknowledge the success. Identify a concept or particular benchmark you liked and why. Share the successes of the staff with the rest of the team in meetings or in e-mails.

As you work toward developing an environment for building effective staff, include elements that enable success. Provide your staff with the freedom to accomplish projects and develop a sense of ownership in their areas of responsibility. When setting goals with staff on projects, allow them to choose how they will reach the objective; let them choose the goals that will work best for their work flow and incorporates their ideas. Do not micromanage the staff. Do delegate the final objective, but leave them the freedom to choose how they create the project. Think ahead and decide what you want with the project, brief your staff, communicate your goals and objectives, and follow through with them. Explain what you expect, focusing on the final outcome. For example, tell them, "I want the display up next week," but allow them to choose the materials, the type of display, the style, and similar. If you choose all elements of the project, do it yourself. Give your staff the freedom to create their work and to achieve success. Trust your staff, and give up control of the project to them to execute. Try to avoid excessive monitoring of the project at every step, and instead focus on coaching staff through the project as they need it or as the project hits benchmarks along the way. Micromanaging creates stumbling blocks and squelches creativity and project ownership. Leave the minute details to the staff, and give them the space to explore their work, be creative, and have unobstructed time to meet their objectives. The most challenging part of this philosophy is backing off when you dislike a way a staff member is doing something. When faced with a difference in opinion, ask yourself, "Will the way the staff member is doing this have a negative impact on the final objective?" If the answer is no, allow the staff to continue. I learned this early on when I had a staff member doing displays for me. I did not care for the colors she chose; the font she picked; and the way she typed, printed, and cut the papers for the display. However, the display was done, and the staff member was pleased with her work, and that was my overarching objective. I learned that I needed to be satisfied with the staff member's work without doing the entire project for them.

Delegate to Empower

Finally, work to choose the best staff member or team for the task or project at hand. Delegating successfully means more gets done and leverages the organization's overall effectiveness. There is a satisfaction in doing, taking ownership of a project, and seeing it to conclusion. Empowering your staff to succeed helps them realize they are appreciated and valued by the library.

Just as important as letting your staff succeed is the importance of letting staff members fail. Coach staff as necessary, and when objectives are not met, discuss why the outcomes occurred. Failures are often learning opportunities, so encourage a thought process that learns from projects or programs that do not work out as planned. Discuss what happened, and guide the staff members in discovering how the negatives occurred and what could have been done differently. Was it a matter of poor timing? Low resources? Overburdened work flows? Poor time management skills? Help the staff to see where different decisions could have resulted in different outcomes. Permit failure as long as assessment and learning occurs. However, in cases of consistent failures, it is best to offer training, regular meetings to keep projects on task, and other managerial methods to determine if the staff member is suited for the job at hand or the library as a whole. Assessment is a key element and will help you identify unnecessary work, programs, or projects that are irrelevant to your library's mission and goals. Preach the value of assessment of every project undertaken, and encourage the thinking and establishment of assessment in planning to your staff. Make it a priority, and ask, "How will we determine if this project is a success? What are the necessary benchmarks the project needs to hit? What ways will we determine if the cost of this project is worth the value?" Including ongoing assessment will help your library execute and complete projects in an effective manner, helping reach an overall state of effectiveness.

Nurture Budding Leaders

When you identify a potential leader in your staff, do what you can to enable them to lead. Encourage them through training and literature and facilitating their leadership on projects. Give them responsibilities and additional governance over procedures, programming, or projects in small doses to facilitate their leadership development. As they grow and improve, continue to provide more freedoms with decisions and additional responsibilities. These leaders will become the backbone of your staff and will alleviate small-project management from the administration. In addition, your leaders will be well groomed for future positions moving up the organizational structure as those positions become available. Help your leaders to establish the facets of your effective management style of communication, feedback, and the like, as they will mirror the developing work environment of an effective staff.

Establish Peer Mentoring Programs

Another way to build effective staff is to set up mentoring programs. If you have someone who is really good at a task or a new project, choose them to act as a point person for help. This is especially helpful when introducing new technologies. If you begin a gaming program and you have one staff member who has his or her own Xbox and knows the tool really well, ask him or her to provide training, answer questions, and create guides. Acknowledge their expertise, and use it for the library. Pairing up staff members to work together to problem solve and think of solutions is great. Find those who are aware of the trend you're implementing, and pair them with someone who is less familiar. Each person's perspective will help the project grow. And as you hire on new staff, make sure they have a more experienced staff member to help them along the way. Mentors do not have to be the trainers but can be people who will answer questions, offer advice, and help new staff understand policy and procedures. Choose your mentors from your leaders and your known experts, and help them develop their role. Offer training and meetings as needed to ensure the mentors do not become overwhelmed or feel overextended.

Cultivate Creativity

Create an environment that cultivates creativity. Allow each staff member a little bit of time every week, maybe an hour or two, to dedicate to a new project or idea. Allow experimentation, and let your staff find things that inspire them, and let them try things out. Set up a rubric for assessment of these projects so that everyone sees successes and where things might be done differently. Again, use failures not as negatives but as learning opportunities. Maybe the Lego-maker space didn't work very well because it was at a poor time of day. Look at the projects the staff create, keep the ones that succeed, and cease or modify the ones that do not do as well. When discontinuing a project, work with the staff member in charge to help them understand how it is not meeting the assessment metrics. Make sure your lines of communication are clear to alleviate hard feelings. Allowing staff to do things that excite them and inspire them promotes good feelings toward their workplace and encourages them to take their jobs very seriously. Experimentation and creativity will bring passion, and with passion, staff will work harder to make things successful and positive.

Encourage Professional Development

Professional development opportunities are very important. Ask staff what conferences or training they would like to attend. Create a line for travel and training in your budget, and encourage staff to "get out there and learn." Opportunities for learning engage staff. Attending conferences reinvigorates and encourages everyone to bring new things back into the library. Learning new concepts helps to cultivate enthusiasm and innovation, and it enables your staff to learn. Look for small, regional conferences; training opportunities; and major conferences. Let staff identify where they'd like to go and what they'd like to learn, and help make it so they may attend. Create a structure that requires a presentation or a report for things learned at conferences so ideas for innovation are exchanged with those who did not attend the professional development event. New projects brought to the organization should be led by the initiator; it is their project, and they ought to be given ownership of it. Help them as necessary, but allow for experimentation and learning throughout the process, keeping in mind the value of assessment.

Create a Nurturing Work Environment

Once you have your innovators, your leaders, your superstars, protect them by providing them a healthy and happy workplace. Some people are not good fits for libraries, and when we come across a staff member who does not do well in the dynamic and changing environment, cannot complete projects as assigned, and disturbs the staff with poor behavior, we remove them from the library or move them to a more suitable area. It is far more important to eliminate negative staff members in order to find and cultivate the superstars that will make your library a success than to allow an ongoing stagnant state of unproductiveness that dampens your effectiveness.

Ample training ensures that everyone has an understanding and awareness of work flows and requirements. Make sure policies and procedures are communicated clearly, made available for consultation, and enforced. Follow through with the staff so that all are on the same page about how things are done, how rules are enforced, and what the library's expectations are. Follow the staff handbook, and if there isn't one, write one. Make sure expectations are made clear, and if expectations are not met, offer training and guidance. This is often a difficult and tenuous process, but work within your means to cull the staff in order to make room for those who are effective, passionate, and in line with the mission of the library. It is imperative to fix, confront, and solve problems when an issue is brought to your attention. This practice cultivates trust among your staff and helps staff feel their work environment is safe and secure. A healthier organization is happier and more effective.

Tip: This process requires a committed investment of your time, but in the long run, having a smoothly running library with each staff member in his or her perfect job will result in a tremendous savings of your own time and energy.

Conclusion

There are low-cost options using time and attention to develop effective staff. Determine your strong staff and where they fit best into the library's programs, services, and projects. Set up lines of communication, and keep those lines open and functioning to ensure that all staff members are on the same page regarding the development and implementation of projects. Create a feedback structure with regular reviews, assessing staff and projects alike. Acknowledge staff successes, and provide regular recognition for positive accomplishments and behaviors. Enable your staff to succeed and learn from failures. Ensure your work environment is healthy and happy. Cultivate a workplace of play, exploration, and experimentation. Encourage your staff to learn and share new concepts and technologies with the organization. Most important, set the example for the behavior you want to see in your staff. Listen. Try. Assess. Fail. Communicate. Remain positive. Remain calm. Envision for yourself how you want your staff to behave and how you want them to be effective, and model those behaviors to your staff. Make work a positive and happy experience. Invest in your staff; they are important and valuable. Make sure they know it. If it helps, map out the behaviors you desire so you've got a set structure to operate within. Ask yourself, "Who do I want to work for?" and be that person. You are the ultimate leader of any staff you manage, and you are an example for peers and coworkers. By making yourself the ultimate wizard, genius, explorer, you set the tone for your workplace. Cultivate your passion, as your passion will be infectious, and that passion will spill over to your community of library users.

Further Reading

Blanchard, Kenneth, and Spencer Johnson. 1982. *The One Minute Manager*. New York: William Morrow and Company.

Lubans, John, Jr. 2009. "The Spark Plug: A Leader's Catalyst for Change." *Library Leadership & Management* 23 (2): 88–90.

Moran, Robert F., Jr. 2009. "What a Great Place to Work!" *Library Leadership & Management* 23 (1): 47–48.

Piegza, Amanda. 2008. "Delegation 101: The Basics for Library Managers." *Indiana Libraries* 27 (1): 77–79.

Roberts, Wess. 1985. *Leadership Secrets of Attila the Hun*. New York: Warner Books.

Schroeder, Harold. 2013. "Post Project Assessment: An Art and Science Approach." *Academy of Information and Management Science Journal* 16 (1): 37–45.

References

"Anythink Staff Manifesto." Anythink: A Revolution of Rangeview Libraries. Accessed October 25, 2013, http://www.anythinklibraries.org/sites/default/files/imce_uploads/Anythink_Staff_Manifesto.pdf.

Chapter 3

How to Effectively Manage Work and Time

Elizabeth Martin and Lynn Sheehan

Overview

Imagine this scenario: The carillon on your small university campus is chiming 8:00 a.m. as you reach the entrance to the campus library. As the library director, your mind is on the busy and fully scheduled day that lies before you, including a meeting with the university's president and executive team that begins in less than an hour. Upon reaching the library doors, you are met by a line of anxious students, including two library student workers, lined up in front of the sign that prominently displays the library's hours, including the 7:30 a.m. opening time.

You hastily unlock the doors, and you ask the student workers to begin the opening procedures while you try to discover what is happening. Checking voice mail and e-mail provides no explanation for the absent staff member and delayed opening, and your mind returns to your first meeting of the day that now begins in forty minutes.

The important meeting with the university president has been on the calendar for over a month. In preparation for the meeting, you and the staff have worked tirelessly preparing a sound presentation. Instead of reviewing your notes one more time, you are left to wonder why one staff member is inexplicably absent and quickly need to find a replacement from your short list of staff members prior to the beginning of the meeting. The time crunch leaves you feeling flustered and ill prepared for delivering the detailed program proposal to the president and executive team.

This scenario may seem a bit extreme; however, it is not an unlikely challenge for the administrator or manager of a small academic library. It reflects the importance of balancing administrative duties with the daily operations of a library; of hiring a reliable, competent staff; and of the necessity of strong managerial and time-management skills.

This chapter defines work management for a small academic library administrator. It discusses the balance of managing the day-to-day operations along with long-term projects and goals and is organized around three important attributes to work management: process, people, and ideas.

Process, People, Ideas

Work management for administrators of small academic libraries revolves around three main concepts—process, people, and ideas. These three attributes, first mentioned by Andrew Berner (1987) and echoed by Judith Siess (2006), bring to light the most essential components in managing work. Within those components there are two practical ways of measuring the best usage of time: being efficient and being effective. According to Siess, "doing the right things well is the epitome of efficiency *and* effectiveness. This is the Holy Grail of time management" (Siess 2002).

Process

An administrator in a small academic library is never bored. The opening scenario reflects the challenges in managing the day-to-day operations of the library as well as the long-term administrative duties. Situations like this scenario make the issue of work management important for small academic libraries. The scene implies that the library manager's shortfall is solely due to that of an absent employee. That said, weak time management skills also play a role in the scenario. Timely preparation by the manager would have diminished the stress felt as result of a late or absent employee. In continuing the focus away from managing time to managing work, it is more import to review how the process of work is managed.

Administrators in small academic libraries are what Roberta L. Pitts refers to as "generalists in an age of specialists," where workload may range from routine tasks like reshelving books to administrative functions like budget planning. Pitts sums up what a day can look like for an administrator of a small library in a 1994 article in *Library Trends*:

> Duties may include everything from administrative work to the most menial of
> tasks. In the course of a day, the director may draft a policy for use of the library

by outside groups, help a patron locate information for a report, edit catalog records, select new titles as well as placing the order for them, and handle the circulation desk in the absence of a volunteer or clerk. (Pitts 1994, 127)

Not much has changed in regards to managing a small academic library. With these varied tasks, it is easy to get lost in the minutia of the day to day as well as to quickly become discouraged. In her article, Sarah Engledow Brown (2012) describes her own struggles, claiming that prior to developing a process for work management she "would arrive, look around, feel overwhelmed, and spend most of the day reacting, rather than acting. The end of the day would come, and I would wonder what I accomplished." To avoid this style of haphazard work management, the development of a process is essential for leading a small academic library.

The concept of designing a process for work management may seem daunting to initiate, which is why the authors suggest dividing the process into three categories: planning, goal setting, and delegating. If you attempt to conduct your workday without a plan, then it can seem is as if every task is immediate. To avoid the pitfalls of becoming overwhelmed with work, begin by strategizing a plan of action for work management. Going back to the discussion of effectiveness and efficiency, these two concepts remain important when designing a prioritized work plan.

In regards to being effective, it is best to begin to look at work in a hierarchical fashion. As any administrator will tell you, there are tasks that demand a higher precedence than others. A high-ranking task may appear differently to administrators in larger and smaller libraries. Workload in a small library fluctuates from more complex tasks to more menial, but each task is critical. The way in which the tasks are prioritized is crucial when looking at effective ways to handle workload. When referring to a hierarchical structure, it doesn't necessarily reflect larger tasks taking higher priority. It may be the case where short-term projects are accomplished, while long-term projects still being addressed are not as high of a priority. All of this is individual to each situation and fluctuates daily, which is why the authors recommend that you continually reassess work management.

The restructuring of a plan also speaks to the efficiency of work management. Efficiency in work management means to conduct your work as productively as possible. To free up time and give a sense of accomplishment, the completion of small tasks may seem counterintuitive with wanting to place as much energy into larger, more innovative projects. This is not to assume that task completion is the goal of designing a work plan; and as Siess states, it is necessary not to confuse "busyness" with being efficient (Siess 2002). Efficiency attributes more to working with purpose and keeping in mind the larger vision of the library.

In addition to planning, it is important to discuss goal setting in relation to the process of work management. Goals create a structure to the library's visions and mission. They are essentially the backbone of planning in the work process. Goals may vary from library-specific to university-wide projects, such as updating subject guides, weeding, or developing a collaborative program with other student services organizations.

When designing new goals, it is best if they are demonstrative in nature as well as measurable and, most important, attainable. Numerous publications speak to developing specific, measurable, achievable, realistic, and timely goals, or better known as SMART goals. It is important to write out goals, regardless of size and scope, in order to examine and revisit them (Siess 2002). They should be clear in their intention, which determines attainability.

People

Most, if not all, time management systems discuss of the importance of delegating work. In an article relating this topic to libraries, "Time Management in Academic Libraries," authors Helen M. Gothberg and Donald E. Riggs state, "The ability to delegate work is frequently mentioned in the literature on leadership as a key element in managing time effectively" (Gothberg and Riggs 1988). Central to the importance of delegating work is the reality that there is someone in place to do the work, either library assistants or a professional librarian.

In a small academic library, there is no shortage of tasks at hand, and it is unrealistic for a library director to feel a need to complete them alone. If you have efficient, trained staff, it should be easy to assign them tasks or projects. Siess (2002) provides a list of guidelines for successful delegation to staff members:

- Delegate to the "right person" based on skill set, knowledge area, and current workload;

- Ensure the staff member has all of the "necessary resources" to succeed, and plan for time needed for learning new skills, for task completion, and for regular updates;

- Give the staff person the entire project, and "assign both responsibility and authority, then hold the person responsible for the outcome"; and

- "Make sure delegate gets the credit," which is important in staff morale and development (Siess 2002).

Personnel Recruitment

The opening scenario for this chapter realistically describes a morning that most small library managers have experienced. It illustrates the challenges of doing while also managing. As time and priorities evolve, so will the skill sets needed by the library staff. Some may be attained by staff development, while others may be added by new hires. Few library managers have the opportunity to hire all new staff library assistants and librarians, but sooner or later a change occurs—someone moves on or retires, or a new position is funded. When the opportunity arises, it may come as something of a mixed blessing to the small library manager. The opportunity to hire someone with a new skill set and different experience from existing staff is balanced by the recruitment and hiring process itself. In her book *Managing the Small College Library* (2010), Rachel Applegate includes a detailed chapter on "Personnel Recruitment," but basically the process is similar at all sizes of academic institutions.

Small institutions do not always have a dedicated human resource department, so the manager of a small library may be on his or her own for much of the hiring process. In any institution, whether hiring for a new or vacated position, approaching the task with a plan is key. The opportunity to add staff is also an opportunity to review the position description and adjust it if necessary. If no clerical staff is routinely available to the library manager, he or she may be able to negotiate for support from the institution for the hiring process. It may also be helpful to recruit a search committee in order to receive input from library and faculty colleagues to round out the evaluation of candidates.

In thinking about staffing, it is helpful to turn to resources like members of the college section of the Association of College and Research Libraries and discussion lists available to participants in the College Library Directors' Mentor Program. Additional information on the program is available at http://www.ala.org/acrl/about/sections/cls/collprogdisc/collegelibrary. Positions at smaller institutions often involve a myriad of responsibilities compared to those at larger institutions. If one does not have the advantage of working with the groups mentioned here, reviewing organizational charts for similar institutions and reading position announcements on the American Library Association's (ALA) job list (http://joblist.ala.org) and other websites offer model descriptions.

After a new librarian or library assistant is hired, orientation to the institution and library may be accomplished by creating one plan. Using a form or a checklist ensures that the new employee knows what will be covered and allows them ownership of the process. A good orientation aids in retention of new hires and initiates the groundwork for future performance reviews. It helps to establish expectations and gives the employee hope and confidence. By establishing a process for orienting new hires, the manager will be able to delegate the process to staff and others at the institution.

Managers should always make sure they are aware of the institution's hiring policies and procedures as well as the support other offices may provide. For example, if background checks are required, the department in charge of safety and security may do them. Payroll may aid in setting up automatic deposit, and the benefits office may explain health insurance and other benefits and aid in enrolling the new employee.

Staff Development

The opening scenario for this chapter also illustrates the important of staff development and training. In a library with a large staff, the absence of one person is not felt so keenly. In smaller libraries, it's important that all staff, including librarians, library assistants, and student workers, have mastered the basics and are cross-trained. Staff development and training add flexibility to providing library services and factor in staff retention, but it comes with a cost of time and money. Managers of small libraries may feel that neither resource is available. However, A. Ann Dyckman observes in *Developing Library Staff for the 21st Century* (1992) that "library supervisors and managers today are often overworked, and harried as they struggle to carry too much of the burden." While it may be easier to do than to delegate, this strategy does not work in the long term. Dyckman further observes that "ways of providing increased opportunities for continuing education and professional growth for all staff must be found despite the cost in dollars and work time. Given scarce resources, this change will demand creative solutions" (Dyckman 1992).

The creative solutions suggested by Dyckman may take a number of forms. Fortunately, resources are available in a number of formats, and costs vary from free or low-cost webinars and workshops to conferences requiring travel budgets. State, regional, and local consortia groups may also offer training to members or those located within the boundaries they serve at little or no cost. Cooperative planning with other libraries may result in more reasonable costs by purchasing a site registration for a number of librarians or library assistants. This arrangement has the added benefit of discussion and networking for those in attendance.

Online webinars and workshops are another option. Resources offered electronically may include the option of self-pacing so that librarians or library assistants may work on content during quiet times. These options range from simple purchases, like Dewey Easy 2.0 and LC Easy 4.0 software (available from http://librarytools.com), that may be used to train library assistants to webinars dealing with a variety of topics, including reference and technical systems. While not currently updated, the Ohio Reference Excellence (ORE on the Web, found at http://www.olc.org/ore) offers a thorough self-paced tutorial in all aspects of offering reference services.

A library manager may find it worthwhile to send one staff member to a conference with the idea that he or she will return to the library prepared to share. For librarians, especially recent graduates, there may be funding available to attend out-of-state conferences and annual meetings.

Time Management

While it is true that we elected to speak about managing work rather than managing time, the term *time management* has become the accepted way to refer to the concept and has become a popular subject for numerous books, blogs, and articles in everything from popular magazines to business publications. One should note that there is no magic bullet or one fool-proof, guaranteed system for managing one's work or time. Most time-management systems are alike in that they support managing priorities, planning, and process.

In her 2012 column, Jennifer A. Bartlett provides information on a few recent library-specific resources for managing time and work. Two of these resources, Judith A. Siess's *Time Management, Planning, and Prioritization for Librarians* (2002) and David Allen's *Getting Things Done: The Art of Stress-Free Productivity* (popularly known as GTD; 2002), are publications that we believe stand out because they represent two different views on managing work.

In her book, Siess (2002) emphasizes the importance of working smart, and she includes a discussion of efficiency versus effectiveness. She bases her discussion on the work of a number of authors but in the end simply states, "In short, efficiency means doing things right, whereas effectiveness means doing the right things." Additionally, Siess includes chapters on people, job stress, strategic planning, and prioritization and an appendix of forms to be used in managing a number of different aspects of work (time) management, including procrastination.

Robin Hastings (2011) recognizes the applicability of Allen's GTD method in her column, saying that "GTD gives library workers ways to keep tabs on what they are doing while keeping their goals in sight." Hastings continues by pointing out the basic principles involved in GTD and how it can be useful for small library directors:

[GTD] combines to-do lists, projects management, and organizational skills to allow workers to do their jobs effectively. . . . The lists that workers make . . . go from a high-level view of the goals of your job . . . to "next action" lists that state, in concrete language, exactly what the next action is that will move your project forward. In GTD projects are any items of work that require more than a single task to do. (Hastings 2011)

Tip: Complete small tasks first. This gives a sense of accomplishment and frees you up for larger tasks.

Tip: Cross-training is critical in a small library.

Tip: Make your goals attainable.

Tip: Whenever possible, delegate.

Conclusion

Work management is critical in a small academic library. If one piece is missing or falls out of sync, the library staff and patrons feel the impact. It is best to approach work management in a systematic way to promote a balanced workload not just for the library manager but the entire staff.

Bibliography

Allen, David. 2002. *Getting Things Done: The Art of Stress-Free Productivity.* New York: Penguin Books.

Applegate, Rachel. 2010. *Managing the Small College Library.* Santa Barbara, CA: Libraries Unlimited.

Bartlett, Jennifer A. 2012. "New and Noteworthy: Making Every Hour Count: Librarians and Time Management." *Library Leadership & Management* 26 (3/4): 1–4.

Berner, Andrew. 1987. "The Importance of Time Management in the Small Library." *Special Libraries* 78 (4): 271–76.

Brown, Sarah Engledow. 2012. "Tips for a Solo Librarian." *American Library Association's New Members Round Table* 42 (1). http://www.ala.org/nmrt/news/footnotes/august2012/tips-solo-librarian.

Dyckman, A. Ann. 1992. "Library Assistants in the Year 2000." In *Developing Library Staff for the 21st Century*, edited by Maureen Sullivan, 77–90. Binghamton, NY: Haworth Press.

Gothberg, Helen M., and Donald E. Riggs. 1988. "Time Management in Academic Libraries." *College and Research Libraries* 49 (2): 131–40.

Hastings, Robin. 2011. "Using GTD to Get Things Done at Your Library." *Computers in Libraries* 31 (8): 23–26. Academic Search Premier, EBSCOhost (accessed November 1, 2013).

Pitts, Roberta L. 1994. "A Generalist in the Age of Specialists: A Profile of the One-Person Library Director." *Library Trends* 43 (1): 121–35.

Siess, Judith A. 2002. *Time Management, Planning, and Prioritization for Librarians*. Lanham, MD: Scarecrow Press.

———. 2006. *The New OPL Sourcebook: A Guide for Solo and Small Libraries*. Medford, NJ: Information Today.

Chapter 4

How to Successfully Plan Your Work Flow

Deirdre D. Spencer

Overview

Management of a small library is a rewarding challenge for the librarian who is given the opportunity. Small libraries include public libraries that serve small populations in municipalities and rural communities. They may also include small academic branch libraries, as well as departmental, corporate, and special libraries of varying sizes. It is gratifying to plan and deliver services according to one's vision. Conceptually, the librarian must plan the overall program for the library and then, in detail, delineate how services are to be implemented. The librarian must determine what personnel, budget, equipment, and other resources are needed. He or she identifies the primary and secondary clientele and their immediate and future needs by asking the following questions: How does one envision patrons using the library and its resources? How might staff (if there are any) best provide assistance to patrons in their use of the library? Might he or she gather and utilize patron feedback to improve or enhance library programming? Does patron feedback inspire ideas that, if funded, would take the library to a new level or a different direction? How do requirements from upper-level administration affect the library? These are important questions that should guide the management of a small library.

Managing a Small Library

The librarian managing a small library is an administrator, budgeting expert, fund-raiser, and advocate. He or she negotiates with administrative superiors on behalf of the library and its clientele. The library must operate within budgetary guidelines, making the best use of those resources. A good library manager looks for additional funding through grants, gifts, and development opportunities. At a minimum, he or she should also advocate for funding to cover inflation. An evolving list of desiderata should be kept in mind in case the opportunity arises to finance and implement an item from the list.

Using Flowcharts

In planning for library services, flowcharts may be a helpful tool. They can be useful in the formal planning process, using mind-mapping software or templates taken from the Internet to present to staff or administration. Conceptual doodles drawn on notepads for the librarian's personal use are beneficial to visualize the trajectory of services and their components within the library. Library staff may contribute to the flowcharting process during meetings; this can encourage staff to buy into the process and build a sense of teamwork.

Flowcharts can be used for public and technical service planning, including all areas of materials processing. If the library is a stand-alone library, materials processing includes acquisitions functions, such as ordering, invoicing, receiving, payment, physical processing, and making materials available to patrons. The tasks of availing patrons of materials involves in-house processing, such as sorting, securing with tattle tape, labeling, temporarily placing them in a new-item display area, and then finally shelving them in the stacks or the DVD racks, journal displays, or wherever their final destination might be before patrons use them. If the library is part of a centralized system, acquisitions, receiving, invoicing, and payment are performed centrally.

It is important to build flexibility into the planning processes so that patrons are served and resources managed to accommodate new developments. Staff may offer suggestions as to where flexibility can be built into the process based on patron feedback or how their own work flow can be improved. With regard to information technology needs, again, depending upon the structure of the institution, information technology services may be centralized within the larger organization, or they make take place within your unit. This would include such functions as copy cataloging (or even original cataloging); batch downloading of data into the online public access catalog (OPAC); and provision and oversight of computing workstations, printers, scanners, and so on. Increasingly, provision of computer workstations, Internet access (via library computers or Wi-Fi accessed by personal computing devices), printers, and perhaps fax service are publically available technical services that patrons require. After receiving authorization or protected password information needed to access data, patrons may be able to work independently and require assistance only for troubleshooting.

Public services are supported by technical and online services. In this chapter, public services consist of circulation and access services; information and reference; and public outreach and liaison, which are supported by collection development. Collection-building processes, such as automated systems for approval plans, acquiring online cataloging data, CIP (Cataloging in Publication), and shelf-ready acquisitions, help streamline the work flow of acquisitions and technical processing for small libraries. Online journal packages and e-books can alter library staffing and operations to include technical troubleshooting of computers and printers rather than technical processing and storage of hard-copy materials. (As mentioned earlier, technical processing has traditionally taken the form of labeling; securing with tattle tape; and shelving books, journals, CDs, DVDs, computer accessories, visual technology, and so on.). Realistically, technical troubleshooting is added to these tasks. Budgeting for services, personnel hiring, and management is important as are liaison efforts to administrators from whom budgets emanate. It is wise to discover cost information quickly from research or colleagues to determine as quickly as possible if a desired item or service is out of the question or may require a bit more planning to acquire. Delegate basic research online and in catalogs to staff members as appropriate and as a break from their routine duties. Again, this can foster ownership in the process and generate ideas.

Although there does not appear to be an overwhelming volume of information about flowcharting in library management literature, in nearly thirty years of small academic library management, I have found it to be an effective means of planning the flow of library processes and operations. Informal versions of flowcharts have proven helpful and may be easily converted into informative memoranda for administrators and into instructional tools for library staff and patrons.

Initially, flowcharts should be kept simple, especially those that are shared with others. Flexibility should be built into the flowchart for addenda, and the manager should have a more detailed version of what occurs at each stage of the process, be it materials acquisition, budgeting, staff training, patron instruction, reference and information, and so on.

A flowchart allows the manager to know where in the process an item should be; if there are problems, a flowchart can identify a breakdown in the system. This can facilitate correcting problems as they arise and identify where in the process safeguards can be implemented.

Access to Materials and Information

Does the library circulate materials, or is it noncirculating? In either case the manager should have a clear idea of which sources of information patrons should have unfettered access to. Is there open access to general collections, reference collections, journals, or journal articles? Access to the OPAC should be self-explanatory, requiring minimal staff intervention. Does the manager collect usage statistics? Does he or she do this manually, or does checking materials into the automated circulation system record browses as well as check-ins? Does the system run reports, or are reports generated with manually collected data? Would the manager prefer that patrons place materials in a return bin or return them to the circulation desk? Would the manager prefer patrons leave materials on the table where they used them and not reshelve them? Determine what would be best for the staffing levels of the particular library. If there are rare or special collections items, of course they must be paged and used within view of the staff desk.

Clear signage and instructions enable patrons of small libraries to help themselves so that skeletal staff may assist in less routine interactions. Instructions should be easy to read and understand. Universal signs with simple images crossed out could be helpful in conveying messages, such as no food or drink. As much information as possible that can be conveyed without intervention allows staff to attend to other duties and provides opportunities for follow-up exchanges with the patrons at the circulation desk or other information portals. One of the advantages of managing a small library is getting to know the clientele, and while there should be access to some information that does not require staff intervention, it does not preclude librarian or staff from interacting with patrons informally or on deeper informational levels.

Reference and Information Service

Reference and information provide more opportunities for patron interaction and for learning their information needs, especially through the reference interview. Information and reference service may be delivered in person at a library information desk, by e-mail, by phone, or even by the postal service. The librarian may be connected to a larger infrastructure of libraries that utilize "Ask a Librarian" chat services, and some small library data could be made available via chat staff. Some queries directed to the library could be answered by data on a well-designed website. If the community is one that is underrepresented in terms of Internet access, however, then an up-to-date phone tree can be effective or a well-informed staff member or volunteer with accurate information at his or her fingertips. Another way to inform patrons of basic information about the library is to publish brochures and make them available not only to library visitors but also to others by distributing the brochures around the community on bulletin boards, kiosks, and other public spaces.

Although information services are traditionally divided into two sections, three sections are actually more accurate in the current climate. The first is basic information consisting of library hours of operation; directional questions, such as where facilities and resources are located within the library; and the names of the librarian and staff members.

The second is ready reference (as it was referred to in the 1980s). Ready reference requires more in-depth use of basic tools that are on hand. Such tasks include looking up call numbers, authors, titles, and dates of publications in the OPAC; finding information from the staff version of the OPAC; locating URLs and basic information on the Internet; and essentially helping patrons find information that they will soon be able to access themselves with practice.

The third information service is in-depth reference. It engages the librarian and the patron in a detailed reference interview where the librarian asks probing questions to determine what the patron really wants and the librarian answers the questions based on the structure and the availability of the resources to answer the query. The reference cap is one of many caps worn by the small library manager. The librarian may have a subject background in the fields related to the library's content. The manager may also wear a cap entitled "collection development" or "bibliographer." The library manager who occupies this position is well aware of the resources he or she has acquired. The library manager may have the capacity to turn what was an in-depth, complex query into a ready-reference question based on his or her knowledge of the collection. It is useful to discover as soon as possible the time frame in which the response is needed and to include it in the work flow. If the library manager has staff to whom he or she can delegate reference queries, a flowchart of the reference interview and a trajectory of strategies to approach various types of questions could prove helpful in answering reference queries in a timely manner.

Collection Development

Collection development is the basis of the library. While some patrons come to the library to use the computers, printers, and obtain Internet access, the main reason for the existence of the library is the information it acquires and makes available to patrons in the form of books, journals, CDs, videos, DVDs, and other electronic formats. Building a collection is a rewarding enterprise in that the library manager helps to shape knowledge and information to which patrons have access. The small library must have a clear, working collection-development policy that has built-in flexibility. The library manager who performs collection-development duties knows the types of information his or her clientele requests to have on hand or need for their work. Hopefully, these requests fall within the scope of the library's collection policy. If it falls a bit outside of the scope, it may be within the budget to provide the resources as a gesture of goodwill. Cooperative access and resource-sharing alliances regarding collection development expand the accessibility of resources to your patrons. Interlibrary loan consortia among institutions can ensure that the small library clientele has access to resources beyond their library. Exchange and gift programs can also augment your collection, and development efforts can be used to build the collection. Donors may be honored with a book plate for hard copies and electronic book plates to display in OPAC records. Electronic book packages that can be downloaded on e-readers and electronic journal packages that enable patrons to print or download articles can expand holdings and save physical space. Deselecting items from the collection on a regular basis (based on circulation data, subject criteria, or publications that have been superseded) are necessary within a small library in order to create an evolving collection for an expanding group of users. Sales of the deselected items may garner a small amount of revenue to add to the collection budget or library slush fund with the support of your administrators. Collection budgets should at least receive annual increases for inflation. Maintain a desiderata list of resources to add to the collection if the opportunity arises to acquire them. Always be prepared to make a convincing argument of how the resource would benefit the collection and the users.

Liaison and Outreach Efforts

Liaison and outreach are important to community relations. Staffing and budget at the library manager's disposal may influence the scale on which the library can entertain, but events can still be successful with less-than-optimal staffing or budgets. Liaison and outreach efforts may consist of tours of the library, open houses, receptions, and exhibits of the library's collections. Exhibits of materials outside of the collection can be of interest to library patrons and the larger community. Exhibits of books by special donors, accompanied by a reception and notice on the library website, is a way to encourage donor involvement and reward their contributions. Sponsoring lectures, cultural programs, traveling exhibits, readings, and film screenings, as well as allowing appropriate outside groups to book available meeting space, can open the library to a wider audience and result in positive press, which administrators view favorably. Offering instructional sessions on how to use the library may be of interest to patrons as well.

Liaison efforts also take place between the small library manager and higher administration. The library's mission should be supported by the administration, and there should be regular communication between the two. The librarian should exhibit confidence and enthusiasm for the library that he or she manages. It is the manager's job to lobby for resources in support of the library's mission, the good of its patrons and staff, and the library's standing in the community (including the community of libraries). Outreach and liaison efforts may encourage giving to the library in terms of trust fund establishments and monetary and in-kind donations.

A final word about liaison and outreach relates to popular media. If the library has a small staff, it might not be wise to engage the library in social media activities that would be difficult to keep current. Also, it would be unfortunate if the social media sites became inadvertent alternatives to established lines of communication between library and patron. Library mobile applications are available and can make your collection continually available, but that would be an undertaking for a larger library system and not one for a small, independent library staff to launch on its own without sufficient technical support. Social media changes quickly in terms of popularity, and using it to communicate with the public may not be a wise expenditure of staff time (unless the library invests heavily in teen and young adult services; if that were the case, significant staff resources invested in social media would be ideal).

Staffing

Staffing in a small library can influence the quality and quantity of service. It is important for the library manager to know what duties the staff member is to perform and that the written description of the position indicates those specific required skills, desired skills, experience, and qualifications that the applicant needs. The library manager should ask open-ended questions during the interview process and conduct a thorough check for references. A new employee requires orientation and training; he or she should understand the mission of the library and be able to work with the librarian to facilitate that mission.

Dependable staff can free the librarian to tend to such matters as planning, budgeting, and lobbying for library improvements. Excellent staff members are assets to the library and its patrons, but a poorly performing staff member with an uncooperative attitude can be a problem for the librarian. In a small library, the staff should work collegially and support each other in the service of the library, its patrons, and the reputation of the library. True collegiality and esprit de corps beyond basic workplace civility can take time to develop among staff members. There should be, however, a willingness of all staff to contribute to developing that spirit, with the library manager setting the example. Staff should be willing to follow the librarian's instructions with a respectful attitude, and the librarian should listen to staff with an equally respectful attitude. The input of the staff could help make a good idea better. Yet there are also times when the librarian's knowledge of the larger picture must prevail. It is advisable for library managers to present the staff with as much of the big picture as possible without divulging confidences or violating library policy. The small library manager and staff are a team with a common commitment to the library they represent.

Tip: As the manager of a small library, you are deluged with information and tasks. Although it may seem old hat, a flowchart is an effective device to manage and control your work.

Conclusion

By virtue of excellent planning and resource management, a broad base of collegial relationships, and personal resourcefulness, the small library manager is in a unique position to offer excellent service on a smaller scale. Building a supportive clientele that appreciates the work the library manager and staff do on their behalf can be effective in securing resources. As the small library continues to evolve, the small library manager is at the helm, improving existing services, identifying new services and information needs, keeping abreast of the profession, and developing new skills to raise the profile and expand the possibilities of the small library.

Bibliography

Mouyval, Katalin Fay. "A Balancing Act." *Collection Management* 30, no. 4 (2008): 43–57. doi:10.1300/J105v30n04_04.

Nelson, Paul, and Jane Pearlmutter. "When Small Is All: The Successful Small Public Library Director Wears Many Hats Smartly." *American Libraries* 42, nos. 1/2 (January–February 2011): 44–47. http://www.americanlibraries magazine.org/issue/januaryfebruary-2011.

Roberts, Joni R., MLS, and Ford Schmidt, MLIS. "Reference Alternatives: Para-professional Staffing at a Small Academic Library." *College & Undergraduate Libraries* 5, no. 1 (1998): 81–90. doi:10.1300/J106v05n01_09.

Watkins, Cynthia A. "Using Flowcharts to Streamline Document Delivery Services in an Academic Library." *Journal of Interlibrary Loan, Document Delivery and Information Supply* 10, no. 2 (2000): 77–88.

Chapter 5

How to Network and Build Partnerships

Robin Shader

Overview

In order to be successful as the managing librarian in a small library, you need to be self-motivated, informed, creative, and resourceful. Networking with other library and information professionals and community leaders and partnering with them to meet community goals is absolutely essential. Networking and developing partnerships will enhance the visibility of your library and will further your professional growth.

If you want your library to be considered a vibrant and important part of the community, *you* need to be an engaged and involved member of your community. A vibrant library doesn't just happen; it is developed over time. Library leaders can contribute toward the success of the library by learning what the community needs and providing it through the use of library resources. The key to identifying and meeting local needs is getting to know the people who have the ability to make things happen and working with them to solve problems and accomplish goals. My colleague, Gene Coppola, director of the Palm Harbor Library (Florida), calls this "having a seat at the community table."

In a Twitter post on November 8, 2013, Syracuse University's School of Information Studies professor R. David Lankes wrote, "We don't save libraries by saying 'look how important we are,' we save them by being important." So how do libraries become important? Most of the librarians I know are passionate about libraries and feel strongly that libraries are essential, but what do other people in the community think? Is your library an important part of your community?

If there were a threat of a significant budget reduction or closure, would hordes of angry people take to social media, flood commission chambers, or start an e-mail campaign to protest? When there is a community issue that needs to be addressed, are you included in the discussion? Do other group leaders call you with partnership ideas? If the answer is less than a resounding yes to any of these questions, you have work to do.

Consider the most influential people in your community. What characteristics do they share? These people tend to be well respected, trustworthy, and have the ability to get things done. These are characteristics of a good library manager and will serve you well as you work to improve your library and your community.

Networking

Building Relationships

The formation of strong relationships built on a foundation of trust is absolutely essential if you want your library to reach its full potential. Start by greeting and talking to the people you see each day. Managers in a small library often spend a lot of time on the service desk and so are already meeting and building relationships with regular customers. Talk to them, and find out what they like and what they don't about the library. When appropriate, use this information to make positive changes to services and procedures. Be open, honest, and approachable.

Getting to know your customers is a great start, but you must get out and meet the people who do not use the library, especially community leaders. It's important to realize that community leaders are not just the people in leadership positions. Everyday leaders are found everywhere. These are the people with influence in your community. It's your job to figure out who they are and get to know them. If you are not an outgoing person by nature, create a list of networking objectives to push yourself. An objective might be to reach out to one new person each week or each month. Go to the person's office or call him and introduce yourself. Let him know you are new in town and just wanting to get to know people. If you are not new to your current position, use this book as inspiration to refocus your energy on community relationships. Attend meetings of the county commission or city council, community improvement organization, school board, and other key groups so you can meet community leaders and learn about the issues they are tackling. Making these connections helps build trust, the foundation for a lasting relationship.

You can find out when community groups are meeting by reading your local newspaper or visiting the organization's website. Open meetings allow anyone from the local public to attend, so attend as many as you can. Go early, and greet the members in attendance. Let them know you are working toward a greater understanding of how the library can meet community needs.

Tip: Be prepared to speak! It is not unusual in a small town for the group leader to give you, the visitor, an opportunity to say a few words during the meeting. If you do get the chance to speak, keep it brief. Don't make them sorry they asked!

One of your goals in meeting and learning about community groups is to add the library to their mental short list. Plant the seed in their mind so that, when a project is in the planning stages, the library is considered as a potential partner. Any community projects related to literacy, workforce readiness, and education (among many other topics) are a natural fit with the library mission. Make sure the groups in your community know that.

Community Involvement

Managing a small library might present challenges to attending meetings and joining organizations. You might be the only staff member and therefore cannot leave during operating hours to attend meetings. Find creative ways to participate. Maybe there is an opportunity for the meetings to be held at the library. Groups that are made up of business professionals often meet before work hours, during lunch, or after hours when you might have an opportunity to participate. The chamber of commerce might have after-hours meet-and-greet receptions for members. Consider having the library join the chamber if your budget allows. This will provide you access to information and events that will put you in contact with business and community leaders. Find out if the library's governing body is a member and whether the library falls under the umbrella of the membership.

Tip: This process of building and maintaining work-related relationships is often referred to as *networking*, but that is a very cold and technical term. It is important to note that, in all your interactions with the community, you must be sincere. Join a group because you believe in their mission. Honor your commitments, and participate. Your participation must be heartfelt and enthusiastic.

Small communities many not have as many organizations as large cities, but there will be plenty of opportunities. The cost of joining, in terms of money and time, should be something you carefully consider. Service organizations usually require a membership fee, and there can be multiple times per year when additional donations are expected. Some employers will pay the librarian's membership, so explore that possibility. If you cannot afford to join a particular group, then don't, but you can reach out to them and let them know you believe in their mission and would be interested in partnerships. Establish a channel of communication, and keep it open. By developing and maintaining sincere relationships, you will build trust.

Service organizations, such as Rotary, Kiwanis, and Lions Clubs, often support initiatives that are important to libraries. Community leaders and business owners are often members of these groups. Meetings often include guest speakers, so you can learn a lot about your community by attending these presentations. The fact that they need guest speakers means there is an opportunity for you to make a presentation about the library. This is an excellent way for the members to get to know you and for you to share details of library services. Even if you cannot join the group, you can still reach out to them and offer a presentation. If you are invited to a meeting, be sure to take the opportunity to talk with members before your presentation.

Tip: Prepare your elevator speech. How do you describe your job? Is your description of the value of libraries compelling? Are you enthusiastic when talking about the library? You only have one chance to make a good first impression, but you will have many opportunities to share the library message with the people you come in contact with. Be prepared to give a short, enthusiastic, powerful summary of issues when asked how things are going at the library.

Know When to Say No

If you attend meetings and maintain a friendly and enthusiastic attitude, it's very likely you will be invited to join the group. Be honest with yourself and with the group if you cannot afford it or simply don't have time right now. If you join a group, you need to participate, so only join if you know you can fulfill your responsibilities as a member. You need to know when to say no. Being an active part of the community does not mean saying yes to every invitation. Inevitably you will need to deal with a group who presents an opportunity that is not a good fit for the library. Always be open to ideas, but simply say no when appropriate. As you become more involved in the community, you could easily become overwhelmed. After all, you do have a library to run. Don't feel obligated to join everything, but do stay informed and involved if you can. If a partnership opportunity or grant comes to your attention that you simply don't have time or resources to handle right now, alert other groups who might be able to take advantage. Maintain a community mind-set, always on the alert for opportunities that could help your community partners. In some cases your involvement can be as simple as writing a letter of support for another organization's grant request.

Library Associations

As a librarian you are part of many communities, not just the one where you live. Library staff members and supporters are eligible to participate in a plethora of library associations and member groups. Research these groups, and join the ones that seem most relevant. Often membership includes access to the group's e-mail list and newsletter, as well as discounts on training sessions and conference attendance. Take advantage of the opportunity to connect with your library colleagues. Librarians are a very collaborative bunch and are usually willing to share what they know when asked. Don't be afraid to ask questions via the e-mail list or reach out to members who have experience that could help you with your project.

In addition to basic membership benefits, these groups also provide opportunities for members to join committees. Committee membership is a great opportunity to meet other librarians with similar interests and delve deeper into a specific area of librarianship. If you do become a member of a library association, get involved. Join a committee, and actively participate. It's a great way to learn from your colleagues and share what you know with others in the profession. Associations to consider are: your state library association, American Library Association (ALA), Association for Rural and Small Libraries, Special Libraries Association, and a multitude of others based on your type of library and interests. A list of ALA-affiliate organizations can be found on the ALA website.

Tip: Usually these organizations require a membership fee, so if you are like most librarians, you will likely not be able to join all of them. You can, however, "friend" or "follow" their social media sites at no cost to learn about major news and events of interest.

Partnerships

Partnerships = Ideas + Relationships in Action

The best partnerships combine a great idea with an established network of like-minded people with shared goals. Where do the ideas come from? Everywhere. Be in the know by being informed about what is happening in the library community and your local community. Read as widely as you can. Pay attention, and be ready to pursue partnership opportunities. If you have already begun your regular routine of connecting with people in your community, then forming partnerships will be much easier. Begin by identifying your natural allies, and reach out to them.

Newspapers

Newspapers and libraries are natural allies, both sharing a desire to have a literate community and both caring about free speech and intellectual freedom issues. You should already be sending press releases or otherwise sharing information about library programs. If allowed by your governing body, consider periodic letters to the editor during National Library Week or Library Card Sign-Up Month or other times when you have an important message to share. Newspapers also sometimes need "filler" and might want to cover, for example, a story time or craft program where they can get some photos of cute kids. Share with them your list of upcoming programs, but also send photos of past programs. Many papers have a society or scrapbook section where they will publish photos submitted by the public. This is a good way to share accomplishments and highlight successful partnerships. Keep newspapers in mind when considering partners for literacy programs. Get to know the editor, the publisher, and the people who can assist you in crafting effective press releases. There are many different ways to partner with newspapers. A few examples are provided here.

GUEST COLUMNIST

It might be possible for the librarian to write a regular column for the newspaper. The column could focus on library programs and services, reviews of new materials, or could take a Q-and-A approach, providing answers to questions submitted by the public. Talk to the publisher or the editor, and discuss different approaches. You might write some samples to illustrate what you have in mind. The caution here is that newspapers have deadlines and so you need to make sure you can deliver on your promise. If one article per month is all you have time to write, do not agree to produce one per week. You do not want to sour your relationship due to missed deadlines or burn yourself out due to late-night writing sessions. If you already produce a library newsletter, you might want to test this idea by including the column there. Practice meeting a regular deadline, and see if you can handle the workload. This experiment would also provide samples to show your contact at the newspaper.

READING CONTEST

In Liberty County, Georgia, my library partnered with *The Coastal Courier* newspaper to offer a contest called "Get Busy Reading." The goal of the project was to encourage children to read during their summer vacation. Library staff selected book titles for three age groups so that pre-K through twelfth-graders could participate. The selected titles were ones where the library owned multiple copies and, as part of a regional library system, we had access to additional copies from other branches. We then created multiple-choice quizzes to test the comprehension of the reader. The newspaper published a promotional ad with contest rules, and the quizzes were available in the library. Library staff checked each quiz, and the names of the children who answered all the questions correctly were entered into a drawing. Winners received a one-hundred-dollar check from the newspaper and their picture in the paper. Through this project the library received free publicity all summer long. Both the library and the newspaper publisher were happy with the results. The winners were thrilled.

Schools

Schools, pre-K through university level, offer unlimited opportunities for partnerships. The Bay County Public Library (Florida) works with Bay District Schools to prepare students for their annual "Battle of the Books," a multischool competition to see which team can answer the most trivia questions about specific books. Staff members from the Library Youth Services Department visit several schools and provide book talks to get kids excited about reading the selected titles.

Many high school students are required to volunteer for a specific number of hours in order to obtain scholarships or simply to graduate. Make sure school administrators and teachers know about the volunteer opportunities you offer students. Encourage teachers to share information about upcoming assignments so you can be prepared with a list or display of library resources. Offer to make presentations to media specialists, parent–teacher groups, and home-school groups. Consider inviting college professors to provide short presentations. The Panama City Beach Public Library in Florida has offered "Lunch and Learn" series programs in partnership with the local college. Attendees were invited to bring a bag lunch and listen to one-hour presentations by professors from the local community college. This partnership promoted the college's continuing education program while offering quality, no-cost programs for the library.

Art Groups and Other Organizations

Do you have any wall space that could be used to display works of art? Partnering with local artists is a great way to bring beautiful exhibits to your library at no cost. There will be some start-up costs to install proper display hardware if you do not already have it, but the cost is reasonable. It's a great investment. Some art groups and artists are willing to sell their work and provide the library with a small percentage of the sale price. Whether or not it is a fund-raiser, it's just great to have the art, and it might attract people to the library who might not otherwise visit. It's also wonderful to provide local artists with a place to exhibit their work.

Another way to partner with art groups is to create displays in support of their exhibits. If the local art gallery is putting on a Postimpressionism exhibit this month, for example, the library could do a complimentary display of materials that could be noted at the gallery.

The same idea can be applied to other local groups. If the local Woman's Club is promoting a campaign to encourage the proper use of child car seats, maybe the library could offer a child safety class or a materials display, or at the very least, a poster could be displayed in the library to help market the program.

Tip: People want to work with people who are easy to work with! The best partners are those who will do their share of the work and will do it with a positive, professional attitude. Be sure to be a good partner when you have the opportunity. It will make future partnerships so much easier.

Marketing Benefits of Partnerships

A true partnership requires involvement of all parties and must benefit all parties. One of the benefits is that, by developing the program with one or more other organizations, you will immediately increase your audience. You will interest not only library users but also the community of people associated with the other groups. The Charles Whitehead Public Library in Wewahitchka, Florida (population 1,800), is partnering with the local 4-H to offer craft classes in the library. This is a fantastic partnership that pairs 4-H and library staff and combines these two participant pools. The work is shared, and both organizations promote the programs. Attendance has been strong.

Consider the benefits of partnering with the newspaper. What is the readership of the paper? Depending on the size of your community, potentially hundreds or thousands of people have the opportunity to learn about the library if an ad, photo, or article appears in your local paper. That's a lot of positive exposure, and it's free.

No matter how small your community, there will always be people who have no idea what your library offers. Even people who do visit are often surprised to find out about services available. When you participate in community groups, you learn about local needs and have the opportunity to share ideas about how the library can help accomplish community goals. If you are present during the meeting when the group discusses wanting to help people find jobs, improve workforce readiness skills, or tackle illiteracy, you can explain why the library is an obvious partner. Use networking and partnership opportunities to communicate what the library is doing. It's possible that the people you meet have no idea, so educate them.

Conclusion

What is your library's purpose? If you have vision and mission statements, they probably include something about connecting people with information, improving people's lives, and enabling success. In order to ensure the broadest impact of library services, you need to know what will make the greatest impact. The best way to gain this knowledge is to be aware of what is happening around you: by reading the paper, watching the news, talking and connecting with people, and asking questions. As a library manager, you are very busy, but the time you invest in your community will pay many dividends. By being involved and engaged at the leadership level, you will have access to more information and be able to make better decisions. Although this means extra work, your efforts will be rewarded and your goodwill appreciated, and you'll help build a better community for all.

Chapter 6

How to Create Functional, Flexible, and Forgiving Library Spaces

Paul Glassman

Overview

Whether a library renovation is a bane or a blessing depends on its responsiveness to patron needs, its recasting of the library image, and its improvement of the built environment. This chapter addresses the essential components of the users' role in commissioning an inviting set of library spaces that accommodate the cosmic effects of virtual collections on library design.

Why Renovate?

Libraries introduce renovation for several reasons. Some address the changing uses of library space and identify the need to reinvent the library as a destination and physical environment. This increasingly frequent repurposing of traditional spaces is the result of diminishing numbers of print items acquired and housed, the increasing number of electronic resources purchased and subscribed to, and the resulting need for more computer hardware and a more ubiquitous technological infrastructure. Others see an antiquated physical plant and have the opportunity to correct the decay caused by extended periods of deferred maintenance. Yet others introduce the concept of the electronic library, one that some playfully call a technology sandbox. In other cases, the current building design presents barriers to patrons with disabilities, and the library administration has committed to correcting that deficiency. And finally, the decision to renovate may stem simply from a desire to improve the appearance of the facility, to make it more attractive, more inviting, maybe even to make it beautiful; thus the renovation is in part a marketing tool in service of an effort to retain a constituency of readers and information seekers.

Given the cosmic changes in both the publishing industries and their related outlets, many libraries, both public and academic, see themselves as subject to an uncertain future. That future—and how it shapes the library, both as an organization and as a place—will evolve as readers' relations to the printed word and its mediation changes. The Pew Research Center reports that, while a great majority of readers favor electronic books for their speed of access, the same number (82 percent) favor the printed format for reading with a child. Thus, the tactility of the physical book dominates in a shared reading experience.[1]

Changing use, insufficient space, and deteriorating building condition are the three most fundamental reasons to renovate. In both public and academic libraries, changing use results from the need for meeting spaces, social spaces for collaboration and group work, and the trend to house aging print collections either in compact shelving or off site. Insufficient space results from either greater demand for meeting and social spaces or for more housing for collections (the latter more frequently the case in research libraries). And problematic building condition stems from deferred maintenance; an antiquated physical infrastructure; insufficient physical accessibility for users with disabilities; the need to provide support for technology; and, perhaps the most abstract reason of all, simply the appearance of the environment. (Public relations and marketing professionals understand that responsive design, attentive physical plant maintenance, and the aesthetic experience communicate the value of the institution to its public.)

Thus it is likely that a comprehensive view of the renovation will result in a radical reconfiguration, of which there are two types: collection centric and people centric. Despite the people-centric trend toward converting space for collections into social spaces, some projects focus on creating long-term, environmentally advanced conditions for the preservation of materials and are thus collection centric. At the University of Chicago's Joe and Rika Mansueto Library, for example, a glass-domed reading room rests above its fifty-foot-deep subterranean, robotic storage facility based on commercial inventory systems, which can hold 3.5 million volumes.[2]

Planning for Change

Typically, the need for change in libraries centers on growth, technology, and flexible space. Collections and staff may increase in number but often not at the same time. Technological advances bring challenging questions, such as whether to rely wholly on a wireless network. And the desire for collaborative spaces suggests a discussion of the nature of multipurpose space. These are the types of conversations that precede and energize the planning phase.

Making the Case

The impetus for renovation may come from an upper-administrative level, but if library staff members see the need, it is critical to present persuasively the benefits of renovation. Six questions can form the outline for making the case:

1. Who benefits? Who are the constituents who will gain the most from improved facilities?

2. How do we preserve the library as a destination? How will a renovation bring the library closer to that goal?

3. Do we want to improve the library as a place, and if so, how?

4. Will a renovation achieve economies of scale by, for example, consolidating service points?

5. Will services improve as the result of a renovation?

6. Will the library mission be served better?

If the facility is an academic library, you might observe that academic libraries are marketing tools for prospective students. The Association of Higher Education Facilities Officers supported studies indicating that 53.6 percent of prospective students during campus tours consider the library extremely or very important in the selection decision process, 48.4 percent want to see the library, and 19.3 percent reject the institution because of a poorly maintained library.[3] And the condition of the library is likely to influence parental impressions even more deeply.

Types of Spaces

A taxonomy of library spaces has emerged with people-centered facilities. They comprise space for quiet study and reading; small-group study rooms; lounge areas with new books, popular titles, and periodicals; and social spaces, such as cafés, conference rooms, and auditoriums. The challenge of providing space for working in isolation as well as in collaboration will add complexity, depth, and energy to the problem.

Developing a Proposal

Key to making the case for renovation to upper-level administrators, elected officials, or municipal appointees is a well-composed proposal that includes a rationale for the project. Be sure to outline the benefits, identify which users will be positively affected, identify the client (who within the organization, agency, or municipality has the final say in decisions), and suggest a planning group. A strong but concise proposal improves the odds for approval and allows fund-raisers to articulate the need successfully to prospective donors.

Design Development Process

How can library staff be involved in the process? A management plan follows a successful renovation proposal. In developing a management plan, be sure to answer these questions:

1. Who will be consulted when the designers, contractors, and vendors have questions?

2. Who will handle communications? How will library staff participate in them?

3. Who will review architectural drawings, specifications, and other documents?

4. Who will make final decisions on behalf of the institution?

5. How will the work schedule be defined? Will the library close during renovations?

6. How have other libraries gone about their renovations?

In the course of answering these questions, be sure to identify a management team that will meet frequently to review project needs and challenges, which include the impact of technology, security of patrons and collections (which designers, vendors, and consultants are unlikely to appreciate), maintenance of the physical plant, the specific needs for furniture and equipment, and other special needs, such as exhibition cases and highly regulated climate for special collections. Be sure to identify to whom design plans are submitted, who reviews them, and who ultimately authorizes them.

Space Inventory

If you are not sure where on campus the facility should be located, conduct an inventory of all possible sites. This exercise helps identify all of the options for adjacencies and possibilities for renewal. List features of each option, such as square footage, basic geometry, structural and spatial intrusions (e.g., columns and ducts), lighting, ceiling heights, type and level of climate control, and the condition of surfaces.

Do You Need a Professional Designer?

If the organization has limited experience with architects and other design practitioners, the assumption might be that a modest renovation proceed without professional design services. For a modest refurbishing with a small budget, that approach may suffice. However, there are benefits to engaging a professional architect or interior designer. The design professional

1. can ask questions that the clients and users may not. For example, if the design professional has had experience with a certain type of wire management, that knowledge may be valuable to even the small project.

2. coordinates the implementation schedule. This is helpful if there are multiple work groups, vendors, or contractors.

3. will supervise implementation. A design professional has experience identifying potential installation problems.

4. estimates costs with accuracy. Cost estimation is time consuming for the layperson, and this benefit might for that reason be cost effective.

5. is familiar with sources for furnishings, equipment, and materials. Especially if there are state contracts, the design professional can assist with generating requests for proposals so as to find the best price for furnishings. Rather than rely on library supply catalogs, the design professional interacts with sources for materials and furnishings on a daily basis and can offer a much broader range of styles and prices.

6. develops specifications for furnishings, equipment, and materials. This is very helpful if you are requesting bids from multiples vendors.

Do You Need a Project Manager?

A project manager is an architect or specialist who serves as a client representative to the designers, architects, vendors, and contractors. Serving as a client and user advocate, the project manager coordinates communication between the various participants in the process.

A small project may not need a project manager, and in fact many large projects do not employ them. Despite the added expense, there are nevertheless several benefits to adding this level of coordination to the process since an effective project manager ensures communication, coordinates schedules, and therefore can minimize the number of change orders. Schedule coordination is especially critical if the project includes architects, contractors, and separate furnishing and millwork orders. For example, early delivery of furnishings can result in unnecessary storage charges, and late delivery can delay installation of technological equipment and opening of the facility.

Do You Need a Technical Consultant?

If the project introduces new levels of technological tools, it may be advisable to hire a technical consultant who can talk to vendors, in-house information technology staff, and other consultants so as to ensure full integration of not only personal computers but also of scanners, copiers, video-editing software, print stations, vending machines for smart cards, and classroom control software. With an eye for advances in technology, the consultant might offer economies unknown within the organization and introduce superseding equipment. For example, the consultant may suggest inclusion of coaxial cable so as to allow for television at every station. Similarly, the limitations of the interactive whiteboard might be addressed productively by a consultant who has tested Apple TV.

The Role of Library Staff

Including library staff in the design process will help address the diverse needs of the library constituents and staff members. The library director must ensure, whether through personal appeal or a formal proposal, that the perspectives of library personnel are integral to the process. Users know better than anyone else what they need, but upper-level administrators, elected officials, and municipal appointees may overlook you if the library leader is not assertive. Be sure to infuse yourself into the process as fully as possible.

Renovation Phases

The three phases of renovation planning are programming, schematic design, and design development. For a renovation to be successful and responsive to user needs, the library staff must participate in each phase.

The program is a tool that defines project objectives and goals. It serves as a device for decision making and a guide for the design team throughout the design process. It also provides a checklist—one that the users can refer to once a design is presented to assess whether it addresses all user needs. Providing scope and parameters, the program lists functional requirements. A good program does not offer a solution; rather it states the core design problem. It quantifies rather than qualifies.

A program is also important to the client and users because it provides an opportunity to evaluate goals, the spaces selected, service and operational concepts, staff size and collection growth, as well as adjacencies and internal organization. In providing an opportunity to examine organizational structure through spatial relationships, the client can offer a more comprehensive and articulate statement of need to the designers.

In addition to a summary of goals and objectives, a program identifies key issues and assumptions. It outlines fundamental planning criteria, such as the amount of space needed for each personnel function, for collections, for patrons, and for storage. It recommends functional adjacencies and may even list technical criteria, room by room.

Remember that, although a program is an essential tool for getting started, it is neither a contract nor a rigid set of rules. And although ideally the architects or designers will create the program in close consultation with the client and users, some architects, for the sake of saving time and lowering fees, will skip this essential phase of the process. As the user, you are in a good position to fill that void. If there is a project manager in the early stages of the project, feel free to suggest collaboration. Alternatively, an independent library consultant might be retained to assist in the programming phase.

Examples of Architectural Programs

In 2005 the Joan and Donald E. Axinn Library of Hofstra University pursued a renovation of the public spaces on the main floor of its nine-story building containing access services, reference services, the reference collection, and a computer commons. The head of access services and the assistant dean for reference and collection development wrote the program in table 6.1 to guide the architects.

In 2013 Felician College applied to the State of New Jersey, under its Building Our Future Bond Act, for $4.3 million to support renovation of the abandoned Messler Library on the original Fairleigh Dickinson University campus in Rutherford, which it purchased in 1998. Although additions over time made the building noncompliant with guidelines of the Americans with Disabilities Act, two grand spaces offered the promise of an Education Commons, to be operated by library services, and a Nursing Skills Laboratory, to be operated by the school of nursing. For the Education Commons component, the director of

Table 6.1 Hofstra University Library Joan and Donald E. Axinn Library Renovation Program

---

Electronic information commons (public computer terminals)

- Include space for four dedicated online public catalog terminals and one printer, three to be positioned at standing height and one to have ADA-compliant accessibility.
- Provide seating and connectivity for thirty-six electronic resource terminals, twenty-two of which can have wireless access to the network. One of the hard-wired terminals should have ADA-compliant accessibility.
- Include space for two public printers.
- Allow adequate space at both sides of each work station for note taking and mouse movement.
- Equip work tables with median dividers to preserve privacy.
- Preserve 210 linear feet of shelving, with consideration given to half-height shelving units.

Reference room

- Provide 3,351 linear feet of shelving.
- Include a double-width atlas stand, and retain flat-file shelving for atlases.
- Retain as many carrels as possible for quiet study, giving priority to perimeter carrels.
- Provide visual access to the south windows.
- Ensure quiet study throughout the area.
- Avoid a seating configuration that positions readers back to back.

---

library services and public services librarian for the Rutherford campus created the program in table 6.2.

Schematic Design

In the schematic design phase, an initial set of floor plans invites discussion about alternatives. Often the most dynamic phase of the process, schematic design allows for the exchange of ideas about overall concept, spatial configuration, and adjacencies. Even if there is only one scheme presented, this is the point in the process for intensive review of and feedback on what the designers envision—or what they forgot. Examples of what designers forget include:

- space for book trucks,

- sorting shelves,

Table 6.2 Felician College Library Plan

Education Commons				Program Areas Summary
Program Component	Collection # of items	Shelving (l.f.)	Seating #	Technology
Public spaces				
Vestibule				Digital sign; drinking fountains, 2; 6 l. f. of fabric-covered bulletin boards
Exhibit space		50 in cases		
Lounge: booths with tables & chairs; café tables & chairs; open/lounge seating			50	Power (data?) outlets in floor; 3 rolling two-sided whiteboard easels; 6 l.f. of fabric-covered bulletin boards
Service desk, desk height			2	Sliding slings for 2 computers; monitors with articulated arms; printer
Cell phone booth				
Conference room			16	Wall-mounted 80" LED/ LCD panel; monitor on articulated arm; computer; cabinet for computer; wireless keyboard; laptop connection; whiteboard; speaker system; telephone & jack; installed video camera & microphone at ceiling level
Cultural events space (can be co-located with lounge—3 above)			75	Data projection with large screen & computer cabinet; laptop connection
Charging stations			5	

Information services		
Help desk, desk height	3	3 computers in sliding slings; monitors with articulated arms; printer
Computer lab with extra power & data outlets	50	50
Printing stations/copy center/ scanners		3 printers & scanner; copier
Group study (2 @ 8 occupants)	16	Wall-mounted 46" LED/ LCD panel; monitor on articulated arm; computer; cabinet for computer; wireless keyboard; laptop connection; whiteboard; speaker system; telephone & jack
Group study (6 @4 occupants)	24	Wall-mounted 36" LED/ LCD panel; computer; monitor on articulated arm; computer; cabinet for computer; wireless keyboard; laptop connection; whiteboard; speaker system; telephone & jack
Consultation room (2)	6	Computer in sliding sling; monitor on articulated arm; cabinet for computer; laptop connection; whiteboard; telephone & jack
Offices, library faculty (3)	9	Computer in sliding sling; monitor on articulated arm; telephone & jack
Office, library director/manager (2)	8	Computer in sliding sling; monitor on articulated arm; telephone & jack
Staff rest room, solo		
Instruction		

(continued)

Table 6.2 (continued)

Program Component	Collection # of items	Shelving (l.f.)	Seating #	Technology
Smart classrooms/labs (1 or 2)			50	85" SMARTboard; teaching station with podium/ cabinet for computer & monitor; wireless keyboard; laptop connection; whiteboard; speaker system; telephone & jack
Materials (shelving)				
Print resources	6,100	800		
Media collection	1,000	60		
Digital Media Lab			8	Plotter; scanner; color printer; cabinet for computer; iMac station; laptop plugin; 46" HD screen; cabinets for equipment (12 l. f.); wireless keyboard; installed video camera; tripod; wireless microphone; DVD recording capability; control panel; speaker system; whiteboard; headphones with microphones
All-hours study with after-hours entry			~50	Wall-mounted 80" LED/ LCD panel; teaching station with podium/cabinet for computer & monitor; wireless keyboard; laptop connection; whiteboard; speaker system; telephone & jack; ~50 student work stations
Lockers			20	
Café/coffee kiosk/cart			~15	Plumbing; digital sign
Rest rooms				Ensure good exhaust system; manual paper towel rollers or high-velocity hand dryer

- staff lockers,

- sensible placement of light switches,

- bulletin boards and signs,

- closets and storage units, and

- wastebaskets.

Design Development

In the design development phase, the decisions are finalized, resulting in a complete set of construction documents that include not only architectural components but also mechanical, electrical, and plumbing design (MEP). Specifications indicate types of hardware, fixtures, and millwork. And detail drawings show the design at a much smaller scale. This package is known as the bid set and is sent with a request for proposals (RFP) to all general contractors who wish to be considered for the job of constructing the design.

Furnishings

Often separate from the architectural contract, furnishings can be acquired through an interior designer or design agency if not requisitioned by the institution's purchasing agent. Keep in mind the ergonomics of your selections, and incorporate anthropomorphic data, which are useful for plotting human dimensions and adding ergonomics to your criteria.[4]

Optimally you will be able to choose from several options for seating. If possible, ask the designers or vendors whether an example of each can be lent for a few weeks to allow a focus group to provide feedback on user preferences. The stimulation of interest in the project and generation of goodwill is likely to surpass the information collected.

Utilities and Practicalities

Examine the lighting design carefully, and if one is not offered, request a reflected ceiling plan. Note the two fundamental types of lighting: ambient (general, atmospheric) and task (focused, intense). Look at wall elevations to assess the locations of light switches. Are they near entrances and duplicated in large rooms? Does the ambient lighting have controls to allow for lowered light levels but sufficient illumination for note taking during image projection? Are there separate controls for the ambient and task lighting?

Ask about electrical power. Examine whether there are outlets near each workstation and workspace. Until mobile devices come with better and longer-lasting batteries, users will look for power wherever they find themselves in the space. Conveniently, customized furnishings often integrate power. And remember to ask whether there are sufficient outlets to accommodate printers and other peripheral equipment.

If it is not being replaced, the current HVAC (heating, ventilating, and air conditioning) system must be able to manage increased heat loads from computer equipment. Since most spaces were designed for lower heat loads, the design may need to introduce larger-capacity air handling units and compressors. Thermostatic controls in each space ensure comfortable temperatures if the zones vary in use and amount of equipment. Multiple zones, however, result in more complex climate-control systems.

Last, keep in mind the needs of technologists who install computer equipment and of the housekeeping staff. Dust-collecting surfaces twenty-five feet off the floor are not reachable, and moveable furnishings make equipment installation much easier.

Shelving Space

Whether or not you expect the print collection to grow, library shelving should be easy to relocate and reinstall for optimal flexibility and future rearrangement. Some libraries acquire compact or high-density shelving when consolidation of less frequently used material results in freeing space for users and services. Compact shelving, which moves over narrow rails suppressed into the floor slab, may be automated or manually operated. Both systems ensure the safety of fallen books as well as readers by means of sensor-activated safety brakes. However, since compact shelving results in nearly double the floor load, most floor slabs will need to be thickened with steel-reinforced concrete at great cost. The most practical location, from the structural perspective, therefore, is the ground floor, which is unlikely to require reinforcement.

Lighting for shelving may be cantilevered off of the top surface of each face or, as is more customary, suspended over the aisle in between each range. Although lighting that runs parallel to the long axis of the shelves results in even distribution and greater legibility of call number labels, that approach assumes a fixed aisle location. With compact shelving, and with shelving likely to be relocated, parallel lighting is therefore undesirable, and most designers now suggest that lighting fixtures be positioned perpendicular to ranges. Request a visit to a site with a similar installation to ascertain whether bottom-shelf end-of-range call numbers are in fact readable.

Although structurally unnecessary, end panels can provide refinement. They can vary in type and cost, from economical acrylic panels to expensive matched-grain wood. Sign holders for call number ranges are essential for item retrieval. Since shelf shifting is inevitable, avoid permanent range signs.

Office Space

Although open-plan offices are less expensive to create—and although they may nurture collaboration and exchange—some library employees may work more comfortably and productively with a certain degree of privacy. Indeed, some offices (human resources, for example) may require privacy. If private offices are provided, optimally each will have its own thermostatic control to satisfy the thermal comfort zones of the individual occupant.

Regardless of which approach you select, enroll the office space occupants in the specifics of the designs. Although interior designers may be experts in selecting office furniture, architects tend not to be. Therefore, user participation—whether in testing chairs, recommending the number of linear feet for file drawers, or explaining how the desktop needs to be configured (the accounts payable manger may need an unobstructed L-shaped surface, for example)—is beneficial.

Workspace

If the library has any processing of collections, whether for cataloging, preparation for shelving, or conservation, the behind-the-scenes workspace needs to be tailored to the work flow patterns of the particular institution. As with office space, be assertive in communicating staff needs to the designers. The result will be more usable if the designers know that book and documents processing needs a four-foot-by-eight-foot work surface with space for a supply truck.

Be sure to poll staff members as to preferences for chairs with or without armrests. Caster chairs add little to the cost but offer much-appreciated mobility. And adjustable seat heights can make the difference between a workspace that is ergonomic and one that causes back pain.

Final Recommendations

Assume nothing! Review each drawing carefully, and even consider making paper mockups of desks and other service points. Learn to use an architect's scale to assess the dimensions of spaces, furnishings, and equipment. Notify the architects and designers in writing of problems, concerns, and suggestions. This is the time to use electronic mail rather than the telephone. And refer to the architectural program as a functional checklist.

Try not to let the architects prevail if you strongly disagree with aspects of their design. The quest for a rational design may oversimplify the problem. Don't be easily convinced that storage is unnecessary or that pearl gray silk is a durable upholstery textile.

And finally, exploit the project as a promotional opportunity. Post "before and after" images at entrances. Photograph the work in progress frequently, and acquire a three-dimensional rendering from the designers. Develop a website or blog with design and construction updates.

Conclusion

Shaping library space is an energizing experience for those privileged to participate. Therefore, engage as many of the library's staff members as you can in the planning and design development stages. Gather and review information thoroughly. Plan the job to take twice as long as anticipated. And be prepared in the end to settle for less, bearing in mind that any improvement to the library environment adds value.

Notes

1. Lee Rainie, Kathryn Zickuhr, Kristen Purcell, Mary Madden, and Joanna Brenner, "The Rise of E-Reading," Pew Internet: Pew Internet & American Life Project, April 4, 2012. http://libraries.pewinternet.org/2012/04/04/the-rise-of-e-reading.

2. Adam Gordon, "Books Are the Widgets of University of Chicago's Mansueto Library," *Forbes*, June 24, 2011.

3. Gary L. Reynolds, "The Impact of Facilities on Recruitment and Retention of Students," *New Directions for Institutional Research* 135 (2007): 67–70, doi:10.1002/ir.223.

4. Henry Dreyfuss, *The Measure of Man: Human Factors in Design* (New York: Whitney Library of Design, 1967).

Further Reading

Gisolfi, Peter. "Melding Minds to Make a Library: Successful Libraries Are Designed Collaboratively." *American Libraries* (September/October 2013).

McNamara, Paul. "Teaching and Learning Spaces: Refurbishment of the W. K. Hancock Science Library at the Australian National University 2011." *Australian Academic & Research Libraries* 43, no. 1 (March 2012): 46–55.

Nelson, Mark S. C. "Tools for Space Analysis and Design." PowerPoint presentation, University of Wisconsin, Space Studies Department, Madison, WI, 2011.

Redesigning the College Library Building. New York: Primary Research Group, 2014.

Chapter 7

How to Rejuvenate a Neglected Library

Jeff Guerrier

Overview

Over the last twenty years I have managed, at different times, three small art libraries: two in small art museums and one in a department of a major art museum. I have also worked on four small private collections, one of which was exclusively an art library. In all these positions I was the sole librarian; in some I was the only person in the library and, although my official titles varied—library manager, head librarian, librarian/archivist—the essential job was the same: to run it and make it better.

I began each position following some sort of organizational disconnect between the time or work style and perceived efficiency of my predecessors' performance. Each of the libraries was limited by budget, space, and support staff. My personal experience spans a fiscally difficult period for most cultural institutions as they faced severe cuts in government funding and then, worse, the Great Recession. Even as the economy began to improve, many of the positions that were eliminated as well as much of the traditional funding allocations were not reinstated, mostly because new technologies called for reprioritized spending.

In each instance, my job was to build or rebuild a small, underfunded (or newly funded) art reference library with a history of less-than-enthusiastic institutional support. This chapter addresses the experience of an incoming solo head librarian in a small museum library, addressing many simple organizational tasks and responsibilities, and the challenges of building on and maintaining a collection, its accessibility, and services.

Challenges to Job Satisfaction in Art Museum Libraries

There are some issues that may be obstacles to accomplishment as well as job satisfaction in an art museum library, but you should consider them to be challenges that can provide positive interaction through the process of change:

- These positions, because of limited budgets and/or lack of prioritization by the museum, are often part time.

- There may be situations where the museum has not previously employed a librarian for its reference collection, which often means that there is a very weak or no digital catalog, no bibliographic control, or no formal organization of the materials.

- It is likely that volunteers and/or staff members from one of the administrative divisions have been responsible for basic library maintenance. These individuals with little or no library or bibliographical knowledge or experience most likely created a very eccentric system of management.

- All too often the professionals and support staff of museum administration have a rather simplistic concept of what is required to maintain a research library. They usually base these simple assumptions on their own user experiences in academic and museum environments where all their research and reference needs are readily provided by a mostly untrained staff of student-workers.

Beginning to Rebuild

After you've been introduced to primary museum staff, had your once-over of the museum facility, and looked around the library itself, it is essential that you begin to assess the library's overall situation.

In the transition period of your new position, you must try to maintain the day-to-day services of the facility. Assessment of every aspect of the facility, both functional and physical—the business and the "being there"—are all important, all at once. Where to begin?

The three steps or phases of initiating the process of assessment and familiarization are: (1) perusal of the "books," (2) establishing relationships, and (3) taking control of the operation.

Perusal of the "Books"

The "books" are the operating, procedural, policy, mission statement, and budget "books," as well as the library's and the museum's strategic plans. You must also execute a cursory scan of the collection catalog itself, whether an online public database, a physical card catalog, or some of both.

Normally, there will be documented procedural guides for every aspect of managing the library: acquisitions, cataloging, style guide, patron access, opening and closing, reference, and any aspect of the library that requires consistency of operation. Hopefully, these will easily be found in or around the librarian's workspace, or they may be in digital format in the office PC (hopefully there *is* an office *and* a PC). These documents are invaluable to you as tools to bring you up to speed as to operations. The lack of some or all of them is another kind of useful information, indicating, perhaps, that the library has likely had a fairly low priority with the museum's administrators, the staff, and other potential users. It suggests a loosely regulated access regime that could mean less-than-reliable collection data. Do not jump to conclusions. This is one of the issues you can address when you meet with the organization's principals, as I discuss later. It also creates an opportunity for you to exercise your management skills, as you will have to be the one responsible for codifying the procedural rules.

There may also be various policy guides for users, researchers, students, and visiting patrons. You may find that some guides are printed hard copy and some in digital format available on the museum's website or simply the in-house workstations. That depends on who created them and when. At this early stage of your new position, it is only necessary for you to read through these in order to understand your responsibilities and user history.

As policy is an intrarelational factor in library management, its lack indicates an inconsistency of staff access, public relations, and administrative participation. The policies that govern the operations of a library and the work of the staff are both essential guidelines and histories of the processes and user expectations. A policy statement delineates the regulations, the dos and don'ts, of who, when, and how the library may be used. Again, at the beginning of your new job, you will not have the time for a thorough study of these documents; however, a quick once-over will give you an introduction to what you need to know to keep the library up and running while you are assimilating your new responsibilities. They will give you an idea of the level of material respect that your predecessor, the museum's administration, and staff have for this research and reference collection.

The funds available for the library's operations are almost certainly spent as regards any projection you can make once you have compared the money budgeted with the various procedures and designated expenditures as well as where you currently are in the present fiscal year. So you are going to have to understand how the available funds are proportioned for the several facets of the library's current operations. The budget is not only about the amount you have to spend; you must also consider the presently due invoices. This is where the remaining fiscal year's budget is going. Before you can begin to consider your own plans for building the collection and expanding services, you will have to pay the bills.

If you have had limited budgeting experience prior to this position, you will need to talk to the museum's chief financial officer for instruction or, if available, your predecessor. In most small museum libraries, the library's manager does not process invoices directly. Accounts payable are usually sent to the finance office for payment.

The museum's strategic plan will help you to understand how the organization sees the function of the library therein as well as the level of their commitment to that role. An organization's strategic plan is usually a five-year projection of its development and growth plans, considering every aspect of its operations, exhibitions, collection development, and so on and the budget entailed. The plans are not immutable, and it is understood that there may be alterations as circumstances change.

Each division of the museum will have produced its own section of the strategic plan, and that may include the library as either a separate entity or as a subdivision of another division, such as education or development. Whatever the arrangement, your predecessor certainly participated in the plan. From my personal experience, I suggest, as you progress past the early days of your tenure, that you should continuously be creating a strategic plan; make notes of realized issues and relevant ideas.

A document that every cultural organization must have is the mission statement. Even a small art library needs to state its purpose, its reason to exist. Most mission statements are one paragraph. The mission should be clearly and concisely worded and should not include policy, procedure, or protracted explication on any of the many aspects of the organization. It will be helpful to you to first read the mission statement of the museum, which may be available on the website. If the library has no mission statement, make it a priority to create one as soon as possible with, of course, the cooperation of the relevant museum administrative staff.

There are plenty of other factors to consider, but you've got to become fairly fluent in the library's present "business" as well as its recent functional history as quickly as possible. But at this early stage, just shoot for a general familiarity. You don't have to completely immerse yourself, at least not yet.

Establishing Relationships

Introduce yourself to your staff, paid or volunteer, if any, as well as to the department heads of the museum. With regards to your staff, get a sense of their personalities, their background, and their experience working in the library. Support and volunteer staff can be an invaluable source of information; they may be able to fill you in on the procedures and policies that are lacking, have insights as to the user base, and give you a history of the place of the library in the administration's level of support.

Next, you need to speak with the curatorial staff, who would likely be the biggest users of the library. Ask them about how they use the facility. Get their perspective on what is good and what is lacking there as regards collection quality and relevance and need for online reference and research tools (usually accessible via paid subscriptions). Let them know that you will work with them on improvements and consider possible projects. These conversations will provide you with the foundation on which to begin to build the collections, improve and develop services, and even expand the facility. In a small museum, especially, speaking with and liaising with other departments' supervisors and staff can lead to particularly constructive cooperation and collegiality. In a museum setting, you should meet with the director of each administrative section and/or department: finance, development, operations and facilities, education, registrar, volunteer, museum shop, and any other. Again, their policies and perspectives, as well as their attitudes toward the library, are very important factors in your understanding of how the library fits into the museum's life and business, as well as guiding your immediate and long-term management and development. Be professional and collegial, and make friends.

It is likely that the first administrative representative you have already had a meeting with was the museum's director. He or she will have shared perceptions of the library's role in the organization and probably also delineated a mandate with which you are to execute his or her vision as well as setting some parameters for making your own contributions.

In the case of a departmental library, your colleagues—the curators and administrative assistants—are the people to talk to.

Taking Control of the Operation

The library cannot run itself, and more to the point, the museum or department cannot manage it at anywhere near an efficient and professional level, or they would not have hired a professional manager. Don't be afraid to make mistakes, but it is probably best to simply make sure that it is, in the beginning, at least business as usual. Until, that is, you catch your stride and begin to make constructive improvements and develop more efficient procedures.

Next Steps

There are several other factors to consider as you begin to orient yourself into the life of the library. Some may be, or have been, in place and some not. Some are rather ordinary, and some may push the envelope a bit. You will need to determine, in the course of time, what and whether to reinitiate or introduce.

Online Public Access Catalog (OPAC)

One of the tasks that may have been emphasized in appointing you library manager may well be the development of a publically accessible electronic "card" catalog of the books and other research materials of the collection. You might have to start from scratch, researching and developing a plan, selecting a service provider, and working with the finance department on a budget. The budget would not usually be available until the next fiscal year, so you will have some time to plan before having any money with which to execute.

In some cases, there may be an electronic catalog that includes only a small portion of the collection with the difference still in card format or other incomplete condition. Converting a card catalog to a digital format, called retrospective conversion or RECON, can be rather expensive, and you need to research services, compare prices, and write a proposal for the administration to consider.

Electronic Reference/Research Resources

Through your discussions with the museum staff, you will discover to what extent they would like to have more access, or any at all, to web-based bibliographic tools, visual resources, and journal indexes. The library, or the museum itself, may already have subscriptions to some of these services, or the library may have some disk-format reference materials. You will need to evaluate these with the assistance of, particularly, the curatorial staff and then research the various services and their cost and, again, write a proposal.

Library Committee

Having a small group of supportive people who can bring you ideas for expansion of services or space is invaluable for validating library initiatives. If there is not one already established, you should discuss the subject with the museum's director. Candidates for the committee should be drawn from concerned staff, trustees, and community members who have expressed an interest in the library's well-being.

Newsletter

Although not a common feature even among large special libraries, newsletters are an efficient and open medium for communicating with and engaging the museum's staff and community. Include announcements of new book acquisitions, events, exhibits, and services.

Collection Display

Exhibits are low-effort and low-maintenance, invaluable ways to showcase various special objects, collections, and thematic surveys. They can feature supporting material for museum exhibitions. They are a tool for attracting museum staff who may not be aware of the collection's depth, as well as library and museum visitors. This is where your positive liaising with the curatorial department pays off. The registrar's—often a division of curatorial—expert advice in object description is indispensable. The department's art handlers may be willing to provide display cases, proper mounts, and framing. There will probably already be protocols in place that would require the approval of the curatorial department for any sort of exhibit, especially when related to a special museum exhibition.

Information Kiosk and Signage

A few signs placed in contextual locations throughout the museum may be an effective tool for advertising and drawing in new library users. A kiosk may be placed by a museum entrance or the museum shop, featuring an interactive touch screen with all of the aforementioned newsletter items. An effective signage program may help to justify the library's funding and help to increase the budget by increasing patronage.

Suitable and Sufficient Research Hours

Internal museum staff should have ready access to the library's collections and must somehow be accommodated even when the librarian is not on duty. But this kind of loosely monitored open-access precedent can undermine every aspect of the collection. Consultation with staff and administration should produce rules that are workable to all parties. Recruiting volunteers to cover more library hours is a practical solution.

Archival and Rare Materials Management

This may or may not be an immediate priority, depending on the condition of archival and rare materials. If they have been stuffed into labeled file boxes and stacked in the museum's basement or stored off site, the librarian should make a priority of arranging and preserving the collection and creating finding aids.

Conservation/Preservation Services

It is more than likely that your predecessors dealt with book conservation and preservation and book binding and repair through an outside contractor. For major conservation services, you may wish to continue that policy. For simple repairs, however, setting up a small, dedicated preservation workstation is fairly easy and inexpensive to maintain basic usability.

Physical Plant

A library in a small art museum is usually going to have very limited physical space and not likely to have any place into which to expand. The same applies to small departmental libraries in larger museums. In most situations you will be acquiring more books and other research materials as expected by the administration as well as according to your own self-directed expansion of the collection.

There are three ways to approach the problem of limited space: (1) creatively identify areas within the library's footprint that can be rearranged to create more shelf, file, or cabinet space or workspace; (2) initiate a weeding project with the dual goal of freeing up space as well as deaccessioning outdated information; and (3) lobby the administration or supervisor for more external space and/or relocation. Ultimately, your ability to think and act creatively when it comes to spatial expansion and management will provide you with a sense of self-satisfaction, organizational respect, and a palpable legacy.

Tip: If the library has no mission statement, make this a priority.

Tip: Quickly establish relationships with staff, volunteers, and library users.

Tip: Take control; don't be afraid to make mistakes.

Tip: Promote library awareness with newsletters, displays, signage, and an information kiosk.

Conclusion

As a solo librarian in a small library within a larger organization, such as a museum, you may not be absolutely in charge of every aspect of, but you are certainly completely responsible for, management style and overall management.

Part II
Finance and Budgeting

Chapter 8

How to Devise a Fund-Raising Plan

James Anthony Schnur

Overview

Libraries provide access to resources and services that have value to their patrons. Public libraries sustain operations through some combination of ad valorem taxes, special assessments or taxing districts, allocations by consortia, state and federal aid or recurring funds, a variety of grants and external funds, and donations directly to the institution as well as to nonprofits with a mission to support the institution (such as "Friends" groups). Archives and special libraries often serve as specific clientele and may impose limitations on access based on the types of collections available, the provenance of those collections, and any proprietary restrictions (such as a corporate archive that maintains sensitive market research data). Funding for archives and special libraries may come from a variety of sources, including genealogical and historical societies, public funds, foundations, or budgetary allocations within a company or organization. Small college and university libraries derive funds from a blend of external sources and internal funds that may come from tuition and student fees. Each of the library types must operate under a budget that accounts for a variety of expenditures related to the physical plant, personnel (both paid and unpaid), collection management (both physical items and electronic resources), and other operating expenses. Budgetary challenges in recent years have, generally speaking, forced libraries of all types to reevaluate services, staffing, and collections as traditional funding sources have declined. In such an environment, the small library manager must recognize possible fund-raising strategies within the organization as well as through external partnerships and relationships that will allow for uninterrupted continuity of operations.

This chapter suggests practical advice that hopefully will assist smaller public libraries, academic libraries, and archives. Rather than offer a shopping list of websites or grant resources that may no longer exist a few years from now, this chapter outlines a variety of personal approaches and organizational strategies that will assist managers of small libraries and archives as they confront budgetary challenges.

Be Proactive

Oftentimes, library managers have to react to budgetary crises and immediately investigate fund-raising opportunities without having a chance to develop a proactive game plan. As you review the suggestions outlined on the following pages, consider the adage "A little planning can go a long way," as it applies to so many things in life. For those who live in areas prone to hurricanes, stocking up on drinking water, canned food, batteries, and other essential provisions before the hurricane season allows those who plan ahead to move forward with their survival plans while others struggle to find an open store or gas station. In similar fashion, some proactive planning allows library managers to have the data, guidelines, constituents and their resources, and support organizations in place before the warning signs appear on the horizon.

Gather Measurable Data

Library managers must compile or gain access to relevant data. As resources have diminished and budgets have tightened, funding and granting agencies at all levels now emphasize quantitative research, measurable outcomes often tied to assessments or survey data, and descriptive narratives that paint a clear image of the information presented. While generic appeals, such as "The library is the heart of the campus," and anecdotes, such as "All residents benefit from our public library," might have carried some emotional value in the past, these general statements do little to impress funding authorities and other external groups unless measurable proof of the validity of these comments accompanies them. The ability to deliver solid—if not irrefutable—data becomes even more important if the library manager senses any antagonism or skepticism on the part of those who will pass judgment on funding based upon information provided to them. One must walk carefully across the data minefield so that the information presented does not seem too overwhelming or have a patronizing or condescending tone, lest those who we share the data with dismiss our efforts as an attempt to "confuse them with statistics."[1]

How do we gather data, what do we do with it, and how do we keep it handy? In smaller libraries where managers also serve as reference librarians, one must view the process of locating data in similar fashion to answering a challenging reference question from a patron. Primary source documents, such as demographic data, and statistical measures compiled by other bodies (e.g., statistical abstracts and statistics compiled by the state library association) offer an obvious starting point. The library management system, database vendors, online tracking software (such as Google Analytics), and the "numbers" collected within the building—such as daily door counts—also give library leaders data that can assist with short-term initiatives and long-term fund-raising efforts. For example, if a small library faces pressure to expand evening hours while funding declines, having hourly door counts may offer strong evidence that the demand perceived by some parties does not correlate with the actual usage patterns. Remember that some jurisdictions may consider any data collected by institutions receiving public support as a government document subject to public records requests, so make sure that any annotations or commentary regarding this data remains separate (i.e., not written alongside) from those documents until it moves from a "draft" form to something shared with governing bodies or other constituencies. Digitized versions of the data, if from public sources, may reside in a digital archive in similar fashion to the way paper public documents may occupy space in the reference or government documents area, but links to and collections of data may also reside in a shared drive or other place where the library manager can retrieve it without delay.

Develop Strategic Plans and Missions

With data that supports the library's mission, library leaders should then reevaluate strategic plans and missions, as well as policies and guidelines that govern operations. In most cases, the library's official strategic plan may require involvement and approval with other bodies, such as a college's board of trustees or a city council. Although the strategic planning process often seems frustrating or an unnecessary diversion when the limited library staff has more pressing things to do, a strategic plan developed with a wide variety of stakeholders provides the library manager with evidence of a mission, defines the library's role and scope, and enumerates its constituents. While many plans include overarching statements about "fostering community literacy" or "supporting the academic mission," strategic plans revised from this point forward should also illustrate how these things will occur by citing measurable protocols and objectives. In addition to ensuring that the strategic plan is vibrant and vital, the library manager should work with staff, patrons, and other stakeholders as is appropriate to ensure that various policies and guidelines reflect present realities rather than idyllic dreams. For example, libraries use a variety of approaches in crafting their collection development and management plans. Some libraries create encyclopedic documents that define acquisition practices and collection intensity by detailed call number ranges, while other libraries have a document that fits on a single page. Regardless of the path taken, the important thing library managers must consider is that guidelines and policies in places reflect—as much as possible—the present financial reality so that, if funding sources dwindle, we can explain this circumstance to our patrons and key supporters in a way that they can serve as allies rather than angry antagonists.[2]

On many college campuses, library leaders have to explain why their budgets cannot cover the cost of providing copies of the required textbooks used on campus. Sometimes library leaders have to repeat their explanations every semester as new student government leaders plead for us to find a solution to a situation we did not create, especially since the selection of texts usually falls upon the faculty teaching the class or academic departments for common courses. By having guidelines in place—especially if student government wants to launch a textbook program—as well as having verbiage in place that supports open access for faculty who wish to explore less-expensive alternatives for students, we may "fund-raise" by finding other partners to assist in funding an expensive project or reducing costs through open access.[3]

Consider the Influences of All Constituents

Managing data and envisioning our strategic role will mean little if the library manager fails to consider the influences of internal and external constituencies and the resources they control. In the earlier examples, students, faculty, and members of the community served by a public library serve as obvious constituents. Other constituencies also play a role in the library's operations: From the governor and legislature or college president and board to the county commissions and city councils, the library manager must understand how various executive and representative bodies affect our pocketbooks directly through allocations or indirectly through unfunded mandates and expectations that fall into our laps. We also need to understand how we can reply to their actions, both in the political and practical sense. The suggestions provided thus far help us prepare our "survival kit," and in most instances we can reply through appropriate channels to the budgetary and policy-making decisions that affect the library's operations.[4]

However, in some jurisdictions, public employees—including library managers, directors, or deans—may face restrictions or prohibitions on the use of public assets, such as computers, e-mail accounts, or telephones, at work if they want to "state their case" or otherwise lobby for resources. Private and public academic library leaders may have to articulate their message through a provost, dean of academic affairs, or other intermediate step rather than directly to the school's president or trustees. If a library manager is uncertain of both the legal and practical boundaries they must adhere to, and oftentimes those are measured differently, it behooves them to talk with colleagues or others familiar with knowing where their advocacy should reside and where it should never take place.[5]

While securing resources from external constituencies often seems daunting, it becomes almost impossible if the library manager cannot influence internal constituencies, those closer to home, such as public library boards, faculty governance groups, or obvious community and collegiate leaders. Just as our data should clearly articulate the present-day realities under which we operate and our plans, policies, and guidelines should reflect current best practices for the library, our local governing boards become most effective when they represent the diverse interests our facility serves at the present time. While strategies for dealing with uncooperative boards and irrational members often require individual interventions rather than a generic approach, the time and effort necessary to have internal constituencies buy into advocating for the library's present and future fiscal needs may be one of the most difficult challenges with developing the infrastructure to carry our plan forward. The administrator of a small academic library will require similar efforts while working with student and faculty leaders. Library managers have to take a proactive role to inform faculty of the services the library offers; for example, some faculty who rely exclusively on databases and electronic resources the library pays for out of its materials budget may not understand that budget cuts could require the cancellation of those subscriptions. Likewise, we must educate faculty at regionally accredited schools that any plans they have for new course proposals and academic majors and minors should involve an evaluation of their impact on library resources. A public health minor may seem appealing to college enrollment managers seeking students and faculty hoping to diversify their course inventory, but adding that program will have a heavy impact on library spending.[6]

The Role of "Friends" Groups

Finally, the library manager must assess the role of support organizations in the context of the evolving political and economic circumstances affecting the library. For most public and many academic libraries, the "Friends" of the library represents this group. With some archives, a local historical society or similar group may serve in the same role as the "Friends." Similar to everything previously mentioned, the library manager will have an easier time establishing a fund-raising regimen with a "Friends" group that is aware of library usage patterns, the institution's plans and guidelines, the resources we have available, and how the decisions of others may affect their allocation and disbursement. Almost always voluntary in nature and usually nonprofit and tax exempt in status, these "Friends" groups offer library administrators an alternate conduit for holding funds, for securing resources, and for collaborating with other groups in a way that often provides more latitude and fewer institutional restrictions.[7]

Similar to building a case with local governing bodies and nearby constituencies, the library manager needs to articulate the library's mission and to explain the role of the "Friends" in supporting our operations and fund-raising initiatives. This may be easier said than done if the leadership of the "Friends" or the most active members in the group have grown accustomed to following the same path and become unreceptive to new ideas. In such circumstances, the "Friends" may devolve into the "Enemies" of the library's fund-raising efforts. While the scholarly literature and professional organizations, such as the American Library Association, offer helpful suggestions for working with "Friends" groups and keeping their members engaged (such as targeting "empty-nesters"), the small library manager will, at a minimum, want to consider a few important first steps. A "Friends" group, historical society, or similar entity that lobbies on behalf of and offers support for a library or archive must observe any local or state regulations involving fund-raising, such as securing and maintaining a charitable solicitation permit, registering with the state's Department of State or similar office, and acquiring whatever permits may be required for it to sell materials and collect (and report) sales tax. If the organization maintains tax-exempt status in the United States, it should also provide evidence of filing appropriate documents with the Internal Revenue Service and equivalent office(s) at the state and local levels. Since the "Friends" group operates in an established relationship with the library, it must provide evidence that it stays in compliance with any laws or regulations that govern its conduct. Bylaws should reflect the organizational needs of a "Friends" group, configured in a way that it serves our library's present needs, not the library of yesteryear. This may mean that revisions of the bylaws remove ineffective or outdated provisions, such as "lifetime" memberships for a one-time fee of fifty dollars. The library manager should encourage the cultivation of new leaders, including succession planning, so that a single person or group of officers does not have, in effect, a "life sentence" in the "Friends." We need leaders who understand our ever-evolving mission rather than just those who became involved because they "loved books" or sought a social outlet. Some of our work with the "Friends" may require that we observe rigid boundary issues, especially if the bylaws state that the library manager's role remains ex officio in practice.

After gathering data, clarifying the library's mission, evaluating constituencies and the resources they control, and understanding the potential for support organizations to advocate on our behalf, the library manager can consider appropriate grants, "shovel-ready" initiatives, and obvious marketing and lobbying efforts, as well as paths and plans to avoid. In addition to the groups already mentioned, the library manager may explore interim or long-term partnerships with specific constituencies who have an interest in a certain area of the collection or facet of library operations. Thus, a local genealogical society may offer to provide volunteers and even monetary donations to preserve and expand the genealogy materials in a public library. A campus club or student organization may partner with the college library's "Friends" group during a book sale. One important point we should remember: Volunteers may give of their free will, but nothing in life is "free." In some cases, volunteers may need to go through some sort of screening, training, or other clearance. Also, we need to have a reliable mechanism in place to track their hours since the sum of their efforts, if calculated by the wages and benefits of a person who would perform comparable duties for pay, helps to put part of their effort into an actual measurement in dollars and cents.[8]

In most jurisdictions, volunteers at all levels—including members of the "Friends"—can help in another way. As residents and taxpayers, they may have the ability to lobby on our behalf in a way that regulations and statutes prohibit library managers and their staffs from doing.

The Role of Civic and Cultural Organizations

As library managers evaluate possible grants and external support as well as make their case to constituencies that offer resources, those working in public libraries should also consider other allies and the expanded expectations placed upon our facilities. In addition to the "Friends" group, public librarians may want to strengthen their ties with cultural heritage organizations or civic groups that value their service (such as a Rotary group that enjoys use of the community room). While public libraries have long supported the educational needs of schoolchildren, outreach to homeschoolers may also bring us allies willing to write letters or otherwise advocate on our behalf as private citizens. The growing demands and expectations of "e-government" services, a move in which many agencies with reduced staff now refer their clients to our libraries to apply for unemployment or other benefits, represents the latest phase of public libraries assuming the role of facilitating other government services. Before many agencies went paperless, most public libraries participated in initiatives such as BPOL (banks, post offices, and libraries), a program in which public libraries served as a venue that carried an array of state and federal tax forms and booklets. The point is clear: Public libraries have assumed a growing number of duties once handled by other governmental and social service organizations. Library managers must emphasize that inadequate funding jeopardizes those efforts.[9]

Academic libraries at small colleges and universities also face unique challenges. Most schools have a foundation or university relations office responsible for "prospect cultivation." The library manager needs to know when pursuing external resources (including library collections) requires the involvement of this office. For example, we may acquire a small donation of rare books from a donor, but if that person is "targeted" for a larger gift or has special status, such as a notable alumnus, we may have to forfeit our plans for a gift that will go to another part of the campus.[10]

Tip: Be proactive. Know who your support groups are before an emergency arises.

Tip: Develop meaningful strategies and guidelines that reflect best practices for your library.

Tip: Be friends with your "Friends" group.

Conclusion

As small libraries adjust to the so-called new normal of flat or declining budgets, managers of these institutions must seek new allies, resources, partnerships, and revenue streams. Rather than seeing this important challenge as another inevitable step toward our demise, managers of small libraries should reflect on the talents we have long had as educators, information professionals, liaisons to various information-seeking constituencies, and masters at diplomacy and collaboration. Instead of overextending ourselves in search of the mythical four-leaf clover that will save us, we should initially invest some time gathering data, strengthening our plans and operations, understanding those who influence the resources we receive, and those who can partner with us so that when clouds of uncertainty approach, our disaster-planning activities can get us through these financial storms.

Notes

1. Collecting accurate statistical data allows us to confront "phantom" budget cuts. See Terrance (Terry) Cottrell, "Three Phantom Budget Cuts and How to Avoid Them," *The Bottom Line: Managing Library Finances* 25, no. 1 (2012): 16–20, doi:10.1108/08880451211229171.

2. As the nature of "value" in libraries continues to evolve, sound planning works to our advantage. See Anthony McMullen, "The Value of Values," *The Bottom Line: Managing Library Finances* 26, no. 1 (2013): 4–6, doi:10.1108/08880451311321519.

3. Whether with textbooks or other resources, managers of small academic libraries must maintain communication with faculty and students, share

data, and explain how budgetary realities may affect the strategic mission. See Mary Ann Trail, "Evolving with the Faculty to Face Library Budget Cuts," *The Serials Librarian: From the Printed Page to the Digital Age* 65, no. 2 (2013): 213–20, doi:10.1080/0361526X.2013.802268; and Lynda James-Gilboe, "Raising the Library Profile to Fight Budget Challenges," *The Serials Librarian: From the Printed Page to the Digital Age* 59, nos. 3–4 (2010): 360–69, doi:10.1080/03615261003623112.

4. Grassroots advocacy only works if we know our communities. Though dated, this brief overview may inspire some ideas: Janet L. Balas, "Looking for Funds in All the Right Places," *Computers in Libraries* 26, no. 8 (September 2006): 23–25. Effective targeting of baby-boomers and empty-nesters may yield results as well. See Beth Dempsey, "What Boomers Want," *Library Journal* 132, no. 12 (1 July 2007): 36–39.

5. Federal and state regulations may prohibit nonprofit groups and professional organizations from certain types of advocacy. The creation of Every-Library (http://everylibrary.org) marks a new chapter in library activism. See John N. Berry III, "A New Weapon for Budgets," *Library Journal* 137, no. 16 (1 October 2012): 8.

6. Knowing our constituencies strengthens our ability at the task of "prospect cultivation," something we need to do more of today than in the past. See Susan Summerfield Hammerman, "The Basics of Prospect Research: Increasing Library Funding Opportunities," *College & Research Libraries News* 73, no. 10 (November 2012): 610–13; and Thomas Wilburn Leonhardt, "Key Donor Cultivation: Building for the Future," *Journal of Library Administration* 51, no. 2 (2011): 198–208, doi:10.1080/01930826.2011.540550. Although written more than a quarter century ago, at a time when "electronic resources" resided on mainframes, a quick glance at this source may refresh us on earlier trends on budgeting for academic library collections: Richard Hume Werking, "Allocating the Academic Library's Book Budget: Historical Perspectives and Current Reflections," *Journal of Academic Librarianship* 14, no. 3 (1988): 140–44. The newer trend of fees, including those levied on students, captures more recent literature: Cheryl Cuillier and Carla J. Stoffle, "Finding Alternative Sources of Revenue," *Journal of Library Administration* 51, nos. 7–8 (2011): 777–809, doi:10.1080/01930826.2011.601276.

7. The American Library Association offers helpful advice at the *United for Libraries* site maintained by the Association of Library Trustees, Advocates, Friends, and Foundations, (http://www.ala.org/united). See also John Eye and Vik Brown, "Establishing a Friends of the Library Advisory Board," *The Bottom Line: Managing Library Finances* 26, no. 1 (2013): 25–30,

doi:10.1108/08880451311321564; and Sara S. Lowman and Mary D. Bixby, "Working with Friends Groups: Enhancing Participation through Cultivation and Planning," *Journal of Library Administration* 51 (2011): 209–20, doi:10.10 80/01930826.2011.540551.

8. Libraries with local history and genealogy collections have long benefited from the presence of local genealogical organizations. See Donald S. Litzer, "Library and Genealogical Society Cooperation in Developing Local Genealogical Services and Collections," *Reference & User Services Quarterly* 37, no. 1 (1997): 37–52, http://www.jstor.org/stable/20863212.

9. A growing body of literature assesses the growth of e-government and its impact on public libraries. For example, see Paul T. Jaeger, Natalie N. Greene, John Carlo Bertot, Natalie Perkins, and Emily E. Wahl, "The Co-evolution of E-government and Public Libraries: Technology, Access, Education, and Partnerships," *Library & Information Science Research* 34, no. 4 (2012): 271–81, doi:10.1016/j.lisr.2012.06.003; Paul T. Jaeger and John Carlo Bertot, "Responsibility Rolls Down: Public Libraries and the Social and Policy Obligations of Ensuring Access to E-government and Government Information," *Public Library Quarterly* 30, no. 2 (2011): 91–116, doi:10.1080/ 01616846.2011.575699; and John Carlo Bertot, Paul T. Jaeger, Ursula Gorham, Natalie Greene Taylor, and Ruth Lincoln, "Delivering E-government Services and Transforming Communities through Innovative Partnerships: Public Libraries, Government Agencies, and Community Organizations," *Information Polity* 18, no. 2 (2013): 127–38, doi:10.3233/IP-130304. Regarding the decline in public library book budgets, see Steve Coffman, "How Low Can Our Book Budgets Go?" *American Libraries* 44, nos. 9–10 (September/October 2013): 48–51.

10. Development officers at colleges and universities often target units besides the library. We need to make a case for our corner of the campus. See Steven Escar Smith, "If No One Graduates from the Library, Then Who Are Its Donors? Some Reflections from an Accidental Academic Fundraiser," *College & Research Libraries News* 73, no. 10 (November 2012): 608–9. For a short discussion of fund-raising in academic libraries, see Samuel T. Huang, "Where There's a Will, There's a Way: Fundraising for the Academic Library," *The Bottom Line: Managing Library Finances* 19, no. 3 (2006): 146–51, doi:10.1108/08880450610682563. For a discussion of "Friends" groups in an academic library setting, see Frank D'Andraia, Jessica Fitzpatrick, and Catherine Oliver, "Academic Libraries and Friends Groups: Asset or Liability?" *Journal of Library Administration* 51, no. 2 (2011): 221–30, doi:10.1080/ 01930826.2011.540553.

Chapter 9

How to Write a Successful Grant Proposal

Sheila A. Cork

Overview

The thought of writing a grant proposal can be intimidating, yet as librarians we are often called upon to raise funds by writing a grant. These requests range from simple to complex: They can be a simple request to a "Friends" group for funding for a new piece of equipment, a request to a government agency for programming help, or a request to a private individual or foundation for major funding, such as new construction. Fortunately, grant proposal writing is a process, and with experience the process becomes easier.

In this chapter I start by briefly discussing the grant review process and then look at the elements that make up a grant proposal. The purpose of the chapter, however, is not to walk you step by step through the proposal-writing process: There are many free or subscription websites that can give you that information, and I have included URLs for some of them later. Rather, it is to give you general information about grant writing, information about planning your proposal, mistakes to avoid, and tips to make your proposal shine.

The Grant-Writing Process

The Grant-Review Process

In many private foundations and government agencies, grant proposals are often reviewed by several different people in a peer-review process. These people are grant reviewers or "readers." Reviewers will usually be well-educated professional people, but they may not be an expert in your particular field. They will not be aware of the specific jargon, acronyms, or "buzz words" associated with your type of librarianship. For example, if you talk about ILLs, they may not know that you mean interlibrary loans.

Readers may be assigned to one section of all the proposals received, for example, the narrative or the budget, and sometimes each reviewer will read the complete proposal. In either circumstance the reviewer then sends the best proposals forward for further discussion with a larger group of reviewers. Following this discussion, a percentage of the grants forwarded will be awarded funding.

During this process, their time is a valuable commodity. Grants that are clearly written, simple to understand, and to the point will have a greater chance of moving forward to the next stage. If the reviewer does not understand the proposal or thinks it has unrealistic goals or expectations, then the grant will be left behind. The grant reviewer has many applications to read, so cover all the requested information but keep your proposal short and concise. It is not the reviewer's job to make a compelling argument in favor of funding your grant; it is your job to do that.

There are many types of grant proposals and applications with more or less specific requirements, but most will contain some or all of the following elements.

Letter of Inquiry to a Private Foundation

This step is only applicable if you wish to apply to an organization that only accepts grant proposals by invitation. This does not mean that they will not fund you; in fact, they may be a perfect match for your project. This is the time to ask them to consider funding your project by writing a letter of inquiry. Your letter should describe your organization, what the need is, how you will resolve it, and how you will accomplish your program. If you have any partners for this project, mention them, and include the financial help that other organizations have promised to give you. The conclusion of the letter should be a request that the funder invites you to apply to them for funds for your project. If you are unsure of what to include in your letter, call the funding organization and ask. They will be happy to let you know.

Cover Letter

The cover letter is often your first introduction to the people who are funding your grant. It should be short and to the point; it should contain:

- The amount of money you are asking for and the reason you are asking for it. For example:

    The Library of Anytown requests $10,000 in funding to update the library's science resources. The library will partner with local school-teachers and school librarians to select books, journals, and electronic resources and make them available to local students and educators during the next school year.

- Brief background information about your organization, an explanation of why your organization is doing this, and how it fits in with the mission of the organization.

- The name, title, and contact information of the people who will be involved in the project funded by the grant and also for the project administrator.

- The name, signature, and contact information of your organization's director. Even if we run a one-person library we do not operate in a vacuum. Your library will have someone that you must report to. It is this person that I am referring to when I use the term *director*.

The Narrative

The narrative is the section that answers the questions Who? What? Where? When? Why? and How? Who are we? What are we going to do? Where are we going to do it? When are we going to do it? Why are we going to do it, and how are we going to do it? It is the description of everything to do with your project. It includes the needs statement, the abstract or summary, the goals and objectives, your evaluation methods, your project activities, and budget.

Statement of Need

This states what the problem is and what you will do to correct it. For example:

    Twenty percent of the science books in the Anytown Library are more than twenty years old. Sixty percent of the collection are books more than ten years old. The library can no longer effectively support the curriculum of local schools. Anytown Library has entered into a partnership with the local school corporation, teachers, and school librarians from local middle and high schools to remove outdated books from the library's collection and replace them with newer titles, journals, and electronic resources. The electronic resources will be available via the Internet to students and educators in Anytown Library, in their schools, and in their homes.

Abstract or Summary

Think of the abstract as the "elevator pitch" of your proposal. Develop a brief statement about your organization, the project that needs funding, and why it is important to your community. Put the amount of money you need in the first sentences of your abstract:

> Anytown Library needs $10,000 to replace outdated science books (80 percent of the library's science collection). The library serves 1,500 middle school and 1,000 high school students and is a resource for students and educators in local schools. Local public library and school funding have been cut, and neither the school library nor the public library has the money to update this section of the collection. The librarian has partnered with the heads of the science departments and the school librarians of the local high school and middle school to identify outdated books and select current books and science databases for Anytown Library's collection.

When you have completed the abstract, give it to someone completely unrelated to the project to read. Ask them to describe your project to you. If they have any difficulties, edit!

Goals and Objectives

This is where you describe the main purpose (or goal) of your project and the measurable steps (objectives) that you will take to make the project a success. For example:

Goals:

> The goal of this project is to provide current scientific resources to middle and high school students and educators.

Objectives: Objectives are the measurable steps you will take to achieve your goal. As you are writing them, make sure that you know how to evaluate their success or lack of success. These objectives are the way you will evaluate your project.

> Working with the school teachers and librarians, the Anytown librarian will:

- Order one hundred new science books for the collection. These books will have publication dates not more than three years old.

- Catalog, process, and make the books available to the students and teachers by the end of the fourth month of the funding period.

- Select and purchase four age-appropriate electronic databases for use in the library, the school, or at home.

- Track use statistics for books and electronic resources.

- Promote the new collection within the school, the library, and the community.

- Meet with teachers and school librarians quarterly to review the impact the new material has had on the student's grades.

Project Activities

What do you need to do to make the objectives happen? When do you need to do them by? This should be as detailed as possible and describe all the activities related to your proposal and time needed to accomplish them. For example:

> During the first week of the grant period, the librarian will meet with school-teachers at the Anytown Library and look at reviews of new science books. The librarian and teachers will then select approximately one hundred books to replace the outdated ones in the library's collection.

It is helpful to make a simple timeline for your personal use, and some funding agencies require a timeline as part of the proposal. Make sure that other program participants know of and approve the timeline, especially when the activity is something that they have to complete.

Evaluation

What are the ways in which you will know if your project has been successful? The evaluation should relate to your objectives (the measurable part of your proposal). They should be "outcomes" based: not how much of a thing you did but the effect of the thing. For example, your program may provide free nutritional supplements to toddlers. Your evaluation should not only include how much of the supplements you distributed but also how much healthier those children are. As you write your objectives, ask yourself "How will I measure these? What is the difference this project will make to the community?" Remember, your evaluation will be based on your objectives.

Information about Your Organization

This can be a boilerplate history of the organization. Include any major developments and achievements and community partners that you have worked with during past projects, and mention any previous grant-funded projects that have been completed, especially if they were with this organization. If you have a good track record with an organization, you are more likely to be funded again.

Budget

You will often have to write proposals for grants that have a matching-funds requirement. Usually those matching funds can be met by in-kind funds as well as the cash funds that your organization or partnering organization will give to the project. In-kind funds can include goods and services that your organization and your partner organizations will provide. All in-kind matching funds should be given a dollar value, for example, 18 hours' use of the auditorium at 150 dollars per hour (see table 9.1).

As well as a stated monetary contribution to the project from your library and partners, cash funds can include salaries of people involved in the project. It should show the percentage of time that each person will spend on the project and how that is worked out in terms of pay. Your grant guidelines will tell you if this should be the number of hours and dollar amount per hour or if it is worked out as a percentage of salary. Do not forget to add in social security payments and any other payments made on the employees' behalf. If you are not sure what or how to include this information, ask the funding agency.

Attachments

The attachments may include: biographies of the people who are working on the project, budget forms, census tables, samples of any survey forms, a copy of your organization's 501(c)(3) status (available from the IRS), a copy of your mission statement, and copy of your library's annual budget. If you have a community partner, you may have to provide this information from them as well. The best letters of support state exactly what contribution your partner will make to the project.

Whatever you include, your attachments should be well organized. Include them in the order in which they are mentioned in the application, and provide a contents page for them.

Submitting Your Proposal

You may think that, once your proposal has been completed, you can relax and that the hardest part has been completed. This is far from the case. Submitting the proposal can be one of the most stressful parts of the process. This is why it is important to leave yourself plenty of time (by *lying* about due dates) to

Table 9.1 Example of a Simple Budget Worksheet

Item	Explanation	Your Library	School Partner	Local TV Station	Funding Agency Contribution
School district publications dept. develop and print promotional material for project	Staff 5 hours @ $15 per hour	$0.00	$75.00	$0.00	$0.00
	500 color flyers @ $0.50 per flyer	$0.00	$250.00	$0.00	$0.00
	1/4 page local newspaper	$25.00	$0.00	$0.00	$25.00
	15-second television spot × 6 @ $500 per spot	$0.00	$0.00	$1,500.00	$1,500.00
2 Anylibrary associates supervising project implementation	3 hours each program × 6 programs = 18 hours @ $10 per hour × 2 associates	$360.00	$0.00	$0.00	$0.00
School district bus transportation	6 return rides from schools to library @ $250 per trip	$0.00	$1,500.00	$0.00	$0.00
Schoolteachers to accompany students	18 hours @ $15 per hour = $270 × 2 teachers	$0.00	$0.00	$0.00	$540.00
Whiteboards	6 × $30	$0.00	$0.00	$0.00	$180.00
Notebooks	$1 per student × 200 students	$0.00	$0.00	$0.00	$200.00
Facility Rental	Anytown Library meeting room 18 hrs @$75 per hr.	$1,350.00	$0.00	$0.00	$0.00
TOTALS		$1,735.00	$1,825.00	$1,500.00	$2,445.00

ensure that the application is sent to the correct person in the correct format at the correct time.

Consider these points:

- Do you have all of the necessary signatures and accompanying documentation? It is a good idea to have people sign the proposal in blue ink to make sure that you can easily distinguish between original signatures and copies.

- Have you collated your proposal correctly following all instructions for pagination?

- Did you make enough copies of it for everyone, including multiple copies for the funding organization?

- Does the proposal need to be sent by mail? If so, do you have the correct name and the complete mailing address including the correct ZIP + 4? Do you need to overnight it or get the package insured?

- If you have to send the proposal by FedEx or UPS, do you have the correct street address, name, and phone number of someone in the organization who the shipping company can contact?

- If filing the proposal electronically, do you have the correct e-mail address? Have you saved the different components of your proposal in the requested format? For example, you may write the proposal as a Microsoft Word document but may need to convert it to a PDF.

- If you are applying for federal funding, do you have the correct software on your computer? If you have the software, does it work, or is there a conflict with software already on your computer.

- Have you left yourself enough time to resolve any software conflicts or other problems with your computer?

Initial Preparation

Now that I have covered the review process, the elements of the proposal, and the proposal submission, I will go to the very beginning of the grant-writing process.

Planning

The worst way to apply for a grant is to see a call for funding and invent a project or program that you think will fit it. An unplanned approach like this often leads to a poorly written proposal and, if funded, poorly used funds, with badly planned documentation and methods of evaluation.

To prevent this happening, identify the problems your library needs additional funds to solve before you attempt to seek grant funding. Choose the most pressing issues, and start thinking of projects and actions that will resolve them. These will become funding requests that you develop and can convert into a proposal. Planning ahead will help you to resist the temptation to apply for a grant that has little or no relevance to your situation.

As you are planning a proposal, answer the following questions:

- Does the director of your organization approve of you seeking outside funding?

- Does the director of your organization approve of the project you wish to fund?

- Do you have time to write and administer a grant?

- Can your library legally accept grant funds? If your library cannot, is there another organization that you can partner with that can accept them on your behalf?

- Are you eligible to receive funds from the organization you are applying to? For example, has your organization been barred from seeking funding because previous grant-reporting obligations were unfilled? If so, how can you remedy this?

- Are you able to file the application yourself, or does a company grants officer need to file it for you? If so, how far in advance of deadline do they need to receive the finished proposal?

- Will you need to rely on other people to help with the writing and/or implementation of the project? If so, will they have the time and enthusiasm to do so? Will you be able to continue the project if a key person leaves?

- If you have to hire employees to carry out the project, will the grant cover their salaries, and are there people available to hire?

- Does your library need to provide matching funds? If so are they cash, in-kind, or a combination of both? Do you have the financial resources to match cash funds?

- Is the amount of funds available from this grant worth the time and money you will invest in putting together the grant proposal and implementing your project? For example, if you apply for a grant that brings you $1,500 in funds but you have to submit complex and lengthy monthly reports, have you really gained anything of value?

Making a "Toolbox"

Create a file folder on your computer in which you will keep information about your community, your organization, and your collections. Think of this as a "toolbox," a place to go to pull out facts that you can cut and paste into every proposal you write. Things that you might include in your toolbox are: a history of your library, your mission statement, community demographics, electronic signatures, board members and their affiliations, volunteer hours, brief staff biographies, library statistics, your annual report, and an electronic copy of your organization's 501(c)(3) tax-exempt status. Remember to update the information in your toolbox periodically.

Investing in a Multiyear Desk Calendar

On it put the dates of everything to do with the proposal, for example, when letters of inquiry and finished proposals are due and any webinar sessions or meetings that are required as a condition of application. Mark the dates when anyone involved with the project will be *unavailable*. This is particularly important in regard to the financial officer, the director, or anyone who needs to sign off on the completed application.

Does Your Project Fit?

Carefully review all the guidelines and eligibility requirements of the funding agency. Look at projects they have previously funded. If there is more than one of you writing the proposal, make a copy of these guidelines for everyone. Get together as a group, and decide if your project falls within the guidelines and if it is a truly good fit with the agency. Being ruthless with this will save you the loss of time and funds caused by submitting to an inappropriate agency. Look at the way in which the funders describe the programs they support. What words do they use? Are there any themes that occur frequently? If so, note these to use when you are writing your proposal.

Constructing Folders

Make a physical file folder and an electronic folder that contains the name of the funding agency and the granting period. These folders will be used to keep all the notes, guidelines, drafts, and correspondence with the funding agency, as well as your finished proposal, proof of postage, and reviews (if your proposal is reviewed by the funders). Make sure that you keep copies of all the returned draft copies that have been sent to you and the notes that accompany them. Identify on the draft whose notes they are.

Contacting Other People

Put together a list of people who will be involved in writing, managing, or implementing the proposal. This might be the city comptroller, staff from another local organization, or a department head in your organization. Let them know that you are writing a grant proposal and you need contributions from them. *Lie, lie, and lie* about the date your proposal is due. Make the date early enough to ensure that you to have time to review, edit, and submit it. If you are reluctant to lie, imagine a world in which you are scrambling to get pieces of the proposal together on the day it is due, having no chance to edit, and then your computer crashes (yes, this does happen).

Common Mistakes

The Planning Process

- Writing a proposal without having a properly thought-out project on which to spend it

- Not giving community partners sufficient information to enable them to make informed decisions about participating in your project

- Sending a proposal to a funder who is not the best match

- Promising things that you cannot accomplish

Writing and Submitting the Proposal

- Not leaving enough time to plan, collaborate, write, and submit the proposal

- Not thoroughly reading the instructions. Make sure that you follow the requirements for:

  Format

  Text style

  Text size

Margins

Sections to complete

The number of words

- Not writing in a clear and simple style—the simpler, the better

- Asking for funding to pay for things that are not covered in the grant, for example purchasing food and drink for launch parties when the grant only covers the cost of publications or purchasing computers and other equipment when the grant will only cover software

- Not having other people read the proposal

- Sending the proposal to the wrong person or place:

  What is the correct name and title of the person you are submitting the proposal to?

  Is the name of the foundation or granting organization spelled correctly?

  Do you have the right ZIP code—is the "+ 4" correct?

  Are you sending to a mailing address instead of a street address?

Use of Grant Funds

- Not getting agreements with community partners about the way the money should be allocated

- Not knowing that matching funds are needed

- Not allowing for the fact that the grant reimburses money that has already been spent

- Not spending all of the grant money

Remember:

- There is no such thing as a "small grant." All grant proposals need you to spend time planning, writing, submitting, and reporting.

- Keep track of dates when reports and updates are due and what form they should take.

- *Lie, lie, lie* to colleagues about due dates.

- You will lose credibility with your funder if you do not use all your money that they allocate to you. They would rather have you reallocate funds within the project than have you not use them. Contact them with your proposed changes, and get their approval.

- Buy a multiyear calendar, and put all due dates on it.

- Have other people read your proposal. Ask them to tell you what the project is and why you are asking for funding. If they cannot tell you, edit and rewrite until they can.

- Your proposal may be split up into sections for different people to read, some of whom have no specialized knowledge of your field. Keep your writing simple.

- There may be grant advisors that work for the organizations you are applying to. They are your friends. They want your proposal to succeed. If you have any questions about how to complete and submit the application, ask them for help.

- Just because you are allowed to write five hundred words does not mean that you have to. Keep it as brief as possible; your grant reviewer will thank you.

What Do You Do If You Get Funded?

Grant management is major part of the grant process. For a detailed description of this, please see Sheila Cork, "Grant Management: A How-To Guide," *Mississippi Libraries* 71, no. 3 (Fall 2007): 62–64.

Here are just a few suggestions:

- Write a thank-you letter to the organization that is giving you funding.

- Immediately fill out, sign, and return any paperwork that you have to submit.

- Notify everyone involved with grant writing and implementation. Make sure that they know when their grant activities need to be completed. *Lie* about this as well, especially for your final report.

- Look at all the reporting requirements. Note on your calendar when reports are due and the type of report it is. Make a note of the name of the person who has to write the report, and *lie* to them about the report due date.

- Make sure that you complete the final evaluation. It is for your benefit as well as that of the granting organization. It will let you know how to improve your programs for next time.

For the Future

Make a simple chart of organizations that you have applied to, the name of the project, if they funded you, and how much they awarded (see table 9.2). There are several reasons for this:

- It gives you a quick way to decide the organizations to which you will apply for funds in the future.

- Include this information on your résumé; update your résumé whenever you get another proposal funded.

- There is nothing like saying "I contributed $25,000 in grant funding to the library" during your staff evaluation to give you fuel for requests for pay raises and promotions.

Tip: Plan your grant-writing process thoroughly before beginning to write.

Tip: Collect necessary data in advance of the writing process, and place them in a separate folder for easy access.

Tip: Request funding from appropriate funding sources. Find the best match for your project.

Tip: Remember to spend all grant funds.

Resources

Purdue Online Writing Lab (OWL): Introduction to Grant Writing: https://owl .english.purdue.edu/owl/resource/981/1.

Non-profit Guides: http://www.npguides.org/guide/grant1.htm

The Center for Non Profit Excellence: http://www.centerfornonprofitexcellence .org/files/Needs%20Statement%20Toolkit%20Formatted.pdf

Table 9.2 Example of a Funding Achievements Chart

Date	Funding Agency	Which Staff Member	Program	Amount Requested	Amount Granted
March 2014	Small Library Funders	Children's Librarian	Summer Reading	$2,500.00	$2,000.00
August 2015	Anystate Humanities and Historical Org.	Library/Archives	Archival-Safe Storage for Big Donor Collection	$7,000.00	$5,000.00
	EZ Reading Dists.	Children's Services	New EZ Readers for Children's Dept.	$3,000.00	$3,000.00

The Foundation Center offers free webinars as well as paid courses about grant writing: http://foundationcenter.org/getstarted/learnabout/proposal writing.html. The foundation's publication *The Foundation Directory Online* (http://fconline.foundationcenter.org) is a useful resource if you will be writing a lot of grant proposals. The directory is expensive, so check for other organizations in your community that may have subscriptions, and see if they will let you use theirs.

The Grant Training Center offers some free information about grant-making institutions and has courses and workshops that are available for purchase: http://www.granttrainingcenter.com/workshops_list

The W. K. Kellogg Foundation Logic Model Development Guide is a great one—http://www.wkkf.org/resource-directory/resource/2006/02/wk -kellogg-foundation-logic-model-development-guide.

Part III

Cataloging and Managing the Collection

Chapter 10

How to Acquire Library Materials on a Tight Budget

Miguel Figueroa-Pagán

Overview

You may be familiar with the following situations: A child comes in asking for old magazines to cut out color images for assignments and homework. Your library administrators want to create a special collection of local history, but buying antique photos is too expensive. Remember that awesome database of medical images you saw at your last professional conference? It was the best one you had ever seen; your library needed it, and you yearned for it, but the price shocked you.

Maybe you don't need to buy the images; you can obtain them from free magazines and newspapers or from open images databases. Perhaps you can contact local experts that can lead you to collectors willing to donate, loan, reproduce, or digitize their own historical resources for your local collection. Do you know that one of the best databases of medical images available today, the Visible Human Project, is totally free?

All of these situations are examples of libraries' needs. The need to develop their collections, to add needed resources, to improve on library's deficiencies, to satisfy users' needs, to expand the scope of information resources, to stretch the budget. All of these needs can be categorized under the same label: collection development (CD).

A library of any type depends on several basic things to give a good service, such as a professional staff, a realistic budget, and an adequate building. One of the most important things is a good collection. Without one, it is impossible for librarians to do their job and for the institution to fulfill its mission. But to have a good collection, you should make a conscious and directed effort toward developing it. You can't just leave this to luck and goodwill.

Collection Development

Collection development is a process long recognized as one of the most important aspects of librarians' work. As long ago as 1925, Lionel R. McColvin wrote, "Book selection is the first task of librarianship." It remains one of the most important tasks of professional librarians.

Today, with the economic crisis still affecting library funding and with soaring prices for educational materials (both printed and digital), it is really important to save on acquisitions. This is especially critical for small libraries with their "relatively" small budgets.

I have always worked in small libraries with special characteristics, leading me to adopt several strategies to face the challenge of stretching the acquisition budget.

What Is Collection Development?

Collection development is the concerted effort to evaluate, select, and acquire resources to satisfy the needs of the community served by a library. According to author G. Edward Evans (2000), library collection development "is the process of meeting the information needs of the people (a service population) in a timely and economical manner using information resources locally held, as well as from other organizations." Basically, it is the process of continually evaluating your collection (books, magazines, movies, and all other items present in your library) to ensure that your library has what is needed by your users to satisfy their needs. To comply with this, the library staff must analyze the resources and the needs of the main users to be able to serve them or to correct the weaknesses detected (inappropriate resources or the lack of them) and plan how to address them.

A Collection Development Policy

A written policy is a tool for the staff to constantly evaluate the library collection and to strive to supply what is needed (see textbox 10.1). It serves as a guide and gives continuity to the process, even if staff members change over

Textbox 10.1 Collection Development Policy
_____ Library

I.   Introduction: Purpose and scope of policy

II. Responsibility for implementing policy

III. Guidelines for selection

   A. Criteria: relevant, need, forecasted use, authority, language, similarity to other items owned, cost, format (and special technical requirements), availability, currency, printing quality, shelf space available

   B. Sources of recommendations

   C. Format, language, multiple copies, replacement, retrospective materials

   D. Donations

   E. Special collections

IV. Discarding (weeding)

time. It can also be useful to explain to users and administrators the reasons for buying an item or not incorporating a specific resource type into the collection.

It's important to understand that a collection development policy is not an individual enterprise. It is a group effort, with input from librarians, users, administration, and faculty (if applicable). The policy must be in accord with the institutional mission. It must include the responsibility for implementation and the criteria for selecting and discarding materials.

The CD policy is not a static document but should evolve with time according to changes in composition of the library's community of users, needs, and technologies, among others. For example, if your college adds a new educational program, CD policy should change to accommodate the needs of this new program.

Examples of collection development policies for different types of libraries can be viewed on AcqWeb's webpage (http://www.acqweb.org/cd_policy.html).

Steps in Collection Development

Collection development encompasses several different steps, each one of equal importance. Typically, all steps are completed by the same staff (CD unit/group), and by definition it goes on a circular path: evaluation—selection—acquisition—evaluation—weeding—evaluation.

In other words, you evaluate to identify your strengths and weaknesses. Then you select and acquire resources to address the deficiencies. Finally, you re-evaluate to measure your success and to discard no-longer-needed material.

Evaluation

CD begins with the evaluation of your current holdings. What information resources do you have in the library? Are they enough in quantity and scope to satisfy your users' need? Are your items current or outdated? Are they pertinent to your mission? What additional resources do you need?

The function of evaluation is to show us the strengths and weaknesses of our library's collection. This can be done through several methods. We can compare our holdings against a checklist of core items for specific subjects or against the collections of similar libraries. Another method is the analysis of statistics for circulation or requests of items, which can tell us what our users' needs are. Expert opinion is also a way to analyze if your collection is up to the institutional mission; for this you can ask faculty and other experts to comment on the scope of your resources by asking whether the resources are enough for what the users require. By no means are these the only methods for evaluation. Others may include analysis of bibliographies or vendor sales reports.

A good evaluation tells you what part of your collection is strong and can help the library fulfill its mission. It also tells you what additional information resources your library needs to acquire. In summary, it tells you in what direction your process shall go.

Selection

As stated in the beginning of the chapter, not everything available and wanted can be acquired, and nor should it be. Some items may be too expensive, they may not be pertinent to your needs, or they may duplicate already-owned material. In addition, a resource may not be available in the language used by your community, or your library may not have the shelving space.

In that case, how do librarians choose what items to acquire and what not to? This is called *selection*, a process that needs to be defined beforehand with clear criteria on the written CD policy. To help with selection, there are several tools that can be used, including vendors' catalogs, publishers' webpages, online bookshops, other libraries' OPACs, or review sources. With these, you can see which are the highest-selling items or resources held in other libraries and assess the quality of usefulness of some resources by reading reviews. You can also use your staff's knowledge on specific subjects or publications. Finally, recommendations and requests from staff, faculty, and patrons are also useful.

What will guide you to choose one resource and reject another? This depends on the selection criteria set out in your collection development policy. This may include, but isn't limited to, need, cost, pertinence, currency, availability, similar items in the collection, awards obtained, and format. It is necessary to evaluate each item for each of these factors before making a decision (see table 10.1). This is a time-consuming task but critical if you want to save money by buying only the best and most pertinent material. It is important to notice that this is not a complete list; each library has its own criteria according to individual characteristics (see textbox 10.2).

Acquisition

The acquisition of the selected items can be done through different means. Some resources may be available at no cost, or you may buy locally or from outside suppliers. You may buy through standing orders or by discretionary purchases. Among free materials, you can get donations, free government or

Table 10.1 Checklist for Selection of Library Resources

	Yes	No
Item merit		
Pertinent to the institutional mission		
Needed		
Owning of similar items		
Cost (initial, shipping, and maintenance)		
Currency		
Availability of similar items by other means besides buying		
Physical quality of item		
Format		
Awards obtained		

Textbox 10.2 Taking into Account the Special Characteristics of Your Community

Sometimes, special characteristics can distinguish the community of a library. These can be language, ethnic origin, socioeconomic level, government institutions in the neighborhood, and so on. All of these must be taken into account when planning the collection development.

Language: Sometimes English is not the first language of a considerable part of your community. As you may imagine, language is a very important limiting factor, and if that's the case for your library, materials must be bought in the primary language of that group whenever available. If language is an important issue in your community, you should take it into account when selecting new material to add to your collection.

Government and special buildings: What schools, elder homes, or colleges exist in the area? Is your library the provider for these groups? Do the schoolchildren use your library as complementary to the school library? Does the public use your facilities for photocopying documents needed to ask for government services? The presence of all these buildings can impact the users you have and therefore your collection.

Social and economic conditions: You must consider these conditions when developing your collection. If your library serves a community with less-than-average income, maybe it will be the only source of reference books for the local students. What should your library acquire? Textbooks for college students or reading materials for children?

NGO publications, open educational resources (OER), or exchange of surplus material. There is no best way to get resources for your library, but one of the most important and useful things you can do to diminish expenses in the acquisition process is to tailor purchasing to your library's needs. Some libraries need standing orders, while others need to handpick each individual item. Some institutions have a relatively large budget for library resources, while others depend almost entirely on donations. Specific examples of acquisition strategies are discussed on the next section.

Weeding

Weeding is the process of deselecting materials from your collection and retiring them for various reasons. Why you should discard already-owned materials if the main idea is to acquire with less expense? Not all materials can remain indefinitely in your collection. Sometimes it is necessary to replace or discard damaged, obsolete, or no-longer-needed materials. This may be due to the publishing of new and updated materials that supersede old ones or the replacement of a damaged item with a newer edition. It can also be the result of the elimination of an old study program or the need for shelving space. What you need to understand is that weeding is a process as important and professional as selecting and should be done with the same care so you can be sure to retire obsolete materials but not useful ones.

How to Reduce Acquisition Costs

While it seems almost impossible to cope with diminishing budgets, the rising cost of materials, and stronger demands from users, it is possible to reduce costs while building your collection. You may even be able to save money when purchasing materials.

Tip: Discretionary Purchases or Blanket Purchase

While it represents more work, small libraries are better off making discretionary purchases than blanket purchases. The latter can add a lot of nonevaluated materials that may or may not be a good decision. Making discretionary purchases requires more work but in my experience is the only way to buy for a small library with a limited budget.

Tip: Compare Prices

You comparison shop when you have to make a big-ticket purchase for your home; you should do the same when purchasing for your library. Sometimes a simple comparison of prices between two or more vendors can add up to big savings.

Tip: Wait for Special Offers

If you aren't in a hurry to get an item, you can simply check and wait for a special offer from your vendors. Perhaps your local bookshop has a clearance sale for the holidays or a special sale on at the beginning of the school semester.

Tip: Purchase Locally

Buying your books and other materials at local stores can save money on shipping charges. Besides, when you buy directly from local businesses, you can examine the books before paying for them. Remember that the resource description in the catalog or webpage is intended to sell the item; it may not accurately describe its content. Sometimes you can even set a credit line with the bookshop for urgently needed materials.

Tip: Purchase Online

No contradiction here. Sometimes materials are cheaper when bought online, especially if you take advantage of free shipping. Don't hesitate to buy online if it's more cost effective than shopping at local bookstores.

Tip: Standing Orders

Decide beforehand on the convenience of setting standing orders (the automatic buying of updates for serials). For some small libraries, this is often a hindrance rather than an advantage as you will expend a lot and may end up receiving materials that are not essential. However, if your library has a budget for this, standing orders can save you a lot of work.

Tip: Select Formats

Sometimes this means buying hardcover books, which are more expensive but enjoy a longer lifespan than paperback books. If you are getting a book that you know will be heavily used, it may be more frugal to pay for a hardcover instead of buying a cheaper format and having to buy it again the next year due to wear. Another option is to acquire as many literary works from free digital sources, which can save you a lot of money in entertainment materials. Sometimes a digital resource can be an excellent option, but if it comes with the need for additional hardware or software, you will need to rethink it. On this, I recommend the use of common sense: What will work better for me at a lesser cost?

Publications Available at No Cost

You may obtain local publications at no cost, including newspapers and magazines, as well as commercial, NGO, guild, and local government publications. These materials usually cover local issues but often include information on tourism, education, sports, and culture. The collection of these materials often requires an active and focused effort from library staff, who must identify and search for these materials. In the long run, it may be easier to make them available electronically.

Free Government Publications

These publications include handbooks and other educational materials available upon request from state and federal governmental agencies. The themes can be as varied as civil rights, STDs, services for the elderly and the physically impaired, and grants for educational or commercial purposes.

Open Educational Resources (OER)

Open educational resources are materials that are in the public domain or protected by a license that allows for free use when used for teaching and research. These are materials made available by teachers, educational institutions, or professional associations. Often peer reviewed, they contain professional articles and journals, papers, classes, and even complete courses to use at your institution. Some of them may be downloaded, saved, and indexed, or they can be printed or even linked through your library's webpage. You may even modify and adapt many of them to your specific needs. These are an excellent alternative to expensive databases. As proof of the quality of OER resources, you may search at Ranking Web of Repositories (http://repositories.webometrics .info) for the MIT Institutional Repository, Jet Propulsion Laboratory Beacon Espace, Harvard University Digital Access to Scholarship, Europe PubMed Central, Cambridge University Institutional Repository, and RedALyC Estudios Territoriales.

Tip: Exchange, Trade, Barter

Exchanging duplicate or unnecessary materials with other institutions is another inexpensive way of acquiring materials. If you have an extra, unwanted copy of a novel, why not exchange it for a duplicate one from a neighboring library? Someone recently donated a second copy of a biology text to your library; why not exchange it for a chemistry text from a nearby university? This may be a time-consuming endeavor, but it is time well invested.

Gifts and Donations

These can come from individual users, institutions, and even from other libraries. People often want to give their books away to a good home and feel assured that a library is the best home. On occasion, an educational institution needs shelving space, and you can take advantage of this. A recommendation borne out of experience: Conditional gifts and donations are usually a bad idea, so don't accept them unless you have carefully evaluated the collection and its value to your library. You can go even further and promote your library's willingness to accept donations. This is a no-cost strategy that can lead to donated materials and something you can do both through posters at the library and posting on the library's webpage.

Puerto Rico: No Library Is an Island

All of my work experience has been in small libraries in Puerto Rico (junior colleges, colleges, universities, and special libraries). Due to their small size, I have learned to work with small budgets and to do wonders with them.

A U.S. territory, Puerto Rico is a noncontinental Spanish-speaking island. These geographical and demographic characteristics act as limitations that make the efficacy and efficiency of the selection and acquisition process even more important. Among these characteristics or limits are language and transportation costs.

According to the 2010 census, less than 20 percent of population of Puerto Rico is fluent in English. You can understand that language is a very important limiting factor, and materials must be bought in Spanish preferably over English whenever available. Being an island, all imports are dependent on sea transportation, so every domestic purchase of foreign materials includes a very high price increase due to shipping.

How do we cope with these?

Added transportation charges consume a big chunk of the budget, so small libraries either buy online or local in order to reduce shipping charges as much as possible. Online bulk-buying often makes it possible to obtain better prices and take advantage of free shipping promotions. If this is your case, don't hesitate to purchase nonlocally. It is not the library's job to subsidize the local economy. Your job is to get the most resources with your budget for the benefit of your community of users.

Local buying gives us two benefits. Not only does it eliminate shipping charges, but it also allows us to get Spanish materials without having to pay for costly translations. Book publishing in Puerto Rico is done almost exclusively in Spanish. Thus, one strategy can serve to tackle two problems: transportation charges and acquisition of Spanish-language materials.

Free items also represent a way to obtain big savings. In some libraries in which I have worked, these represented almost 25 percent of the acquisitions, so I have become a big fan of them. I never waste an opportunity to get free materials to include in our collection. Right now, four of the six newspapers at my library are free publications. Among other free materials that I collect for my library are brochures, health publications, government educational materials, open educational resources, free PDF books, tourism magazines, city official publications, and many others.

Tip: Your first obligation is to your library, not to local or independent sellers. Shop around for the lowest price, period.

Further Reading

The following are a few additional and useful resources available for study, both on collection development and on small libraries management.

Collection Development Training for Arizona Public Libraries (http://apps.azlibrary .gov/cdt)

> This is an excellent resource from the Arizona State Library. It contains a full training course on collection development for the staff of small public libraries. Materials on the website are organized in several modules that can be studied independently and include books, articles, a glossary, and even quizzes for self-evaluation. It's especially useful for training new staff as well as for the professional growth of collection development librarians.

Johnson, Peggy. *Fundamentals of Collection Development and Management.* 2nd ed. Chicago: ALA, 2009.

> A book on collection development for both students and librarians, it presents information on all aspects of the process, not only on selection and acquisition, but also on policy making and marketing. The interesting thing about this resource is the way it shows collection development not as an isolated process but as part of a whole in library management. Supplemental readings and several appendixes are big bonuses. Among the latter you will find selection aids, policies samples, and contracts and licenses terms.

Pearlmutter, Jane, and Paul Nelson. *Small Public Library Management.* Chicago: ALA. 2012.

> This 150-page handbook from the American Library Association is a complete course on management, specifically written for librarians working in small public libraries. It is organized in nine chapters that cover different aspects of management, including budget, staffing and services, and programs. It has a full chapter on collection development that includes the process of weeding. An interesting feature of the book is the section "Tales from the Field," which offers real-life examples from across the country on the topics discussed.

Bibliography

Evans, G. Edward. *Developing Library and Information Collections, 4th edition.* Westport, CT: Libraries Unlimited, 2000.

McColvin, Lionel R. *The Theory of Book Selection for Public Libraries.* London: Grafton, 1925.

Chapter 11

How to Evaluate, Build, and Maintain a Special Collection

Erica Shott

Overview

Developing and maintaining a collection for any small and special library will be a completely unique experience for every librarian. However, there are several concepts and ideas to consider that can help those unfamiliar with the small library, the industry that it supports, or how to develop and maintain a collection.

From gaining a complete insight into the type and purpose of your library to understanding your users and their habits, what to purchase, and how to create accessibility, as well as knowing how to maintain the collection, there are many important steps in collection management that must be analyzed carefully by a special librarian. Once you feel comfortable with all of the information you accumulate, you will be on your way to creating a comprehensive collection.

Your Library and Its Users

The first thing that you must do to be able to build and maintain a good collection is to know your institution, its role in the field, and the needs of your patrons. Assessing the needs of your library is pertinent to being able to provide the best resources to your users.

Your Library's Mission

First, what is the type and purpose of your library, and what industry does it serve? For example, a scientific library may be more inclined to technical information as well as digital formats. An art library's users may be more visual. They may expect large, colorful volumes full of art, as well as digital resources. Understand the scope of your library's mission statement (or that of the industry your library supports) and how it will affect your collection development policies and procedures. If you do not have a mission statement, this is something that you can create as you collect the valuable information that helps you understand the mission and purpose of your library. If you do not have a collection development policy, this chapter can also assist with that process, which is far more detailed and procedural than a mission statement.

Sometimes, gaining the insight into an industry with which you may be unfamiliar can take time to understand. Knowing the industry type is one thing, but knowing exactly what it means in a professional capacity can be learned through interaction with the employees and becoming familiar with the different departments and areas and the collection itself. Do not expect to become an expert immediately, especially if your type of library supports a field that constantly evolves, such as new breakthroughs in science for a medical library, evolution of laws in a law library, or new techniques or trends available to artists in an art library.

Fulfill the Needs of Your Users

Next, understand the habits and needs of your users. Some small and specialized libraries may have a concise and consistent patron base, but others may have a wider variety of users.

You must determine whether your users prefer to use digital or paper formats or both. How likely are the users to do research on the web for convenience's sake rather than come to the library for assistance? If you find you have electronically inclined patrons, try to find a way you can make the information easily available for these people. Creating an electronic index of your databases, bibliographies, and any other lists that will help the patrons complete their research from afar will increase accessibility and usage.

Other patrons may prefer tangible items and enjoy visiting the library, but some may be restricted due to distance, time, or both. If you find that there is a desire to research in person but it is hard to get these patrons to the library, a delivery service may be a good solution depending on your library's resources. Deriving a system in which you would receive the requests and pull and deliver to them directly to the patron may prove to be very popular with the users.

Tip: Interact with Patrons.

Patron interaction on a daily basis will gradually invite an understanding of the various requisites of your users. It's quite interesting to talk to and listen to the individuals and learn what projects they're working on, classes they're teaching, workshops they're hosting, or research they're trying to collect. Conversing on a one-on-one basis allows you to ask for clarification and sometimes learn interesting bits of information, ideas, and new topics to better understand your patron's needs and how this is applicable to building the collection.

Tip: Survey Your Patrons.

Surveys are a useful tool to learn what your patrons would like to have added to the library as well as helping you gain insight into the users and their habits. When creating a survey, it is best to keep it short, simple, and not open ended. Multiple-choice questions with an optional comment section will usually attract a greater response from a wide variety of users. Your survey can ask questions to understand patterns in Internet/digital use of information, frequency of library use, what topics and formats are most helpful, as well as suggested titles to add to the collection. Also, time your survey carefully. Schedule it when it is not a historically busy season for your institution, and you will receive more results.

Taking verbal or e-mail requests on a one-on-one basis is another option. Objectivity is important when taking suggestions, but on occasion it may pay off to take a chance on someone's idea. This is a circumstance where, depending on the leniency of your fiscal situation and policy, it is best made on a case-by-case basis.

Know the Institution

Finally, becoming familiar with the library's collection development policy and corporate strategy is very important. The policies and procedures, which may or may not be well documented, will include approval processes, budget information, and overall management style. This sometimes means working through the process on a diminished staff or budget. How often does the budget and policy allow for new acquisitions? Is there a policy on accepting donations? Do you have the time and/or staff to handle a constant flow of new materials? The collection development policy and budgetary needs may also help to direct you in your weeding and preservation efforts. Depending on the management structure, you may be required to satisfy the patrons and users as well as the management and what they deem appropriate or necessary for the library.

Building the Collection

Once you have a thorough grasp of the library and its patrons, you may feel confident enough to make major collection decisions yourself. As previously mentioned, this can take a long time before you are comfortable with your understanding of the library, the purpose, and what the patrons expect. Otherwise, some helpful options are available. Your ideas and selections for the collection may or may not always be perfect materials for the library. Having some guidance in this area is not a bad idea.

User Suggestions

As previously mentioned, an excellent way to make selections for your library is to collect ideas from your patrons, especially during the "getting to know your library and patrons" stretch of time. The personal interaction and surveys already discussed can help you understand your users and also what titles they would be interested in having in the library as directly related to their work. Requests from patrons, either formal (through the survey) or informally (through conversation or e-mails), are a great way to add to the collection.

The Library Committee

Another excellent resource that involves your library community is to create a committee with a well-rounded selection of the users. Be sure to invite members from every area or department within your institution so you cover all areas of interest. Keeping the committee engaged in the library is sometimes difficult since the economy has changed and some people are required to take on more work with fewer resources. It is important to hold regular meetings or at least stay in contact with the committee through e-mail updates or reminders that you are always accepting requests and suggestions. Not only can the committee keep you up to date with current trends or happenings within the field, but you can also keep them updated on the status of the library. Circulation numbers, usage information, and administrative changes should be relayed to the committee so these important facts will circulate through the rest of the personnel. This facilitates collection development, as patrons are more willing to make suggestions if they know the library is always evolving, changing, and willing to hear their ideas.

The library committee can also serve as liaisons to others in their departments on behalf of the library to relay the interests and title suggestions for collection development. It is a good idea to advertise your committee, whether it be in a newsletter or website, to let everyone know who they can contact or talk to about suggestions if it is not convenient to contact the librarians every time.

Join Professional Organizations

An excellent way for you as the librarian to work on the collection is to join relevant groups and professional organizations. Subscribing to mailing lists and regularly viewing websites may also assist in leading you to valuable information and titles that can be added to your collection. This will help you not only gain an understanding of the industry that your library serves but also may offer up some titles or other resources. If possible, subscribe to trade publications that provide relevant resources to your field and help you locate current information, titles, and ideas. Many of these professional organizations will provide subject bibliographies and guides that are very inherent to that particular subject matter. Also, national bibliographies and other library catalogs are excellent places to get more ideas on how to expand your collection.

Vendors and Publishers

Contact book vendors and publishers to speak with representatives and browse their catalogs and reviews. Sign up for their mailing lists, and frequent their websites for any new information. These are beneficial for reading reviews, viewing the content of the books, and learning of new items before publication dates. Depending on the scope of your library, blogs and nonprofessional means of information are also useful. Hearing from other users and interested parties and not just the professionals may also direct you to excellent resources that are on trend with the industry.

Adding to the Collection

Now that you have established the needs of your library and patrons, there are several ways you can start adding items into the collection.

Purchasing

Setting up a regular purchase schedule is ideal. It gives you time between purchases to research and collect titles and search out the best costs, whether through your familiar vendors or through publishers. Amazon and eBay are excellent for locating out-of-print, old, or rare books for reasonable cost, as long as you're willing to be diligent and check back with them on a regular basis.

Donations

Another method of obtaining books for your library is to accept donations. Your collection development policy should have a section on how to deal with donations. If you do not have a policy in place, accepting donations should be at your discretion. Many people want to donate their books because they feel they are going to a good home.

The first thing is to ask the donor if, once the books are evaluated and may be found not suitable for the collection, they would like to have them returned. If they have no opinion, consider creating a "free books" section or a book exchange where patrons can take the books home with them. Also, ask donors if they would like to be recognized for their donation, either with a bookplate, an announcement on your website, or in a newsletter.

Depending on your institution's policies, it is wise to create a donation acceptance form with the assistance of your legal department. This form will keep any legal issues from arising. For example, a donor will not be able to request the return of the items once donated, or there will not be any consequences should the donated books be discarded at a later date.

Electronic Resources

Electronic resources should be evaluated for their usefulness and the cost in comparison to the other formats available to your library. Some industries may have more digitally inclined users, in which case adding these resources to you library would be a positive attribute. The methods for determining their suitability is similar to that of other formats; it merely depends on whether your users are digitally inclined.

Maintaining the Collection

Constantly evaluating the institution, the patrons, and their needs and changes in the field are necessary to keep the collection current. This may mean not only adding to the collection but also discarding dated materials. The arrangement, cataloging, and display of the items are all important functions to keep the collection well maintained. These factors can have an effect on your cataloging methods and accessibility to the collection.

Cataloging

Small libraries are often extremely limited in the spectrum of materials, which can sometimes create a lot of duplicate call numbers. When cataloging, make a few very unique identifying decisions that can help patrons use the library's collection to the fullest. Using a Cutter number to help differentiate between one hundred books that are cataloged as Dewey decimal number 741.9062 can help, but sometimes these unique identifiers can get repetitive, too. Using additional descriptors, such as the date of publication or volume number, can help further distinguish certain titles. For example, yearly annuals or publications will often have the same classification and Cutter numbers, but adding the year after the call number will increase accessibility for the librarian as well as the patrons.

Accessibility

The final step in maintaining your collection is to make sure it is easily accessible to all. Are preserved and archived items going to be made available, or will you create strict usage guidelines? Are electronic resources available only through the library or from any location? In addition to creating a good system for your public spaces, a filing and cataloging system for noncirculating items is a must.

Another way to break up a similar collection is to create featured sections and displays. For example, a current or "on trend" section can feature books that were published within a designated time frame, allowing the user to browse the most current information. A "new book" section will direct users to the books that are new to the library that they may have not yet read. Some libraries will benefit from having a certain section of books that have legal ramifications, such as copyright issues when dealing with art. Creating specific display areas featuring one discipline within the scope of the library is also a novel idea that draws in patrons. Making an event out of a new display is also fun as well as educational for you and the patrons.

Weeding

Weeding is an important part of maintaining a collection. There are several reasons an item may need to be weeded. Materials may be outdated or in poor condition, or the library may need to address space constraints by removing duplicate items. Determining what is relevant or what may become relevant again in the future is something you will have to come to know. There is no surefire way to determine these points. Instead, it will come with time, as you keep yourself current with the trends of the library. The library committee is also useful in assisting with weeding, as they are most familiar with the industry.

After you've weeded items, it is also necessary to determine if they will need to be discarded (or given away) or if they are worthy of preservation. This can only be determined by you based on the significance to your library or the field, as well as the budget for the extra cost it will incur having to purchase special materials for preservation. This also applies to damaged items. What is more cost effective: repairing, preserving, purchasing a new item, or removing it altogether? Also take into consideration the space constraints of storing items that will be removed from the shelf for preservation. Not all libraries will have ample, environmentally sound storage space.

Conclusion

The ideas, questions, and suggestions provided in this chapter can be used to help you evaluate, build, and maintain a collection for your small or special library. In addition, the information collected when you delve into this undertaking will build a solid foundation for creating a new mission statement or collection development policy.

Tip: Take the time to discover what is available to you and your library through any creative means necessary.

Keeping up to date with library science trends as well as the field your library supports is crucial in collection development and management. As mentioned, participating in any field-related resources is great, but joining local, regional, or national library associations can result in a never-ending supply of great information. Many of these associations provide free or low-cost seminars that can help keep you current and refreshed on all things library. They also often offer communities with other librarians and information professionals who are willing to help, share information, or point you in the right direction to get the help you need as you embark on your new journey to a fantastic collection.

Chapter 12

How to Manage Electronic Resources

Ashley Krenelka Chase

Overview

Libraries are undergoing rapid transformations, often to the dismay of library managers who are comfortable working with reasonable budgets and (primarily) print collections. As library budgets and resources shrink and electronic collections grow, an electronic resources management (ERM) team must function as efficiently as possible. With a team of one or two individuals, it is entirely possible to manage an entire e-resources collection, one that grows yearly due to patrons' preference for digital over print.

Planning for an Electronic Collection

The difference between managing print collections and electronic collections makes this one- or two-man show practical and easy to implement. The purchase of electronic resources is nearly identical, usually, to the purchase of print, and because of that the purchasing process can be completed by a library's acquisitions librarian or acquisitions team. With purchasing remaining with a librarian outside of the electronic resources team, selecting, implementing, maintaining, and canceling (when necessary) electronic resources can then be completed by any relatively tech-savvy member of the library team. In a small academic library, or any small library, it is likely that the librarian heading the electronic resources team will also have other responsibilities, such as sitting at a reference desk, supervising librarians or staff (or both), and teaching. With that in mind, certain background information and skills make the process of electronic resources management as simple and easy to manage as possible.

When preparing to implement a small electronic resources management team, a library manager must first understand the life cycle of electronic resources. This life cycle typically has eight steps:

1. Discovery of the resource

2. Trial of the resource and request for a quote/additional information

3. Acquisition of the resource and price negotiation

4. License negotiations

5. Implementation of the resource

6. Gathering of statistics and analysis of the resource

7. Testing and troubleshooting

8. Review of usage and renewal or cancellation. (Weir 2012)

While these eight steps are important, remember: As the manager of an electronic resources collection, they can easily be broken down into three essential categories: discovery/acquisition, implementation, and cancellation/renewal. Because librarians tend to be busy, organized multitaskers, checklists for each of these three phases has been included for ease of use (see appendixes A, B, and C at the end of this chapter).

Discovery and Acquisition

When discussing the discovery/acquisitions portion of electronic resources, remember that the acquisitions process involves more than flipping through a table of contents to determine if the resource meets the needs of the library collection. In discovering and acquiring an electronic resource, the manager of the team must, with help from any other professional or paraprofessional members of the library, determine:

- the resource's audience;

- the price;

- the duplication of content, if any;

- the method(s) of access;

- the usefulness of the content; and

- the available methods of ongoing evaluation.

Each piece of the discovery/acquisition process has been included in the checklist in appendix A.

Audience

The single-most important factor in determining whether to purchase *any* resource, whether in print or electronically, is the audience. For academic libraries, the electronic resources team should determine whether the resource is appropriate for students, faculty, staff, and the public (if the academic library is open to the public). Determining whether the electronic resource is available to alumni is important in academic libraries, particularly where alumni work in a field that requires substantial additional research after graduation (such as medicine or the legal field). Finally, if the library is active with interlibrary loans, determining whether the electronic resource can fulfill those requests is essential.

If the resource isn't appropriate for your audience, why make the purchase? Obviously this holds true for all types of resources, but given the parameters of usability for the electronic resources, the audience is of the utmost importance. There's no need to continue assessing an electronic resource if it's not appropriate for the group you're trying to reach, especially in academics.

Price

Budget, budget, budget. If the library has an annual cap of $15,000 for electronic resources and a resource is available with a price of $12,000 per year, that is likely to be an unreasonable purchase. If, however, the high price can be negotiated as a part of a multiyear contract and the electronic resource being assessed is targeted at the library's primary patron base, it may be worth requesting a free trial. When requesting information on an electronic resource's price from a vendor, ask if there are multiyear discounts available, whether the resource is shareable with other campuses (if appropriate for your institution), and if there's a price cap allowance for further negotiations. Keep track of all of this information on your ERM acquisitions checklist, with supporting documentation, such as e-mails or letters, so it can be easily referenced when the resource comes up for renewal.

Content Duplication

If the electronic resource being analyzed is audience appropriate and has a great price, the next step in the process determines whether the content is being duplicated by any other electronic resources owned or licensed by the library. When analyzing e-journals, subscription to a platform, such as Serials Solutions or CASE, can be helpful in determining overlap. Where a resource management product is not available, checking for content overlap is a task easily delegated. A list of titles within the electronic resource or information about what is covered by the resource can be compared to other products to determine overlap. If there is overlap, it may not be for every year or for a full-text resource, so each piece should be analyzed to determine whether the resource is a good fit for the library.

Access

Once an e-resource has been determined suitable for the library, the methods of access must be addressed. In libraries where a method of IP authentication and proxy access are available and where the electronic resources management team comprises one or two people, this method may be preferable. If there is no proxy/IP access, determine how access to the resource is set up, authenticated, and maintained. Does the electronic resources librarian or manager need to add individual e-mail address or usernames to the database? Can you send the vendor an e-mail domain that allows them to authenticate individual accounts? With this information, it is easier to determine how much time will be spent with setup and troubleshooting of an e-resource.

Besides setting up access for the library patrons, find out how the users will access the e-resource. Can it be added to the library's OPAC? Can it be added to the library's list of databases? Will your library receive MARC records as a part of the subscription, and if so, does the library have the resources to add those records? If the library works with a resource management program, such as Serials Solutions, can the e-resource be added to that product? Having all of this information during the initial acquisitions phase can mean less confusion during the implementation phase and will save substantial time when documented.

Usefulness

Often librarians find products useful because it is our job to find them useful, so we must think about how the patron uses electronic resources. Library users today thrive on using products like Google, and when considering a new e-resource, it is often helpful to test the usefulness on a Google-like model. Does the resource require Boolean operators to be useful? In an academic library, is it possible for the resource to be connected to Blackboard or TWEN? By thinking like library patrons, an electronic resource manager is more likely to understand and document the usability of a resource during a free trial to determine whether it is worth purchasing. Asking other library employees, such as paraprofessional staff or student workers, is also a great way to determine usefulness of an electronic resource and can free up some time for the electronic resources team to analyze other pieces of the puzzle (such as the access piece).

Evaluation

The final stage of analysis in the electronic resources management process looks at methods of evaluation available for the resource. If the library is driven by hard statistics, look for databases that provide COUNTER-compliant usage data or SUSHI data that can be harvested. Ideally, usage statistics will be recorded monthly, so a consistent picture of usage across all e-resource products can be analyzed monthly. Looking for similar usage information from each e-resource vendor allows for consistency and keeps usage from being skewed because reporting methods aren't identical.

Besides evaluating statistics, it is important to determine whether full-text databases are sustainable. If a database has all of its journals available in full-text at the beginning of the year but by the end of the year full-text access to some of those journals is lost, it may not be worth licensing. Another important piece of information for analysis is information about canceling and whether the electronic resource will be available after cancellation. If the library determines an electronic resource is not being used enough to justify the licensing fee and the e-resource requires the vendor be notified of cancellation three months prior to the termination date of the license, that is something that needs to be noted during the implementation phase. Missing a cancellation deadline for an e-resource has the potential to completely throw off a library budget, and the electronic resources team must stay on top of these deadlines and make any other members of the library (such as the acquisitions librarian) aware of them, as well.

Implementation

Implementation is, perhaps, the most enjoyable portion of electronic resources management and, with preparation, can be completed quickly by one person. Again, a checklist is included for ease of use (appendix B), and the checklist can be used for reference while the e-resource is being used by patrons should any troubleshooting be required. The general steps for electronic resources implementation are:

* vendor correspondence;

* preliminary testing;

* setup;

- testing; and

- marketing, training, and so on.

Vendor Correspondence

It may seem obvious, but the first step in implementing a new electronic resource is to pay for it. While some of this correspondence can be done by the acquisitions librarian, the vendor may find it easier if the electronic resources librarian begins the initial conversation (which is usually the case due to the free trial requests and questions that are asked during the discovery/acquisitions process). Once payment is arranged, communicate with the vendor regarding the library's IP ranges or e-mail domains, and follow up with the acquisitions librarian to make sure the invoice and payment are being processed and implementation can continue.

Preliminary Testing

When the vendor provides the URL to access your electronic resource, check it immediately. Is it identical to the URL you were given for the trial? If so, is the functionality the same? If it's a different URL, does it work? Does the new URL provide the content you tested during the discovery and acquisitions process? Additionally, make sure that the content being licensed is the same that was accessed during the free trial prior to fully setting up the e-resource.

Setup

The checklist for setup reflects several steps that may or may not be appropriate for your library. If the library uses a proxy server and/or IP authentication for electronic resources, the first step adds the relevant information to the proxy server and resets it to recognize the new addition. If the library subscribes to an electronic resources management platform, such as Serials Solutions, the new e-resource must be added. The new electronic resource will also need to be added to the library's OPAC, either with MARC records or as an individual record created by the electronic resources manager or cataloger. Simultaneous to adding the electronic resource to the OPAC, a tickler should be added to either a calendar or within the library management system to alert the electronic resources management team that termination of the license is impending (three months prior to the termination date is a good time to think about renewal and/or cancellation, which is discussed in another section).

If the library has a subject database, add the new electronic resource to that database and to the list of library databases that is available online, if appropriate.

It is extremely useful to scan the license agreement and to either link it to the record in the library management system or scan it and save it to a networked folder or drive that can be accessed by everyone on the electronic resources team, the acquisitions librarian, and the library director. If usage statistics are kept on a spreadsheet, add the resource to the spreadsheet for easy analysis.

Testing

Once the electronic resource has been added to all of the appropriate sources, check its accessibility. Check the access inside the library/on campus and outside of the library/off campus (if you are working with proxy/IP authentication), through the catalog and database list, and on a variety of devices, from mobile devices to PCs and Macs. After checking these accessibility points, access the statistics to ensure usage is being tracked.

Marketing and Training

The best way to promote new library resources is to "productize," or point to products or services that are being provided by the library (Abram 2007, 46–48). By prioritizing marketing a new electronic resource, you not only help to ensure its use, but you also publicize what is being purchased with the library budget. By marketing a new e-resource and training patrons on best practices in using the new resource, you give the resource the best chance of being used and remaining a part of the collection.

Renewal/Cancellation

The decision to renew or cancel an electronic resource is seemingly an easier decision than weeding a print resource that has been made a part of the collection, and a quick glance at the renewal/cancellation checklist (appendix C) provides the basic information required. With no physical object to add or remove, the process seems simple, but it is important for a library's electronic resources manager to ensure two important steps are followed when an e-resource has been renewed or canceled: correspondence (in both instances) and removal (when the e-resource is canceled).

Renewal

Correspondence

During the implementation phase of electronic resource management, ticklers should be set to alert the appropriate parties that the e-resource is up for renewal. After consulting usage statistics and logs of reported issues with the resource, many electronic resources will be renewed without a second thought. While this makes the process easier than a cancellation, there are still things that must be done, namely correspondence with the vendor that the library would like to renew the resource and extend the current license or sign a new license. Ideally, the decision to renew an electronic resource should be made a month or two before the expiration of the current license so any new negotiations can be completed in a timely fashion and there is no disruption of service. After corresponding with the vendor, negotiating new license terms or renewing the current license terms, and paying for the renewed e-resource, it is important to add a new tickler to your calendar or library management system to address the e-resource renewal again when it comes due.

Cancellation

Correspondence

As with the decision to renew an electronic resource, the decision to cancel should be communicated clearly with the vendor, well in advance of the contract's termination date. In a perfect world, your tickler for a renewal or cancellation decision will alert the electronic resources management team that a decision must be made in an appropriate time frame under the license terms, and all communication with the vendor can occur so the library is not unwittingly drawn into another license term. The cancellation checklist in appendix C makes this process relatively easy. The decision to cancel the e-resource should be clearly communicated with the library's acquisitions librarian and with the vendor; the librarian or administrator who communicates this decision with the vendor may vary from library to library. Consult your acquisitions checklist to determine, at this point, whether you were guaranteed any postcancellation access to the e-resource. If some postcancellation access was promised, follow up with the vendor, and keep track of the termination of access so the removal steps can be completed. Besides communicating with the vendor, communicate with other interested parties, within the library and outside, about the cancellation so there are no surprises.

Removal

The process for removal of an electronic resource from the library's universe will likely vary drastically from library to library. The most important, first step in removal is to suppress, *not* remove, the electronic resource from the library's OPAC. Suppression is the preferred method for "removal" from the OPAC because it allows the library to keep track of the fact that the e-resource was, at one time, licensed by the library. Should the library license the electronic resource again in the future, that suppressed OPAC record can hold a wealth of information, from pricing to methods of access, that may be valuable in further decision making. After the electronic resource is suppressed from the OPAC, add any relevant notes to the suppressed record and to your cancellation checklist. This duplication ensures that multiple sources can be consulted to determine why a particular decision was made about the resource, and reporting information in several places, while a seemingly wasted effort, may prove useful in the future.

With notes added and records suppressed, the electronic resource can be removed from the library website, any database list the library may make public, and from any LibGuides and resource management software, such as Serials Solutions or CASE. Gathering final usage statistics can allow for a complete picture of the electronic resource's use (or lack thereof), which may also be useful should the library circle back to the resource in the future and add it back into the library's electronic resources collection.

Conclusion

These guidelines and checklists are a simple starting point for librarians who are new to the field or who are just beginning to tackle a more formal electronic resources management program.

Tip: Troubleshooting access issues and dealing with vendors are best left to individual libraries to determine best practices; what works for a small academic library may not work for a public or special library.

Tip: The type of electronic resources management described in this chapter is completely manageable by one or two people, neither of whom need be exclusively working on the electronic resources management team. You may determine that, in your library, the team would benefit from additional members; cross-training between departments is always encouraged, particularly as libraries move away from print and toward digital.

Tip: Adaptability is important, and managing a team that is comfortable with electronic resources will benefit not only the employees learning these skills but the library and academic institution, as well. By managing the basics of electronic resources, you will quickly find that the more difficult pieces fall into place and become less challenging, making electronic resources management in any library second nature.

Bibliography

Abram, Stephen. 2007. "20 Tips to Inspire Innovation." *American Libraries* 38 (1): 46–48.

Weir, Ryan O. 2012. "Learning the Basics of Electronic Resource Management." In *Managing Electronic Resources: A LITA Guide*, edited by Ryan O. Weir, 1–16. Chicago: ALA TechSource.

Appendix A

Table 12.1 ERM Discovery/Acquisitions Checklist

Product:_____

Company:_____

1. Audience

Is this resource appropriate/useful for our –

Students	Y	/	N
Faculty	Y	/	N
Staff	Y	/	N
Public	Y	/	N

If there is a specific group/center/faculty member for whom this database would be appropriate, please list:_____

Is the resource available to walk-ins?	Y	/	N
Is the resource available to our alumni?	Y	/	N
Is the resource an option for ILL?	Y	/	N

2. Financial

What is the price?_____

Is there a discount for a multi-year contract?	Y	/	N
Is this resource shareable with other campuses?	Y	/	N
Is there a price cap allowance?	Y	/	N
Can we get a free trial?	Y	/	N

3. Content

Is the information duplicated with current resources?	Y	/	N

If yes, where? _____

What years?_____

Full text?_____

4. Access

Is there proxy access?	Y	/	N
IP authentication?	Y	/	N

If no to proxy/IP, how is access set-up/authenticated/maintained?_____
_____

Is the access unrestricted?	Y	/	N

Who maintains the database?_____

Is customer/tech support readily available?	Y	/	N

What is required for set up by our library?_____

Will we receive MARC records?	Y	/	N
Is the resource in the resource management software?	Y	/	N
Is the resource able to be added to the OPAC?	Y	/	N

If yes, at what level?_____

5. Usefulness

Is the interface intuitive?	Y	/	N
Is it as easy to use as Google?	Y	/	N
Is the resource linkable to educational tools (i.e. Blackboard)	Y	/	N
Does the company provide training or tutorials?	Y	/	N

6. Evaluation

Is there COUNTER-compliant usage data?	Y	/	N
Is there other usage data available?	Y	/	N

How often?_____

Is the full-text sustainable?	Y	/	N

What is the notice period for cancellation?_____

Is there post-cancellation access?	Y	/	N

For how long?_____

Appendix B

Table 12.2 ERM Implementation Checklist

Product:_____

Company:_____

1. Vendor Correspondence

Arrange for invoice or credit card payment	Date:_____	By:_____
Send IP ranges to vendor, if required	Date:_____	By:_____
Send email domains to vendor, if required	Date:_____	By:_____
Confirm payment/invoice with acquisitions	Date:_____	By:_____

2. Preliminary Testing

Is the trial URL identical to the URL for full-use?	Y	/	N
If yes, does the trial URL still work?	Y	/	N
If no, does the new URL work?	Y	/	N
Does the new URL provide the requested/paid content?	Y	/	N

3. Set-Up

Update proxy settings	Date:_____	By:_____
Reset proxy servers	Date:_____	By:_____
Update resource management software	Date:_____	By:_____
Add e-resource to OPAC	Date:_____	By:_____
Add e-resource to subject database	Date:_____	By:_____
Add URL to database list and/or subject guide	Date:_____	By:_____
Guides:_____		
Upload MARC records, if available	Date:_____	By:_____
Add license record	Date:_____	By:_____
Add to database stats spreadsheet	Date:_____	By:_____

4. Testing

Is the e-resource accessible on campus

Through the catalog:	Y	/	N
Through database list	Y	/	N
On a desktop/laptop	Y	/	N
On a mobile device	Y	/	N

Is the e-resource accessible off campus

Through the catalog:	Y	/	N
Through database list	Y	/	N
On a desktop/laptop	Y	/	N
On a mobile device	Y	/	N
Are the statistics available?	Y	/	N

5. Marketing, Training, etc.

Provide info to marketing committee	Date:_____	By:_____
Schedule & provide training, if necessary	Date:_____	By:_____
Follow-up with users, 30-days after launch	Date:_____	By:_____

6. Notes

_____

_____

_____

_____

_____

_____
_____
_____
_____
_____

7. Further action taken, if necessary

_____
_____
_____
_____
_____
_____
_____
_____
_____

Appendix C

Table 12.3 ERM Renewal/Cancellation Checklist

Product:_____
Company:_____

1. Renewal

  a. Correspondence

Alert acquisitions of renewal	Date:_____	By:_____
Communicate renewal to vendor	Date:_____	By:_____
Tickler updated:		Y / N

2. Cancellation

  a. Correspondence

Alert acquisitions of cancellation	Date:_____	By:_____
Communicate cancellation to vendor	Date:_____	By:_____
Expiration date:_____		
Post-cancellation access?_____		
Communicate cancellation to library	Date:_____	By:_____
Communicate cancellation to faculty	Date:_____	By:_____
Communicate cancellation to undergrad library	Date:_____	By:_____

  b. Removal

Suppress OPAC record	Date:_____	By:_____
Add notes on cancellation to OPAC record	Date:_____	By:_____
Notes:_____		
_____		
_____		
_____		
Remove from LibGuides/Database list	Date:_____	By:_____
Guides:_____		
Remove from resource management software	Date:_____	By:_____
Gather final usage statistics for spreadsheet	Date:_____	By:_____

Chapter 13

How to Choose the Right ILS for Your Library

Joy M. Banks

Overview

The process of finding the right integrated library system (ILS) for a collection can seem daunting. As the library world continues to change, some may argue that an individual ILS is obsolete in today's library environment. For the small library, however, a functional ILS may be the best and most effective way to connect our holdings and services with our users. The process of selecting a system, migrating data, and becoming accustomed to new work flows takes a significant investment of time and money. Faced with limited time, staff, and budget, small library managers may be overwhelmed by the process. Changing systems should only happen when absolutely necessary. Some may be forced into migration through a shared consortium system, some through the discontinuation of legacy systems, and some simply to find a better product. This chapter is meant to help guide readers through the complicated process of finding the best system for your unique library situation.

Terms and Definitions

For many who work with smaller collections, the world of cataloging may be the most foreign, filled with a number of strange terms and jargon. This section offers a few definitions and points of clarification to help readers better understand the terms and acronyms they may encounter during the ILS shopping experience.

- For the purpose of clarification in this chapter, the term *library* is used to represent all types of information centers. The steps and suggestions presented, though, should address a wide range of situations for all types of small facilities offering information services to their users. These guidelines could also help steer the selection process for other types of content management systems, including those used for archival collections.

- *ILS* versus *OPAC*. While in today's online environment these two terms may seem interchangeable, they actually represent two very different ideas. The integrated library system (ILS) is a complete package that can offer public and staff modules to facilitate all or most of the library's functions (e.g., circulation, acquisitions, cataloging, etc.). The online public access catalog (OPAC) is merely one portion of the ILS, offering library users the ability to search the catalog as well as perhaps request interlibrary loans, place holds on items, and check their accounts. While not all ILS options necessarily have an OPAC, all OPACs will be attached to some sort of ILS.

- *Digital asset management (DAM):* "Systems designed to organize and display digital content produced in a variety of media types. The content is usually locally owned and controlled, rather than licensed from a third party."[1]

- *Electronic resources management (ERM):* "Systems developed to assist librarians in the control of licensed third-party resources published electronically (databases, e-books, e-journals, etc.), including license management, renewal, legal use, access management, and collection development."[2]

- *Library management system (LMS):* "In automated systems, an integrated set of applications designed to perform the business and technical functions of a library, including acquisitions, cataloging, circulation, and the provision of public access."[3]

- *Open source software (OSS):* "A computer program for which the source code is made available without charge by the owner or licenser, usually via the Internet, to encourage the rapid development of a more useful and bug-free product through open peer review. The practice also allows the product to be customized by its users to suit local needs."[4]

- *Unified resource management (URM) system* "include[s] the integrated management of digital, electronic and printed collections and the services which are associated with academic libraries and their constituencies."[5] In other words, the URM is meant to fully integrate all aspects of library collections' management and searching, including databases, to create one point of entry for all user and staff needs.

Selection Process

Small libraries often have unique needs and requirements for their management systems. Organizations may have very few, if any, professional librarians on staff. The technology infrastructure for the library may be nonexistent or completely out of the control of the library staff. Small libraries may be part of a larger system with little to no say in the selection of a new system. The digital divide may mean some smaller, more remote libraries may have limited access to high-speed Internet, further narrowing the available possibilities for practical, online system solutions. The combination of limited staff, limited budgets, and limited resources may seem like an overwhelming hurdle. The world of ILS options is vast, however, so there is certainly a solution for every situation. Approaching the problem in a systematic way will ensure the most efficient use of resources expended to find the best solution. Faced with so many software options in the marketplace, there are two key questions that you may want to answer before considering specific budget constraints: self-hosting versus cloud hosting and open-source versus proprietary software. Answering these two questions first will help significantly focus your ILS search.

When Internet Access Is Limited or Unreliable

While many libraries in the twenty-first century have reliable access to high-speed Internet, this may not be true in all cases. Many rural and remote communities have yet to gain access to this important technology. This does not mean that libraries must sacrifice access to their collections. Many products in lower price tiers have options for just such situations, allowing the libraries to purchase software packages that can be made available onsite only. Solutions as simple as a detailed spreadsheet or simple database are also options. These systems may not provide the luxury of an OPAC, but creative solutions, such as exporting a simple list of the collection's items that can be added to a website later, may provide basic access that library users will find helpful. This solution has been used by a number of religious and other small libraries that have resources they would like to share with their user groups but lack the infrastructure to support a full ILS.

Self-Hosting versus Cloud Hosting

Self-Hosting

For most small libraries, the ability to self-host anything other than the simplest system is probably unlikely. There may be some collections that serve an internal user group and have no need to have their collections online. For these collections, something as simple as a shared spreadsheet or local database on an intranet may meet your user needs. Be sure to secure these options from editing by anyone other than specific library personnel. These two solutions offer the ability to inventory, track, and search your collection holdings but may also limit your users' ability to perform advanced searching. Small libraries may also choose to host a stand-alone ILS product only available to their internal networks, a solution that may prove appealing with highly sensitive collections.

Tip: If the small library has access to adequate IT support and reliable Internet, self-hosting an ILS system may prove to be cost efficient.

Cloud Hosting

Choosing a hosted option means that you must rely on consistent Internet access to perform daily tasks, such as circulation and updating the collection database; however, users would still be able to search the collection remotely even if your institution's Internet crashes. This solution often works well when libraries have little to no control over access to a server and lack staff that can handle IT tasks, such as networking and programming. When considering a hosted option, be sure to ask about average downtime for the system (it should be very low), the security level for all information, and how your data will be stored and backed up in case of emergency. Also consider the level of customer service that the host will provide. If the company offers anything less than 24/7 support, consider if their hours of operation coincide with your own.

Open-Source versus Proprietary Software Solutions

Open-Source Software

The emergence of open-source ILS solutions is still relatively new to the library world, but this new option in the marketplace has caused quite a stir. According to Marshall Breeding, "The open source movement has disrupted long-established patterns, introducing a new way of thinking about the development and distribution of software, new products, and a new set of companies seeking to compete against the status quo."[6] One major clarification that should be made is that, while open-source ILS solutions are available free of charge, they are not necessarily free to maintain. Library managers should consider the costs of the staff time needed to maintain the systems, to integrate any available upgrades provided by the open-source community, and to manage the server needs of hosting such a system or paying for someone else to do these things in a cloud-hosted environment. If a library has the advantage of access to an expert programmer and a reliable server, open-source solutions can offer the freedom to customize a system for very specific needs rather than waiting for what can be slow development in the proprietary realm. Any modifications made to the system can then be shared (or not) with others interested in the software. Open-source options are now available as hosted options, too, allowing libraries to support the initiatives of the open-source community while benefiting from the customer support of a larger organization.

Proprietary Software

Proprietary ILS solutions follow a model of closed development in which the "original source code is held as confidential proprietary information, made available only to programmers of the organization that created the software application."[7] This often removes the library from the ability to directly customize or otherwise change the original system, but most ILS providers actively seek the input of their customers in order to direct their development efforts. New releases for proprietary options often come on a more predictable schedule, and whether hosted or not, companies usually provide consistent customer support in order to work through those upgrades. Be wary, however, of any proprietary systems that convert your data into proprietary data formats, essentially holding your data hostage. This can cause huge problems and expense in the future if you choose to migrate to a new system. You should always have complete access to all of your data in a universally recognized file format (e.g., MARC21).

Visualize the Process

In order to better visualize the process of answering these two fundamental questions, refer to the flowchart (figure 13.1), and follow the steps to see which combination of hosted versus self-hosted and open-source versus proprietary may work best for your library. While determining whether a hosted or self-hosted solution is best will probably be relatively easy, the question between open-source or proprietary software may be more difficult to answer. There is nothing wrong with exploring both options as you move into selecting specific vendors. You should soon discover the solution that would work best for your library.

Identifying Priorities

Once you have determined the type of system and hosting option that works best for your institution, you should now begin the process of determining the priority features for your system. When you are faced with a strict budget for spending, you will need to know in advance what features you need, what features would be nice to have, and what features you can live without. Here are some examples of questions to consider:

- Do you need a functional way to create original records in your system, or do you mostly import records from elsewhere?

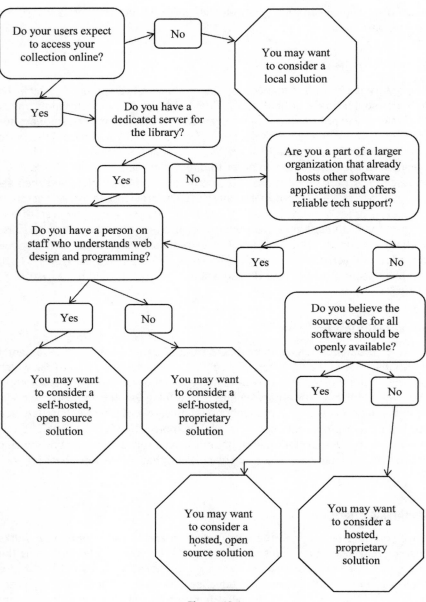

Figure 13.1

- Would you like to use services like Z39.50 to gather records from a variety of sources?

- Do you need the system to be able to import and/or export data in a variety of formats (e.g., MARC21, CSV, etc.) to support the informational needs of your organization?

- Do you process a number of serials and need a serials module to track subscription information?

- Do you need the ability to print labels and/or barcodes from the ILS?

- Would you like to use your ILS to track your acquisitions and/or budget expenditures?

- Do you circulate items and need fully functional patron record–processing capabilities, such as the ability to send automatic notifications?

- Do you need your OPAC to display in multiple languages?

- During searching, would your users appreciate spelling suggestions, the ability to narrow their search results through faceted searching (e.g., only pull books published in a certain date range), or the option to resort search results?

- Would you like a reporting feature that has preset reports for typical reports? Do you need the ability to create custom reports?

- Do you need your system to interact with an authentication software for licensed databases or to allow different levels of authorization, both allowing certain staff or patrons varying degrees of access?

- Do you need the ability to either access or store digital files within the ILS?

- Is it essential that you be able to perform batch processing of any records?

- Does the system allow for customization for local practices, and is it prepared to handle any upcoming changes in cataloging standards (e.g., RDA)?

This is only a representative list of some of the most common features in today's modern ILS programs. The issues of each individual library will vary, and what may be vital to one organization may be unnecessary to another. For example, most music libraries would consider the ability to perform complete authority control, including the importing of authority records, a vital component to an ILS, while school media centers may consider this unnecessary. The best way to develop this list is to consider the way your staff and users utilize your current system on a daily, monthly, quarterly, and yearly basis. This exercise will ensure that you get a system that is able to do everything you need, even if the steps to achieve the end are a bit different.

Shopping for Solutions

Once you have considered the features, make a list of your priorities. Start a spreadsheet to track what you learn about specific systems. This may also prove beneficial if you must justify your final recommendation to administration. Be sure to include the features of your current system in the comparison. Use the Internet to locate a handful of options that may fit into your budget (perhaps no more than ten). This part of the process may seem overwhelming, but this is where your librarian colleagues can help. Contact other librarians with similar collection needs. Use a LISTSERV like Autocat to reach out to an international cataloging community for recommendations. Research individual systems by using a resource like Marshall Breeding's "Perceptions" survey to gain further insight.[8] While pricing information is available online for some systems, you may need to contact some vendors in order to receive an initial quote. As you begin to enter data into your spreadsheet, you should see that some options rise above the others.

Narrowing the Field

Before ever contacting a vendor, you will need a few basic pieces of information about your own system, such as how many bibliographic and patron records you will migrate and what migration timeline you need to follow (e.g., if there are any time constraints due to institutional budgets). Having a list of questions is also helpful to address any pending issues from your research. The process of requesting quotes can be time consuming, so examine your spreadsheet and choose the top three or four options to contact for more complete information and specific quotes. Depending on the size of your library and the size of the vendor you contact, the presentation may be conducted over the phone, through a webinar, or even in person. You may find that, during your conversations with different vendors, questions arise that you had not previously considered. Do not hesitate to reconnect with other vendors to make sure that all have an opportunity to address all issues.

Different vendors will handle the request for quote (RFQ) process differently. Some may grant you access to a sample database, actually allowing you to use the staff side of the system to check work flow and record compatibility. Some may only show you the user side of the interface at first, but be sure to explore the functionality of the staff side, too. Some may clearly be salespeople with limited knowledge of the library world, and others may be degreed librarians. As you work through the process, you should start to see a clear advantage of one over the rest. If you are required to present more than one option to a larger administration, use all of the research you compiled to make a clear argument for your own top choice.

Making Your Choice

Congratulations! You made it through the selection process, and your administration has approved your top selection. You are on your way to migrating to a new system. The migration process could fill another chapter, but you should remember to stay calm, to prepare your staff and users for the changes, and to remain in regular contact with your old and new ILS providers, ensuring that the process goes as smoothly as possible. There will be bumps. There will be a learning curve when the new system goes live. Be realistic with your goals and expectations, and you will soon be using your new system like a pro.

Tips for Success

Tip: Do carefully read any contracts you may be required to sign, and seek legal advice if necessary.

Tip: Do not buy more system than you need unless your library will soon grow. There are many exciting options available, but you should be honest about the actual needs of your library.

Tip: Do contact other libraries that use systems you are considering to hear their honest feedback.

Tip: Do not shy away from asking tough questions and expecting answers.

Tip: Do consider contacting your current vendor to see if your concerns can be addressed, potentially avoiding a migration.

Tip: Do not assume that all ILSs are created equal. Ask questions even if the answers may seem obvious.

Tip: Do remember that, even if you choose the wrong system, you can always migrate later!

Useful Resources

A bibliography of resources is included for further reference. The following three resources provide the most readily accessible information:

Autocat archives (https://listserv.syr.edu/scripts/wa.exe?A0=AUTOCAT).

> The archives to this cataloging LISTSERV provide many conversations concerning ILS migration and software suggestions. You must subscribe to the list to have access to the archives. If you cannot find the answer you seek, ask this very helpful community.

Integrated Library Systems: Planning, Selecting, and Implementing by Desiree Webber and Andrew Peters.

> For a much more comprehensive analysis of this process, consider this book published in 2010 by Libraries Unlimited, available in paperback and e-book format.

"Perceptions 2012: An International Survey of Library Automation" (http://www.librarytechnology.org/perceptions2012.pl).

> The results, typically posted in January, of Marshall Breeding's annual survey concerning library automation systems. The interactive version allows users to see feedback for specific systems. The "libwebcats" tab allows users to search and find what ILS software different libraries are using.

Notes

1. Joan M. Reitz, "digital asset management (DAM)," ODLIS: Online Dictionary for Library and Information Science, accessed November 20, 2013, http://www.abc-clio.com/ODLIS/odlis_d.aspx.

2. Joan M. Reitz, "electronic resources management (ERM)," ODLIS: Online Dictionary for Library and Information Science, accessed November 20, 2013, http://www.abc-clio.com/ODLIS/odlis_e.aspx.

3. Joan M. Reitz, "library management system (LMS)," ODLIS: Online Dictionary for Library and Information Science, accessed November 20, 2013, http://www.abc-clio.com/ODLIS/odlis_l.aspx.

4. Joan M. Reitz, "open source," ODLIS: Online Dictionary for Library and Information Science, accessed November 20, 2013, http://www.abc-clio.com/ODLIS/odlis_o.aspx.

5. "Specification for a Unified Library Resource Management System," LibTechRFP: Open Specifications for Library Systems, last modified August 2012, https://libtechrfp.wikispaces.com/Unified+library+resource+management+specification.

6. Marshall Breeding, "Open Source Library Automation: Overview and Perspective," *Library Technology Reports* 44, no. 8 (November/December 2008): 5.

7. Ibid., 7.

8. Additional information on both Autocat and Breeding's "Perceptions" survey can be found in the "Useful Resources" section.

Bibliography

Breeding, Marshall. "Open Source Library Automation: Overview and Perspective." *Library Technology Reports* 44, no. 8 (November/December 2008): 5–10.

Eden, Brad. "Reinventing the OPAC." *Library Technology Reports* 43, no. 6 (November/December 2007): 13–40.

Kirkland, Anita Brooks. "Six Letters That Count ILS + RDA = A Better School Library Experience." *School Libraries in Canada—CASL* 28, no. 1 (Winter 2010): 114–16.

Matthews, Joseph R. "20 Qs & As on Automated Integrated Library Systems: Are They a Remedy for What AILS Your Library." *American Libraries* 13, no. 6 (June 1982): 367–71.

Reitz, Joan M. *Online Dictionary for Library and Information Science.* Accessed November 20, 2013. http://www.abc-clio.com/ODLIS/odlis_about.aspx.

"Specification for a Unified Library Resource Management System." *LibTechRFP: Open Specifications for Library Systems.* Last modified August 2012. https://libtechrfp.wikispaces.com/Unified+library+resource+management+specification.

Wang, Yongming, and Trevor A. Dawes. "The Next Generation Integrated Library System: A Promise Fulfilled." *Information Technology and Libraries* 31, no. 3 (September 2012): 76–84.

Webber, Desiree, and Andrew Peters. *Integrated Library Systems: Planning, Selecting, and Implementing* (Santa Barbara, CA: Libraries Unlimited, 2010).

Chapter 14

How to Excel at Collection Development

Wanda Headley

Overview

The success of any small special library or information resource center depends on its ability to meet the information requirements of a particular set of individuals. Included among the numerous factors contributing to its success is the quality and timeliness of the research and other relevant items in the collection. Small specialized libraries present distinct challenges for collection development, often because they are run by a single nonspecialist librarian or paraprofessional whose time and resources are divided among all the tasks required to maintain the library's daily operation, conduct special projects, and meet other organizational obligations. Developing a focused or subject-specific collection is a demanding and time-consuming undertaking. But without a quality collection in place, the small research library, its staff, parent organization, and, most of all, the user community suffers.

Special libraries exist to support their parent organization, have a targeted set of users, and provide information resources specific to their subject area. They can be found in a variety of environments, such as corporations, law offices, museums, medical facilities, research institutions, and nonprofit settings to name a few. Special libraries, often referred to as information centers or resource centers, often emerge when there is a need to organize materials scattered throughout an organization into a central location. The size of the existing collection can range from a few seminal studies to hundreds or thousands of titles of various ages in an array of formats and condition. As time goes by, materials are added to a "collection" but not always with a defined sense of direction or logical categorization. Enter the librarian whose task it is to organize the existing material as well as acquire new and supporting material. Once the current collection is reviewed for relevancy and weeded, if necessary, the chore of collecting new material begins. This chapter offers useful tips to help the nonspecialist librarian or paraprofessional in a small institution, such as a research center, successfully create a focused and coherent collection that reflects the needs of the user community.

What Is Collection Development?

In the most basic sense, the term *collection development* refers to the process of building a library collection to meet the needs of its users. Despite the simplicity of that loose definition, building collections requires more than placing books or other items on the shelves. Collection development is a continuous process that requires the librarian to be a subject-matter specialist or at least have working knowledge of the subject matter. The process also involves an understanding of the user community's needs, the creation of policies aimed at defining collection parameters, selection and procurement of material, and an evaluation of the existing holdings, as well as the weeding of outdated titles or those that are no longer pertinent.

Know Your Subject Areas

The more knowledge the librarian has of the subject increases his or her ability to recognize quality items to add to the collection. It may be out of the reach of the librarian to become a subject specialist; however, a good working knowledge of the literature, issues, trends, scholarly experts, and groundbreaking studies in the collection's particular area of focus is a necessity to successfully operate in a specialist environment.

Subject guides are helpful but, depending on the topic, cannot always be relied upon to provide a complete picture of the field. Class syllabi are valuable tools to help build knowledge. Often faculty will post their class syllabus, complete with a recommended reading list, online for their students. The selections listed provide a good overview of the subject matter and are written by prominent scholars in the field. If you are not in an academic environment, recommendations can be sought from knowledgeable coworkers who create a "go to" list of titles when they need to increase their knowledge in a particular area. Other libraries with similar collections can also provide suggestions. It is to the advantage of all librarians working in a related subject area to maintain a wiki or LISTSERV to share professional information and experiences. Using the list of authoritative sources will be of help to the librarian learning the subject matter and will come into use in other areas discussed later in this chapter.

Many lectures and meetings are broadcast on the Internet. Webinar organizers and presenters are well aware of time constraints placed upon attendees so will follow up presentations with an e-mail to participants containing links to the recording as well as handouts or slides that were used as part of the webinar. Blogs, websites, and LISTSERVs are other avenues that offer opportunities to increase subject knowledge. LISTSERVs exist for all types of industry- and academic-related topics. For example, a librarian needing to learn the details of computer science as an area of study can quickly search the Internet and find a number of LISTSERVs, with each providing a forum dedicated to a specific theme or group within the industry.

Academic journals, newsletters, and trade magazines should not be overlooked. Their content consists of the latest research, editorials, and contemporary issues in the field and often includes reviews of recently published books.

Tip: Familiarity with issues and trends is a necessity to successfully operate in a specialist environment.

Know Your User Community

User communities come in all sizes, from a few researchers in a single location to thousands of people who access the collection by remote means, yet they are all connected to the library by the subject matter of its collection. An effective collection depends on the librarian's knowledge of this group. Who are the users? How many are there? Where are they located? How do they access and use the material in the collection? Answers to these and even more questions factor into collection development decisions.

Consumers of a special research collection can include faculty, researchers, students, project staff, practitioners, the general public, or a combination of information users. Regardless of which group or groups the library or information center serves, the user community acts as a guide in collection development efforts. Connecting with community members can be as simple as one-on-one conversations in the hallway or more advanced to include organized focus groups or a comprehensive needs analysis. Conducting a user needs assessment is a worthwhile investment in time and resources. Although not a standard method of conducting a user assessment, informal conversations in the library, at meetings, and at conferences can aid the librarian who has no time or resources to put together a more substantive assessment. Conversation offers immediate feedback but cannot provide a clear picture of the community or its needs as effectively as the focus group and survey methods, which also consume much more staff time and are more costly to produce. Yet, designed correctly, these methods produce data beyond discovering who is using the collection. Focus group and survey data provide answers to how the collection is being used, what items are used most frequently, what are the preferred formats, how individuals use the information, how much the information is valued, and more. The data is also valuable for justifying the need for new technologies, services, and staff.

Tip: Familiarity with users and their needs and desires is essential in effective collection development.

What's in a Collection?

The objective of the small special library is based on the goals of its parent organization. A careful reading of the parent organization's mission statement provides insight into both the range and depth of the collection. It is important that the current collection as well as any future additions correspond with the overall goals of the organization.

Increasingly shrinking acquisitions budgets eliminate the quantity-versus-quality controversy that has plagued librarians in prior decades. Simply put, today's collection development librarian must ensure that every dollar is well spent providing quality resources. An evaluation of the collection does just that. It describes the strength and value of the holdings and provides a means to ensure the library is and remains on track to meet organizational goals and budgetary limits. Additionally, data compiled from a well-planned evaluation will serve as a guide to collection-planning efforts, help frame the collection development policy, determine the quality and currency of the current holdings, determine the allocation of funds for purchases and subscriptions, and justify the need for budget increases.

Citation analysis, list checking, collecting circulation and interlibrary loan (ILL) statistics, and feedback from users are some of the more common methods employed to determine the strengths and weaknesses of the collection. Citation analysis reveals the importance of a publication based on the number of times it has been used in work by other researchers. Frequently cited titles reveal an item's impact on the subject. Tools, such as Web of Science and Scopus, expedite the process by using a computer process to count the number of times an article or author has been cited. When using this method, keep in mind that currency is important in a research setting, so take care to use recent books and journals.

Reading lists recommended by faculty and coworkers mentioned earlier in the chapter or other authoritative sources can be used to compare the lists against the library's holdings. Does the collection contain the titles found on the lists? It is important to maintain a current list of resources for future evaluations to keep the collection from becoming outdated. Look to other libraries that are comparable in size and subject matter. How does your collection compare? Again, keep in mind that the goal is the quality not the quantity of works on the shelves.

Data captured through collecting circulation and interlibrary loan statistics are useful for determining trends and discovering what is missing from the collection. High numbers of interlibrary loan requests may be a sign that a certain section of the collection needs attention, or perhaps the low number of books circulating is due to an increase in remote users who are looking elsewhere for full-text copies in digital format.

Tip: Familiarity with existing resources, keeping up with new publications, and data captured though ILL are all essential to effective collection development.

The Collection Development Policy

The necessity of a creating and maintaining an effective collection development policy continues to be debated in the library science literature. While some claim such a policy only limits the librarian and confines the collection, others believe it can be a powerful tool for driving development decisions. A collection development policy for a small research library serves as a living document that should be continually revisited and updated. Some of the major elements included in a policy are:

- defines the nature and scope of the collection,

- defines the library's mission in relationship to the parent organization,

- states what will and will not be included in the collection,

- helps alleviate personal biases by setting guidelines for the selection process,

- sets standards for determining disputes,

- acts as a training tool for staff tasked with collection development duties,

- explains the deselection policy and disposal of weeded materials, and

- explains how gifts are handled.

The policy not only directs the librarian's attention to the collection but also raises awareness of issues that impact its growth and forces systematic planning when building a new collection or adding to an existing one. A collection policy need not be a lengthy document. Depending on the size and function of the library, the policy can range from a few succinct paragraphs to pages of documentation. The point here is to be concise and include enough information that even an outsider can learn all he or she needs to know about the library simply by reading the policy.

In Search of a Good Book

Once resources have been identified, the work of actually obtaining them begins. Most research is considered "old" if it was published two or more years ago, so, with the exception of historical collections, it is best to focus collection development efforts on material that is less than two years old.

The very nature of a special collection deems most finding aids of little use. Most small research libraries collect items that are highly technical or specific to a group of individuals. Some materials may be restricted by law or company policy. As they do for academic and public libraries, publishers don't produce catalogs specifically targeting the nature of the most specialized collections, leaving the librarian looking toward other avenues to uncover useful material.

For example, consider the research collection that is focused on youth violence. The subject is studied from a number of perspectives. Economists write about the costs of youth incarceration, psychologists study youth behavior and mental health, educators look at the impact of teen violence on child development, crime analysts investigate trends and patterns, and so on. To develop a well-rounded collection focused on youth violence, the librarian must gather research from all trade and academic works associated with the subject, which often involves looking to a number of dissimilar fields of study. So where does the librarian turn?

Traditional publisher catalogs are still a good bet. Produced quarterly, many of the big and small publishing houses offer both print and online versions of their catalogs. Still, it is time consuming to thumb through page after page of a print catalog, hoping to find that one item. Certain publishers produce online catalogs, allowing the librarian to limit the information they receive to only books and items published within their field of interest. This form of direct marketing not only removes the piles of catalogs cluttering your office floor but also allows for timely notification of a publisher work much quicker than having to wait for the next quarterly print catalog to land in your mailbox.

Don't overlook newsletters, journals, blogs, user recommendations, LISTSERVs, Google Scholar, and an item's citations as potential sources.

Newsletters, Trade Magazines, and Academic Journals

Several associations, businesses, and nonprofit organizations circulate newsletters that, in addition to covering news, feature stories, and conferences, also contain a book review section. Since most librarians acquire books based on the title or a short abstract, these longer and more in-depth reviews are more helpful when deciding which book to select. Academic journals and trade magazines often provide the same review service. As an added benefit, subscribers and nonsubscribers alike can submit an online form containing their research interests and be notified when a report or article is published (oftentimes before it is in print).

Blogs and LISTSERVs

The same blogs and LISTSERVs used to help build your subject knowledge can now act as a finding aid. Whether or not they are technically considered a review, bloggers and LISTSERV participants identify recently published and unpublished works and provide a direct link to the items. Comments and feedback from readers can also aid in deciding if the item is appropriate for your collection.

User Recommendations

Users don't always know what they need, but they do know what they want, so you may consider them an active avenue for purchasing ideas. Provide an online form for users to suggest works for the collection. Ask for their input when conversing at the circulation desk or answering an e-mail or phone call. If problems arise, refer to the section of your collection development policy that describes the inclusion and exclusion of material.

Decisions about what will be acquired must not only include the subject matter but take into consideration format, access, and physical shelf space as well as digital storage options. Again, this is where the user-needs assessment and collection analysis come into play. Serious considerations must be made to ensure users have legal and easy access to the collection and the library budget is capable of covering the costs.

Procuring Resources

Small research libraries face the challenge of working with little or no monetary funds available for purchases. Vendor services can prove to be too costly, and the librarian is forced to look elsewhere for quality resources. The goal is to obtain proprietary material at the least possible cost or at no cost if possible. If you must purchase an item, make sure to check Amazon and similar sites, as they offer used copies at a much lower price.

Reports can be obtained for free from government agencies, universities, some national and international nongovernmental agencies, nonprofit organizations, think tanks, or other public entities. Subscribe to receive e-mail press releases from organizations. News releases of recently concluded studies are announced along with a link to the resulting report.

Other free sources include gifts and exchanges. Make it clear to your user community that you accept gifts of appropriate resources. Set up a wish list on Amazon, and publicize it. Offer to write a book review in return for a newly published book, or agree to feature it on your library's webpage.

Despite their popularity and importance in the research arena, proprietary materials like journals and databases devour a large amount of the library's budget. However, if possible, negotiating with publishers to review or feature the journal on your webpage in return for a complimentary subscription is a worthwhile endeavor. If not possible, carefully review each journal for content to ensure it is suitable for your audience. For instance, purchasing a journal that addresses the subject matter from a mechanical engineering perspective will not be useful to users who are social scientists. The costs of journals and databases have skyrocketed in the past decade and may be completely out of the price range for the library. In this case, ILL can be a substitute, but remember: ILL services come with an associated cost.

Despite the type of material, where it originates, or how it is obtained, be aware of copyright restrictions. Fair use is most often cited by librarians distributing content, but in today's changing copyright landscape, that may not always be accurate. While issues surrounding copyright and digital rights management are too abundant to address in this chapter, there are numerous resources that address a host of copyright situations.

Deselection

Collection development involves acquiring new resources and discarding the old. Deselection, or weeding, is the process of removing unused, deteriorated (replace if needed), irrelevant, or outdated items from the holdings. Removal does not necessarily mean sending weeded material to a trash receptacle. Moving it to an off-site storage site, selling it, or donating it to another facility are acceptable methods, though be aware of legal restrictions against selling certain items. Any collection must undergo a periodic review to guarantee its users a dynamic assortment of current, high-quality resources.

Items to be weeded are identified in the collection evaluation process. Criteria for what is to be removed should be determined prior to beginning the weeding process. Even with criteria in place, the knowledgeable librarian's judgment is a valuable asset to any deselection project.

Conclusion

Because of the specialized nature of their holdings and specific user base, collection development in special libraries and information centers differs from academic or public libraries. The process of identifying and procuring resources becomes highly individualized based on the collection's particular subject area and limited acquisition funding, thus dictating a departure from the standard collection development process. Formalized policies and instruction as well as personal knowledge of the research literature, trends, and issues in the subject area all work in tandem to produce focused collections that deliver quality resources to all the library's users.

Chapter 15

How to Choose the Right Cataloging Tools

Beth Dwoskin

Overview

Library cataloging is a moving target. What's state of the art today will probably be behind the curve in five years. Yet the factors that go into deciding how to automate cataloging and build a database will remain constant: mission and scope of the library, circulating versus noncirculating, budget, technical savvy of the librarian, hardware support, and clerical support. These are the same factors that influence other aspects of running a library, and the best approach is one that integrates all librarian functions to the greatest extent possible.

This chapter helps you determine which cataloging tools will work best in your own library.

Initial Considerations

Users' Needs

Before deciding about cataloging, a librarian should refer to her library's mission statement. Who is this library serving? Do the materials circulate? Is it a collection of books only, or are other formats available? Are books checked out when no staff is present, or is the library closed at that time? Are there foreign language materials? Is the collection specialized or focused on only one subject? Will users expect to have web access to the collection from their homes and/or smartphones? The librarian who is choosing cataloging software or an integrated library system will need answers to all these questions before he or she proceeds.

Budgetary Concerns

In addition, the librarian needs to know how much money is budgeted for this expenditure and who the person is in the organization who handles hardware and technical problems if it is someone other than the librarian. It can be helpful to think of this choice as a shopping task. Choosing cataloging software is like shopping for a house or a car. It's a weighty decision, and it can be difficult to compare prices because different vendors present features in different ways. If you make the wrong choice, it will be very difficult, but not impossible, to change.

The cost of automated library cataloging is sometimes presented as an implementation price and an annual price. The implementation is usually only slightly higher than the annual cost, and it will cover the first year, so the main concern is settling on an amount that can fit comfortably into the library's budget every year.

Hardware

Hardware is the next consideration. Does the librarian have a state-of-the-art computer and stations for patron access? Does he or she have time and resources to deal with backups, upgrades, storage, and migration issues? Do the library's users work primarily from stations that are networked with the library's computers?

Before going any further, some definitions may be helpful. A library catalog is a database. In the library world, the database is composed of records. Each record represents an individual title of a work in its particular format. Thus, if the library owns the book *Gone with the Wind*, there should be a record for that book. If it owns a DVD of the movie *Gone with the Wind*, there should be a record for the DVD. Each record is composed of fields—separate data elements containing such data as author, title, place of publication, publisher, date of publication, and so on. Bibliographic file formats—that is, database programs that are set up with fields that can contain data about books—are usually the best choice for a library catalog.

A librarian who is comfortable with the Microsoft Office suite may be tempted to create a catalog in Access or Excel. Any automated catalog is better than none, but these programs will not be as flexible and user friendly as a bibliographic database. It will be harder for users to do granular sorts and faceted searches, and the librarian will have to create a new field every time he or she thinks a data element is important enough to extract. But, the main drawback to the Microsoft programs is that they cannot import shared cataloging.

Shared Cataloging

Shared cataloging is a historic practice in which major libraries, such as the Library of Congress and the largest university libraries, do the original cataloging of all new or newly discovered material and then distribute it to smaller libraries. Thanks to the Internet, this sharing can now be done with one click but not in Excel or Access.

Librarians who have robust hardware and support might be tempted to use a program that is designed for a home library. There are several such options that can be installed on a Mac or Windows platform, and they are very economical. After the initial purchase, the only cost is for major upgrades. These programs are user friendly and have state-of-the-art catalog features, but they have two drawbacks.

Web Accessible

The first problem is that not all of them are web accessible. If you choose a program that is not and you want to share your catalog with users, you will pay for the client/server module of the product. Users will then have access only through networked stations, or from mobile devices if the product offers that service and you work with your users to download the app and synchronize with the database.

MARC Format

The second drawback to using a home library cataloging product is that, if in the future you decide to upgrade to a professional cataloging program, you might have serious difficulty migrating your database to that program because your records will not be in MARC format. At present, cataloging in the library world is done in a format called MARC (machine-readable cataloging). Because MARC is the standard in the library world, it's easy to move records from one catalog to another and one program to another—the process known as import/export. Data in other formats can be exported, but the process of moving it from one program to another is much more complicated.

Network Support

Again, this comes back to the issue of support. In the digital world, nearly everything is possible if you can find the person who knows how to make it possible. Software installation, backup, and data migration are all operations that require varying levels of skill and time commitment. A librarian has to try to envision doing these tasks in the future as he or she shops for automated cataloging in the present.

Cloud-Based Products

A very foolproof way of getting started without the need for a top-of-the-line computer or a big budget is to use a cloud-based home-cataloging product. A cloud-based product stores your database remotely on its own servers and gives you access to your records through the Internet. The one-time cost is typically very nominal, and with web access, everyone who has a computer or mobile device can see the catalog. The interfaces are user friendly with a strong social component. They are geared toward users who want to share their reading enthusiasm and learn about what others are reading, more than those who just want to manage their collections. Nevertheless, many small libraries make use of them because they cost virtually nothing. Importing shared, authoritative cataloging records into your library account is easy, and the support team should be able to work with you if you eventually want to export your records to another product.

Circulation Module

The main problem with these nearly free cloud-based products is that they do not have a circulation module. Circulation is the biggest complication in the purchasing decision. If there is more than one professional librarian involved, they should work together to decide on an integrated library system (ILS) that handles circulation and acquisition as well as cataloging. The ideal automated product is one where each database record is used in multiple ways without being recreated for each module. Circulation complicates this ideal because a record has to be created for each user. Do you have a membership list that can be imported to the system? Is there a list of employees who are users? Who can use your library, and how will you determine whether an individual qualifies? Will you give users a card or an ID number? All these questions have to be dealt with in any circulating library.

Barcoding

The other aspect of circulation that is challenging is the need to barcode the items in your collection. Barcoding is a complicated clerical task, though it becomes easier once it is in place. It requires extra hardware, setup, and staffing. Some small libraries choose to forgo this task and stick with manual circulation—the card-and-pocket method. This, too, is a clerical task.

An ILS for cataloging and circulation is the most expensive investment of cost and commitment for a small library. At present, the overwhelming majority of ILS vendors offer web-based products, known as software as a service (SaaS). If a computer can access the Internet, it can use these products. Therefore, the cost of the product is for the Internet service that you are probably using anyway plus the annual cost for the service itself. These programs offer all the features of a catalog that you see in a public or university library in terms of accessing material in a collection—big libraries also offer access to subscription journals and databases, but that's another consideration.

In each of these categories, there are numerous choices, and they can be difficult to compare. The best approach might be to make a table with categories that are important to you along the top and vendor names down the side:

	Annual Cost	Web Accessible?	Circulation Method	Z39.50?	Quality of Support
OPALS					
LibraryWorld					
LibraryThing					
Readerware					

How to Begin Cataloging

While you are in the process of choosing your automated catalog, you should also be weeding your collection. You don't want to bother cataloging something that has no place in your collection. You also have to decide what you want your catalog records to include. For example, almost all modern catalogs include cover images with each record.

Once your software is in place, you can begin cataloging by downloading shared cataloging records that have already been created for the items in your library. Most cataloging software will give you the opportunity to download records from at least the Library of Congress (LC) and Amazon. A good program will give you a long list of libraries to choose from, and you'll get far more accurate, complete, and consistent records from LC or a university library than you will from Amazon. If your collection consists of modern trade or university press books in English, in most cases all you have to do is enter the International Standard Book Number (ISBN), which is usually found on the back of the book or the back of the title page. If more than one record comes up in your search, be sure to choose the one that is exactly right for your book. If there is no ISBN, you can search by title. Again, make sure you get the record that is as close as possible to the book in your hand. After you download, edit the record to make it match the book you have.

Choose a Classification Scheme

Is there a classification scheme for your library's collection? Almost all libraries organize books and media on shelves according to a classification scheme. The most commonly used schemes are Library of Congress Classification (LCC) and the Dewey Decimal System (DDS), but these are designed for large, general collections and might not be right for yours. Try to use a scheme that you feel is appropriate for your collection. Do research to determine if there is a scheme that matches your needs and a community of users to support and update the scheme. If your library is small enough, you may want to organize books by broad subject categories rather than classifications. Some libraries have begun to use BISAC, the system developed by the Book Industry Study Group. But if your collection is all on one topic, you need a scheme that is specific to that topic.

Sometimes, a small library that has been managed by a lot of different people will have a homegrown classification system that may or may not be written down and applied consistently over the years. Spine labels may or may not be consistent with the scheme. This is the time to decide on whether to move to a better scheme or to try to modify and improve the existing scheme. The decision typically involves money, time, and staffing.

Some of these same considerations are also pertinent to subject headings in bibliographical records. In standard catalog records, these subjects are derived from the Library of Congress Subject Headings (LCSH) or the Sears List of Subject Headings (Sears). Again, are these terms appropriate for your library? Is there an alternative list developed by the community you serve? For example, if you have an education library, you might want to use the list of ERIC descriptors as your subject headings.

Subject Headings

For both classification schemes and subject headings lists, be very leery of trying to create your own. Decades of thought and effort have gone into the published schemes and lists, which in most cases have developed organically with the input of diverse librarians over the course of years of publishing. However much you may know about a particular subject, you'll find it difficult to organize a system that books will fit into. Design of these structures is highly theoretical and time consuming. Most likely you'll find it not only unworkable but also a frustrating waste of time.

One thing to keep in mind when you are adding or modifying subject headings is that they should reflect the subject(s) of the work, not its form or format. In other words, you don't need subject headings such as "Videodisc," "Textbook," or "Fiction." Rather, these are *form subdivisions* and should be in the text string after your subject heading; for example, for *Gone with the Wind*, United States—History—Civil War, 1861-1865—Fiction.

Subject headings and classification schemes are for users who want to browse a subject. Some will prefer to use a computer, while others would rather go to a shelf. The former will be better served by a well-thought-out subject heading list, while the latter need a detailed classification scheme. If your collection is small, you probably don't need to worry about subdivisions for format and historical period. They have to be added to the subject headings in a consistent pattern so that a list of search hits will be useful, and constructing them is confusing to an untrained cataloger.

Though you may not be able to use classification numbers and subject headings from records that you download to your database from the Internet, you will definitely be able to use the names that libraries, such as the Library of Congress, provide, and you should. LC and its partners catalog virtually everything in print in the United States and many other places as well. For decades, it has maintained a list of name authorities (LCNA), correct spellings and forms of names, and birth and death dates in some cases to distinguish between similar names. This is especially helpful with foreign names that are transliterated from other scripts. For example, how are you going to enter a name like Muammar Qaddafi in your catalog? Or Kadaffi? Or Kaddafi?

Using Z39.50 Protocols

If your collection contains older, foreign, or highly specialized materials, you may not find them in online catalogs. If you have foreign or specialized materials, check the list of libraries that your program provides to see if any of them match your collection in terms of their focus. If you know of such a library and it is not in your list, it may be possible to download from that library's catalog through a process called Z39.50. You have to verify first of all that your program will allow you to add libraries. Then, go to the relevant library's webpage and see if you can find information on Z39.50 compliance. You may have to contact the library directly. Adding a library's Z39.50 protocols can be challenging, and a librarian may need assistance from someone with network experience, but if there's a library collection that you need to access, you should add it to your list to make your cataloging program worthwhile to you.

Once your records are downloaded, they are yours to do what you like. The program will allow you to edit them, and you should do so to make them describe accurately the book you have in hand, to modify or change subject headings and classification numbers to make them more useful for your patrons, and to correct errors. There will also be times when you will not find a record for your book, and you will have to create one from scratch.

Don't panic! First, be absolutely certain that no record exists anywhere for the book. Search every catalog that might possibly be relevant. If you find a record in an online catalog that is not in the list your program provides, you can often download the one record or cut and paste it into a blank form in your software.

If you still can't find a record, search for the author's name and all other relevant names as well. You want to make sure that you use the correct form of the name in the record you will be creating. In addition, you may find the book in a different language, under a different title, or as part of a collection. If not, the author may have written something similar, giving you clues about subject headings and classification. Trained catalogers never catalog a book from scratch until they have looked everywhere to find as much information as they can about the material, its author, and its subject.

Consistency in Cataloging

Modern cataloging in the United States is done in MARC format, according to one of two cataloging codes, AACR2 or RDA. The more that librarians use the cataloging codes, the more shared cataloging benefits in terms of quality, consistency, and uniformity. However, the records you create in your local catalog are unlikely to be shared by other libraries, so your main concerns should be the forms of names and the proper use of subject headings and classification. If you find that you have a lot of uncataloged books, if they are in an unfamiliar language, or if you expect to share your cataloging, it's best to consult a trained cataloger.

Cataloging trade books using the ISBN is so simple that you can assign the work to a clerical assistant. However, you should review your assistant's work, ideally by creating proof lists of records sorted by name and title. When such lists are generated, errors typically stand out immediately.

The assistant will often find errors in spine labeling and classification because he or she is handling the books one at a time. For purposes of work flow, it is usually best for the assistant to put the problem book aside with a note. By handling these problem books, the librarian gets a feel for cataloging issues and the state of the collection, without having to spend time on simple downloading. Every situation will be different.

Typical problems that arise with online cataloging are with names. LC and research library catalogers use character sets that can accommodate diacritics—accent and pronunciation marks in foreign names. These diacritics do not translate in the standard coding that most software uses, resulting in strange characters that have to be edited in the catalog record.

Another problem is confusion about editions. Current cataloging practice is to make a separate bibliographic record for each edition of a work, making it easy to accidently download the wrong edition.

The most confusing thing for nonprofessionals is the difference between a bibliographic record and a holdings record. The bibliographic record tells you that your library holds that item. The holdings record tells you how many copies you have, whether they are hard or soft cover, whether they are being circulated, whether you have them in different locations, and so on. Clearly, the two types of records have to be linked, with the bibliographic record being the master record. This is an important interface to look at closely when you are reviewing demos of different products. The link between the bibliographic records and the holdings records have to be clear and easy to use to you, or your clerical assistants will never understand.

A librarian has to stay flexible when approaching cataloging. You may not be able to afford the program you want. You may find that your collection is too large or you can't take the time to start over with the ideal classification scheme. You may choose the ideal software only to have it raise its price dramatically, change its features, or go out of business. You will have inevitable headaches at the beginning when you are implementing your automation program. And many of the previous recommendations may be obsolete in five years, certainly in ten. Just remember, any automated database of the contents of a library collection is better than none. Google-searching *library software* will get you started on your database planning. Good luck!

Conclusion: Tips

Following this chapter are links to some of the most popular, reliable, and recommended products for automation in each category of choice as well as lists of other recommendations. As with any type of shopping, read recommendations and talk to other users. Look at as many demos as you can find, make a list of questions, and call or e-mail the support staffs of the products you are considering to see how responsive they are and if you like their answers. Then, take a deep breath and make a decision to purchase.

Useful Resources

The American Library Association has an excellent overview page on this subject, with useful links: http://www.ala.org/tools/libfactsheets/alalibrary factsheet21.

There is also a page with links to cataloging tools, only some of which are free: http://www.ala.org/tools/libfactsheets/alalibraryfactsheet18.

Home Library Software

Collectorz: http://www.collectorz.com/book.

Primasoft: http://www.primasoft.com/products/library_software_solutions .htm.

Readerware: http://www.readerware.com/index.php.

Free Cloud-Based Programs

Goodreads: https://www.goodreads.com.

LibraryThing: http://www.librarything.com.

Shelfari: http://www.shelfari.com.

Integrated Library System (Software as a Service)

Alexandria: http://www.goalexandria.com/landing.html.

Destiny: http://www.follettsoftware.com/library-automation-software.

LibraryWorld: http://www.libraryworld.com.

Mandarin: http://www.mlasolutions.com.

OPALS: http://www.mediaflex.net/showcase.jsp?record_id=52.

Chapter 16

How to Master the Art of Cataloging

Arwen Spinosa

Overview

We have access to an overwhelming expanse of information, and managing this information is an ever-changing endeavor. Of the tools librarians have developed to help organize and navigate this sea of knowledge, the primary tool has remained the catalog. Cataloging librarians build and manage the catalog and are responsible for accurately representing the library collections. The catalog is built within a software database that has a staff and public view, generally called the integrated library system (ILS) and the online public access catalog (OPAC). There is such a diversity of special libraries, each with their own unique issues, that there is not room here to discuss how cataloging is performed in all of them. There are many books that explain how cataloging is performed in just one kind of special library! This chapter instead gives an overview of cataloging in small special libraries, as well as a list of resources.

The Catalog

The catalog is used by both the public and staff for different purposes. It remains one of the library's primary discovery tools to evaluate and locate library material, regardless of whether it is physically or digitally accessed. In the case of small special libraries, the online catalog may be the only discovery tool. The cataloger's job is to provide access to library materials through accurately representing the collections in the catalog and upholding the organizing classification system. One of their most traditional tasks is creating and enhancing records in the catalog. Many catalogers operate behind the scenes, but their work is often the first aspect of the library that patrons interact with. A library presents itself to the world though access to its online catalog, and the contributions of competent catalogers are essential to making the catalog functional, accurate, and efficient.

Cataloging is not simple data entry, nor is it magic. A wide range of tools and expertise are used to properly manage the catalog. The foundational knowledge is the same across the profession, and it is only after these core competencies are attained that one can develop the specialized knowledge needed for certain kinds of special libraries. Traditionally, cataloging has been behind-the-scenes work. With increasing digital collections and the need for metadata, catalogers are becoming more visible due to their involvement with collections of digital objects. In many cases the person performing cataloging duties has many additional responsibilities and spends a great deal of time multitasking. Traditional cataloging tasks are still very much in demand, but the job title may be vaguer than "cataloger" in order to encompass the range of responsibilities. Performing cataloging tasks in a special library is very similar to those tasks in larger institutions. The principles and goals are the same, but the degree of specialized knowledge and the amount of original cataloging needed will reflect the unique collections of different libraries.

Necessary Software

The primary tool catalogers should be very comfortable with is their ILS, the database that constitutes the library's catalog. ILS software come in many flavors, from massive cooperative, shared catalogs with high functionality to more Spartan but affordable systems designed for small libraries. Explore your ILS to determine its strengths and weaknesses so that a flaw doesn't catch you off guard. Talk to librarians elsewhere who use the same software to get their thoughts on it. Some systems have tool options that do not work because that part of the software was never fully developed. This becomes problematic when, for instance, you need certain statistics and it appears that the ILS software will provide them but cannot. On the other end of the spectrum, older ILS software can be glitchy, and if it is no longer supported by the software developer and doesn't receive updates, the software may eventually develop major issues of data corruption.

The other main software tool to become friends with is a bibliographic utility. Most cataloging work involves importing records from vendors or OCLC Connexion or by using the Z39.50 application. Many libraries use OCLC, the Online Computer Library Center, which is an international cooperative of libraries that produces WorldCat. Because of its widespread use, OCLC Connexion is used as an example bibliographic utility for the rest of this chapter. When copy cataloging, the cataloger will search the OCLC database for an existing record to import into their catalog. When performing original cataloging, the cataloger creates a new, unique record that is added to the database for the benefit of others. OCLC has useful guidelines for when to create a new record. Many basic tools are incorporated into OCLC's cataloging interface, such as authority records and links to MARC field usage guidelines.

Basic Knowledge

Basic cataloging knowledge includes the formalized, international standards used to increase efficiency and promote cooperation. All librarians should know how to read a MARC record, but catalogers need a much deeper understanding of them. MARC21 is the current standard of formatting bibliographic, authority, and holdings information. Become familiar with what information is entered into each of these three kinds of records. When reading MARC records, cultivate a habit of systematically checking each record in the same way, from fixed fields to the end of the record. This way, when information is out of place or missing, it will stand out. It is impossible for anyone to memorize the usage of all the MARC fields! An online reference tool produced by OCLC, the Bibliographic Formats and Standards, explains the use of all MARC fields and subfields for AACR2 and RDA.

Currently, a shift is taking place in the standards of bibliographic description from AACR2 to RDA. RDA is a response to the changing world of information, its storage, and dissemination from print based to digital. It is built on AACR2, so many of the standards are the same or similar. Access to and familiarity with the current standards of description are a must for any cataloger.

All librarians can read call numbers, but not all know how to create them. Most libraries organize their materials using either the Library of Congress Classification or the Dewey Decimal System. There are others, but whatever classification system is used, learn its history and development. This will help in understanding inconsistencies, biases, and limitations of the system and ultimately make the creation of new call numbers much easier. Some formats, exhibition catalogs for instance, have special ways of structuring call numbers. Research the formats in your collection to see if they require special treatment.

Tip: Becoming familiar with your cataloging system will help you identify and understand inconsistencies.

Tip: If you work in a special library, you may need to create special ways to structure call numbers.

Performance

A good cataloger is made of more than technical proficiencies and knowledge. The attitude, qualities, and discipline one chooses to cultivate are equally important. It might seem obvious to say that manners matter, but they are so often neglected that a sincerely respectful person stands out. Act professionally regardless of the behavior of those around you for the sake of your self-respect as well as the respect of others. Build professional relationships outside of your institution, as many of our successes come from the cooperation and collective wisdom of the cataloging community. Many people of this community are often described as "detail oriented." This can be seen as a commitment to personal discipline, an attentive focus on maintaining accuracy, and consistency in their work. We do our best when presenting, and we do our best when no one is watching. Accuracy and attention will build a catalog that is consistently organized and without cataloging errors, duplication, or missing information or items. Patience is essential. Weigh your decisions and imagine their results, and protect the catalog from impatient, uninformed colleagues. Beware the temporary or easy fix, as these solutions can end up generating a host of new problems.

Cultivate a positive attitude toward change. Hard and fast rules are reassuring, but the world of cataloging is a work in progress and always has been. Keep an eye on changes to the profession, do your research, and remain responsive to your professional environment. Records made according to previous standards of cataloging live side by side in the catalog, a constant reminder of our evolving philosophies and standards. Know the rules, but don't marry them!

Finally, *cataloger's judgment* is a term that can generate anxiety in a new cataloger. There is a difference between cataloger discretion and what the cataloger considers to be a perfect record. There is no absolute perfect record because our preferences and needs are too subjective. We use our best judgment when interpreting rules of classification and description, and it can be a gray area without definitive answers. This is an example of why research and cooperation with other catalogers is so vital. Templates sometimes just aren't enough. If you are not a trained cataloger and discover you must become one, seek classes and a mentor, and network with other catalogers who can help interpret cataloging rules and their application. Learn well, for someday you will be counted on to be a mentor yourself.

Tip: Accuracy, attention, and patience are essential to effective cataloging.

Tip: Seek a mentor, and network with other catalogers to become a proficient cataloger.

Cataloging Policies

Many specialized libraries are small, sometimes run by a solo librarian. One of the dangers of a small library is a lack of documentation and written policies. Why should a solo librarian document work flow or make policies that no one else will use? When there is no policy in place, organization breaks down, principles are disregarded, and we compromise our efficiency by reinventing the wheel. Very strange things happen when there are no guidelines, like cataloging books by their color and making collection codes for "upstairs" and "back room." Documentation is very important, perhaps especially for the solo librarian. Without it, processes become difficult to communicate, your reasoning and decision-making criteria remain mysterious to others, phases of projects are accidentally skipped, and work must be continually redone because of repeated errors. Catalogers sometimes are burdened with the stereotype of being rule mongers. We don't love rules, but we love organization! Policies don't have to be perfect—it is normal for them to go through many revisions—but they must be present and applied.

Tip: Even if you are a solo librarian, it is essential to develop cataloging guidelines.

Copy Cataloging Work Flow

Compared to the amount of background knowledge catalogers need, the process of copy cataloging is fairly easy. Copy cataloging is the process of importing a MARC record into the catalog that was created by someone else. The trick is to find the record, which brings up the need for advanced searching skills. In OCLC Connexion there are many duplicate records of varying quality. Do your best not to add to them by finding a usable record instead of creating a new one because the initial search failed. Many records can be found through searching for the ISBN or other standard number but not all. Perfectly usable records are often found that only lack an ISBN. Broad searches tend to bring up all the relevant records, whereas narrow searches might not bring up the record at all. Searching skills improve with practice, and a creative search can reveal fun and quirky aspects of the item you are searching for.

Once the correct MARC record is found, verify that it matches the item in hand. Records are coded for different levels of description, from minimal to full level and everything in between. Some records will be fully populated with all the needed information and be ready for importing immediately. If the record is incomplete or local standards require more information be added, then the record will need to be enhanced before importing. Some MARC fields are considered required access points, provided the information is available. For instance, some records have physical description fields that are incomplete or absent. As this is a required field, you would need to enhance the record by adding this information and saving the changes. Record enhancement benefits everyone.

Most libraries have a minimum requirement for the number of subject headings present in a MARC record. Subject headings are used to describe the people, organizations, places, ideas, and things a book or other item discusses. They are a kind of controlled vocabulary, with authority records to display the preferred form of the subject heading. For instance, an English-language title with the corporate author King Baudouin Foundation will not have this as its authorized heading but rather Fondation Roi Baudouin, the name as it appears in its native language. This control is a way of formalizing our methods of description so that we all describe material using a uniform format. When all the subject headings needed are present, use the toolbar to control all headings.

When all the information is present, the last thing to check is the call number to see if it will put the book in the right area of your collection. The differences in collection strengths are reflected in the call numbers used. A library with a strong subject concentration on eighteenth-century Polish miniature painting will develop call numbers in this range that are very detailed and locally specific. To ensure the new item will be placed properly, its call number must be checked against the shelf list.

Just before exporting from OCLC Connexion, check the spelling of the record. This is one very basic quality-control measure that is often overlooked. Typos are expensive, so be sure to check your English and non-English records. Note that in OCLC diacritics will not import into the catalog accurately if they were copy-pasted from another program—they must be put in through OCLC Connexion. It only takes a few seconds to verify if non-English records have imported properly. When this is done, verify the record through a button on the toolbar. This is another quality-control measure. It is now safe to import the record and attach the item to it through a barcode. Strive for the ideal of cataloging something only once so there are no mistakes to track down and fix.

There have been discussions as to what constitutes "good enough" cataloging, and it differs by local needs and personal preference. Untrained catalogers do tend to make the same kinds of mistakes, like using a record for a similar but different item, using the same call number for different items, and making up subject headings. Templates are very useful for both new and experienced catalogers. They are good as guides and reference, especially for unusual formats like kits, three-dimensional objects, media, and parallel-language records. Templates become a problem only when they are used as a crutch, as a prescription rather than a guide. Feel free to examine the work of others and investigate their choices of MARC fields and description, but be wary of falling into a habit of monkey see, monkey do.

Tip: Creating templates may be useful as guides and references for specialized collections.

Original Cataloging Work Flow

Not all libraries need an original cataloger, but special libraries tend to have unique collections that require one. Original cataloging is more time intensive and requires more focus, cataloging expertise, and doing more research. It includes cataloging non-English–language items and materials in all formats. Creating a record from a blank work form, one generally works from the top down:

1. Choose the format of the item: book, continuing resource, and so on.

2. Fill the fixed fields.

3. From top to bottom, fill all the applicable fields. Be attentive to all the information the item can supply, which might include running through a video to record its length in minutes.

4. End with the routine spell check, verification, and control of all headings.

Subject analysis must be performed on the item to accurately assign subject headings as well as the call number. This requires an investigation of the material and noting the predominant subject and all those involved in creating the item. Many libraries have a minimum of three subject headings per record, but that isn't always possible. All subject headings should control; they will not if there is a spelling error or for uncontrolled personal names. Some uncontrolled headings are inevitable, as not all personal names have birth dates in the authority records and not all institutions or corporations are in the authority files.

Difficulty arises when an item is incomplete, supplies little information, or is printed in a foreign language that doesn't use an alphabet. Incomplete items sometimes have clues as to what they are, but sometimes your best is all you can do. An item with little information is not a hopeless case. Dates, publishers, and country of origin can often be found through online research. If a date isn't supplied, you can at least narrow the date to the time frame when the publisher was at the supplied address. Items in languages that are inaccessible to most people can be cataloged with the help of specialized catalogers at other institutions.

Original catalogers are expected to perform cataloging for all formats of material that come across their desk. Some libraries will not require original cataloging, and some will require a great deal of original work if they collect specialized and obscure material. A backlog of original work can accumulate when there is not an original cataloger or their time is demanded elsewhere.

Tip: A note on non-English cataloging: Most items can be cataloged if they are in a language that uses an alphabet of some kind. There will often be a record for the item in its native language, and the cataloger will need to make an English-language record. Online translation tools can assist in subject analysis, determining dates, the form of the work (biography, for example), and the spelling variations of names. Respectable dictionaries are good to have on hand but not the pocket dictionaries or phrase books meant for tourists.

Resources

There is a wealth of resources available for every kind of special library. LISTSERVs are online mailing lists that discuss every facet of library work. They are a great way to build knowledge and relationships, as they provide priceless access to the collective wisdom of professionals around the world. Search the web for those pertinent to your specialization, and sign up to the group. Always be aware that discussions on LISTSERVs are professional communications with a highly qualified peer group, so choose your words appropriately. A couple general cataloging LISTSERVs to consider are Autocat and NGC4Lib. Library associations relevant to your specialization often have their own cataloging LISTSERVs.

Explore the Library of Congress website for cataloging subject guides and resources, MARC standards, authorities, and so much more. Your specialized needs may be unique, so here are other general resources to explore:

- OCLC Bibliographic Formats and Standards

- RDA Toolkit

- Rare Books and Manuscripts Section of the Association of College and Research Libraries

- Special cataloging reference templates found on many websites, such as special-cataloguing.com

- Translation Cutter tables found online in varying levels of complexity

- Professional associations

- Local organizations

Useful Resources

Intner, Sheila, and Jean Weihs. *Special Libraries: A Cataloging Guide.* Englewood, CO: Libraries Unlimited, 1998, 242.

Myung Gi Sung. "Ten Essential Qualities for Success: A New Cataloging Librarian's Guide from a Supervisor's Perspective." *Public Libraries Online* 52, no. 3 (May/June 2013).

Chapter 17

How to Train Your Staff to Catalog

Charles Ed Hill

Overview

Librarians in small libraries are, by nature, generalists. With one or two people usually in charge of all library operations, it is unthinkable that a person will be doing exactly what their training in library school, or whatever situation they are coming from, prepared them for. For those whose training did not involve extensive cataloging, it can seem akin to computer programming, full of arcane abbreviations, acronyms, and numerical codes that simply refuse to be straightforward. Even if you do have training in cataloging, chances are your library has materials you are not familiar working with. My library at the Natural Hazards Center, for instance, contains books, serials, DVDs, videocassettes, maps, archival materials, born-digital items, items digitized in house, photos, and several other material types, most of which my background in music cataloging gave me no preparation for. Given the variety of special libraries and the limitations of experience, it is almost a given that you, cataloging training or not, will encounter unfamiliar material types and feel out of your depth.

Nonetheless, if you work in a small library, chances are you will have to catalog at some point. The library's collection is its centerpiece, and making sure people can access that collection easily and efficiently is a primary goal of virtually all libraries. As such, you can expect cataloging issues to arise in your day-to-day in a small library, even if you have a rather small collection. With luck, you will be able to copy catalog most of your items, but you will still likely spend time fixing up records to local standards; checking to make sure any volunteers, student workers, or paraprofessionals have made adequate records; or ensuring that your local cataloging policies are best serving the needs of your patrons. In short, ensuring your library catalog is up to par should be part of your daily routine and receive regular "big picture" attention.

This chapter, then, offers some guidance on the difficulties of cataloging, followed by a brief discussion on training paraprofessionals, student workers, volunteers, and other nonprofessionals to help with your organization's cataloging needs. It will not be a full introduction to cataloging, for which there are several book-length examples,[1] nor will it offer detailed analysis of cataloging specific items. Also, I do not cover authority work and classification, which, though integral to the cataloging process, simply would make this chapter longer and more complex than can be presently covered. Rather, I attempt to be general about cataloging; define abbreviations, terms, and acronyms; and offer a road map to help a noncataloger get into the mix of cataloging library materials of whatever type and train others to do the same. The only assumptions I am consciously making are that you are working in a MARC environment and likely using AACR2 or RDA (defined later) for your description guidelines, an assumption I find necessary to meaningfully discuss the topic. If these assumptions do not apply to your library, I hope you can still find something of use here.

Cataloging for Noncatalogers: The Basics

First and foremost, pay attention to your local catalog policy. The guidelines and standards discussed here are robust, powerful tools for describing content and encoding it such that both machines and humans can read it. However, no set of rules will ever be so comprehensive that they will perfectly provide for each library's particular situation. Guidelines like AACR2 and MARC make it possible for records to be standardized across institutions so that they can be easily shared, greatly increasing cataloging efficiency. You, however, know your patrons and their needs, so your catalog policy should reflect those needs, even if they conflict with the guidelines described here. A simple, relatively low-stakes example involves what is known as the "rule of three." This is a statement in AACR2 that, if you have more than three of something in AACR2 (most often authors/editors), you input the first mentioned followed by *et alia* for the rest.

At the Natural Hazards Center we decided that this rule left out information that could be highly relevant to our patrons. We decided to break the rule of three, adding omitted authors back to copy-cataloged records and including all authors on newly cataloged records. This is not to say that you should disregard the guidelines on a whim, as they do make sharing records possible and increase the ease with which patrons can parse records across institutions, among other benefits. Rather, you should simply bring the same sensitivity to patron needs you have in other areas into your catalog and sculpt your policy and local practices to reflect that.

As stated earlier, the whirlwind of codes and abbreviations used by catalogers can present a barrier to understanding, so some of the most important ones will be dealt with from the outset. It should be stated that all these are much more complicated and in depth than they are presented here, but a full exegesis of each is far beyond the scope of this chapter. They are:

- AACR2—Anglo-American Cataloging Rules, Second Edition—The set of practices used to decide how to describe items and where in the item to take this description from.

- RDA—Resource Description and Access—The set of practices currently superseding AACR2 as the guidelines for how to describe an item and where this description comes from. The Library of Congress started using RDA as their primary guideline source in March 2013.

- MARC21—Machine Readable Cataloging—The current input format for catalog records. MARC provides the organizational shell into which one puts the description of an item. MARC records consist of fields that have numerical tags (the field for title is 245, for instance). These fields consist of lettered and/or numbered subfields that are denoted by $ or | before the subfield letter in many ILSs. Many fields also have indicators, numerical codes that tell your ILS how to treat the information, associated with them.

- ISBD—International Standard Bibliographic Description—The set of guidelines that establish a set of core areas of description as well as control aspects, such as punctuation and capitalization.

- LCSH—Library of Congress Subject Headings—The set of standardized subject headings provided by the Library of Congress for subject description.

- MeSH—Medical Subject Headings—Another popular standardized vocabulary specifically for medical topics.

These different standards interact in every bibliographic record. The cataloger opens a new MARC record, uses the guidelines in AACR2 or RDA to describe an item, applies appropriate LCSH, and puts that description into MARC fields and subfields according to the conventions of ISBD. A labeled example of a field from a MARC record from HazCat, the Koha-powered catalog of the Natural Hazards Center library, can be seen later.

Copy Cataloging: The Mile-High Overview

With luck, the majority of materials in your library can be copy cataloged using OCLC's Connexion client (a paid service, Z39.50 targets a freely available transfer protocol[2]) or some other method, such as manual transfer. What method you use to get the records into your catalog will largely depend on your ILS and funding, as OCLC memberships, while incredibly helpful, can be quite expensive and out of range for small libraries. Whichever method you use, when searching for records, keep a few things in mind.

First, make absolutely sure that each record you import is indeed for the item you are trying to catalog. This may seem insultingly simple advice, but with the plethora of editions, variations, formats, and other minute differences, it can be incredibly easy to import a record and only later realize that, while you have the physical item, you imported a record for the electronic version. First, check the 245 field to make sure the title and authors match exactly and see if there is a general media designation, subfield h, stating it is an electronic resource or other format. Next, check the 250 to make sure the record is not for a different edition, and if the item has an ISBN, check the 020 to ensure it matches, but be sure to combine this with the other fields, as records will often include ISBNs for multiple manifestations of an item. If all these fields agree with the item in hand, it is likely that this record is for the same item. This reduces the maintenance work you will have to do from importing incorrect records and save you time as recognizing correct, quality records will quickly become second nature.

Once you've determined which record you want to use and imported it to your ILS, you should check all the fields to make sure they are accurate. Even records from the Library of Congress sometimes have mistakes, so it's best to make it a habit of checking every record you pull in for spelling, punctuation, mistakes in coding, and other errors. If your institution uses authority records to help standardize and collocate names, subjects, and series, those can be verified and made if needed during this checking step as well. Next, you can enhance the record according to your local policy. This will vary greatly across institutions, but making your records reflect your specific situation gives patrons that much more information to work on. Some examples of enhancements include a table of contents in the 505 field, notes in the 500 field detailing physical condition, extra subject headings in the 650 fields, or links in the 856 fields to an electronic version of the item or related materials. This enhancement can be time intensive, as you are usually putting in extra information by hand rather than automated tasks, but knowing your patrons and including information and resources they may find useful can only make your catalog a stronger, more useful tool.

Original Cataloging: The Five-Mile-High Perspective

First, unless absolutely necessary, I would caution against doing original cataloging before you have done a considerable amount of copy cataloging. Copy cataloging develops a familiarity with MARC structure, and some of AACR2 or RDA and ISBD will "seep" into your consciousness. Paying attention to formatting and other patterns while doing copy cataloging will help you later on. I would also encourage having an experienced cataloger review some of your work by sitting down with you while you catalog a few items from scratch. Cataloging has a host of guidelines and exceptions to those guidelines, and sitting down with somebody who has dealt with them and has worked out how to think through making many complex catalog records will help you more in an afternoon visit than a week of floundering on your own. If you find yourself isolated from other librarians and not sure who to ask, there are resources like the Autocat mailing list,[3] a mailing list expressly for library catalogers. It is well stocked with experts in practically every type of cataloging and is an excellent place to ask questions and get speedy, expert opinions. What's more, the archives are a treasure trove of advice on all aspects of cataloging. Like most librarians, catalogers tend to be all too happy to talk about what they do and offer advice and will often be your best resource.

With that in mind, I offer some tentative suggestions to guide your thinking in doing original cataloging along with some basic rules of thumb to keep in mind. First, I would strongly suggest developing some familiarity with the structure of AACR2[4] or RDA.[5] It is not necessary to be able to quote it chapter and verse, but to know where to look if you are not sure how to treat a certain aspect of description. Depending on your collection, you may be able to use a handful of rules to describe most of your items and only refer to the guidelines for corner cases, but regardless of the depth at which you are working, it is beneficial to have the rule set on hand and some idea of how to use it.

Title and Responsible Parties

The specific routine that you use to catalog may vary greatly from the following description, but I like to start with the simplest questions and work toward the more complex. Thus, I typically start by transcribing the title and responsible parties from the title page or chief source of information for the item type being worked on into the 245 field while making sure the indicators are correct. The second indicator here is the easy one; if the title begins with an article, you put the number of characters to skip in order to not include the article in the indexed record. Remember that this is characters, though, so it will always be one more than the number of letters in the word to include the space before the next word. The first indicator states if a title-added entry is made. Typically, if you have anything in a 1xx field (name main entry), the 245 first indicator is 0, and if there is nothing in a 1xx, the first indicator is 1. A rule of thumb for making the decision of whether something is a main entry for a 1xx field or added entry for a 7xx field is that discrete authors that are responsible for almost all the intellectual content of a work are generally main entries, and works without this are generally added entries placed in a 7xx field (this means editors are in a 7xx). If there are multiple discrete authors for a work, you place the first in a 1xx field and the others in a 7xx field, as each record can only have a single main entry. For more guidance on whether something should be considered a main or added entry, consult AACR2 or RDA for information on access points.

Physical Description

Following the 245, remain on the chief source of information for the item in hand, and input the publisher information into the 260 and the physical description into the 300. If unsure about formatting for these or any other fields, consult the Library of Congress MARC guides, which give detailed notes and examples for each field.[6]

Subject Description

After these fields, I typically tackle the authority-controlled fields, which include the 1xx, 6xx, 7xx, and 8xx. Of these, I typically reserve the 6xx for last because subject description typically takes more time than name and title. Subject description is one of those aspects of cataloging that is somewhat subjective in that, barring a heading that has nothing to do with the item in hand (*Spaghetti* for a recording of Beethoven's third symphony, perhaps), there is not a "right" heading, but there are "more accurate" headings that more precisely pinpoint the subject of the work. It is also one of those complicated areas that takes practice and benefits from critiques from others with more experience. Generally, though, if the item has some sort of introduction, synopsis, abstract, or other information about it, you can intuit what some headings will likely be from reading this. You can then use tools like the Cataloging Calculator[7] or the Library of Congress authority search[8] or consult the Subject Headings Manual and its updates[9] to find the authorized version of the heading. The Cataloging Calculator can be especially useful for this purpose, as it allows for dynamic searching of terms, showing a list of possibilities as you type. While subject description can be difficult and certainly benefits greatly from experience and frequent critiques, asking yourself two related questions will usually get you in the ballpark: Would somebody searching on this term expect or hope to find this item? and Would somebody looking for this item be likely to use this term to find it?

Control Numbers and Other Fixed Fields

Finally, I go back to the 0xx fields and put in the various control numbers and fill in the fixed fields.[10] This is also the time when I check back over everything I have done. Consistency will benefit you in upkeep on your catalog and your users by increasing findability. Therefore, checking your work religiously is very important. In small libraries, we are constantly pressed for time, but this attention to detail pays off in a well-ordered, usable catalog. That being said, don't let yourself get stressed over errors, and certainly don't lose sleep over possibly misplaced commas. Errors are inevitable, so we seek to minimize them as much as possible, know we made useful records, and sleep soundly.

Teaching Others to Do the Same

The bad news is that cataloging is time intensive. The good news is that teaching somebody to copy catalog is not insanely time consuming. The rub is that small libraries frequently have little to no staff, and what there is can often be unstable. At the Natural Hazards Center, we rely on undergraduate students with work study to assist us, which means that we typically have high turnover and workers who cannot commit large amounts of time due to school commitments. For this reason, we've developed a very direct method of training that should also work for paraprofessionals or volunteers.

First, we are as direct and procedural as possible. Rather than explain what ISBD is and why that matters, we tell the students, at least at first, that titles are transcribed in a specific way and to just do it that way. This method leaves out a lot of nuance, but you can add that nuance over time if you have long-term assistants. To provide this training, I sit with each new employee, and we immediately begin copy cataloging a work together. I talk them through the process in the most mechanical way I can, explaining every action taken. We do this for several books while I gradually give less and less instruction, until they feel comfortable doing the entire process on their own. At this point, I let them work individually, and they give me their finished works to check. I critique the work and offer feedback as soon as possible, giving them the items back to fix errors. While I will admit this is not an ideal teaching strategy, we have found that our workers pick up the process fairly quickly, and the detail-oriented mistakes, such as indicators, they pick up after a small number of errors. In general, even this short, limited training has allowed new student workers to start contributing to the catalog sometimes by their second day, and with the kind of turnover we have, that is essential. Additionally, we have a short handbook document we give every new employee that provides ILS-specific guidance for every action they should take when copy cataloging an item and provides examples of formatting, which they can reference.

For those assistants who are longer term, there are ways to increase their knowledge of cataloging and have them do more than routine copy cataloging even if they have no interest in being a professional librarian. The first is simply an extension of the previous method but introducing concepts rather than rote routine. With this method we have trained a student worker to be able to critique and offer feedback on other students' work and train new assistants. Additionally, if you can find a time every week or every other week to get your cataloging group together in the same room, you can use this time to go over concepts you weren't able to cover in their initial training. Additionally, they can ask questions about problematic materials so that everybody can learn from each tricky example. This method has been successfully implemented by Oregon State University's cataloging department to help train their paraprofessionals in subject description[11] and provides a model that both cuts down on the time you spend correcting mistakes or explaining idiosyncrasies and allows for growth in your assistants.

Tip: When teaching others to catalog, concentrate on what to do at each step, and save the reasons for later.

Tip: All libraries are different, and so their catalogs may be different.

Tip: Keep in mind the needs of your users when cataloging.

Conclusion

Cataloging is not easy. There is a reason catalogers have specialties and subspecialties because the plethora of materials out in the world simply does not admit to somebody being able to handle everything. However, it doesn't have to be painful or endlessly confusing. There are a plethora of resources out there to help you, including catalogers with decades of experience, even if you've never spent a day of your life in the back end of an ILS. The standards exist for a good reason, but there is no reason the catalog in your library needs to be like the catalog in somebody else's. In a small library, you likely have a good handle on who your users are, so as long as you catalog with them in mind (and hopefully adhere to standards), your catalog will reflect your commitment to serving your patrons.

Notes

1. Arlene G. Taylor, *Introduction to Cataloging and Classification* (Westport, CT: Libraries Unlimited, 2006); and Lois Mai Chan, *Cataloging and Classification: An Introduction* (Lanham, MD: Scarecrow Press, 2007).

2. Information for a large number of Z39.50 targets can be found at IRSpy, accessed January 5, 2014, http://irspy.indexdata.com.

3. "AUTOCAT Home Page," LISTSERV 16.0, accessed January 5, 2014, https://listserv.syr.edu/scripts/wa.exe?A0=AUTOCAT.

4. "Cataloging Fundamentals," Boston College, accessed January 5, 2014, http://www.bc.edu/bc_org/avp/ulib/staff/cat/fundamentals/AACR2pt1. pdf. Another great resource for training and reference materials is "Cataloging Tools and Resources," Yale University, last modified November 1, 2013, accessed January 5, 2014, http://www.library.yale.edu/cataloging/ tools.htm.

5. "Prospectus," Joint Steering Committee for Development of RDA, last modified July 1, 2009, accessed January 5, 2014, http://www.rda-jsc.org/ rdaprospectus.html.

6. "MARC 21 Format for Bibliographic Data," Library of Congress Network Development and MARC Standards Office, last modified September 24, 2013, accessed January 5, 2014, http://www.loc.gov/marc/bibliographic.

7. Kyle Banerjee, The Cataloging Calculator, accessed January 5, 2013, http:// calculate.alptown.com.

8. "Library of Congress Authorities," Library of Congress, last modified December 7, 2012, accessed January 5, 2014, http://authorities.loc.gov.

9. "Subject Headings Manual," Library of Congress, accessed January 5, 2014, http://www.loc.gov/cds/products/product.php?productID=79.

10. For information on fixed fields for various formats, see "008—Fixed-Length Data Elements-General Information (NR)," Library of Congress, last modified March 5, 2010, accessed January 5, 2014, http://www.loc.gov/marc/ bibliographic/bd008.html. Banerjee, Cataloging Calculator, is also useful in this regard.

11. Richard Sapon-White, "Subject Analysis Training for Cataloging Paraprofessionals: A Model for Ongoing Learning and Support," *Technical Services Quarterly* 26, no. 3 (2009): 183–93.

Chapter 18

How to Utilize Interlibrary Loan

Corinne Nyquist

Overview

Interlibrary loan (ILL) is sharing materials between libraries in your region, around this country, or across the world. It is the way we get what is not owned by our library or is currently unavailable and how we respond to other libraries. Since it also involves articles not returned or access to materials online and even cooperative collection plans, a suggested name change is *resource sharing*. *Document delivery* has been used in many ways to explain special services, such as physical materials libraries deliver to faculty offices or to distant learners at home. An "Amazon.com-like future for libraries" has even been envisioned (Coffman 1999). Items purchased from a commercial service to meet patron requests also fall under this term. Yet, the term *interlibrary loan* is still most used.

The Basic Rule

There are rules for this service. A request comes from a library mediated or unmediated, but in either case, the first rule to learn is that the borrowing library is responsible from the time the requested item leaves the lending library until it is received back by the lending library. This is what differentiates ILL from consortial borrowing.

Interlibrary loan is a transaction between two libraries and never between a library and an individual. Even with unmediated borrowing, we must continue review of our patrons because we take responsibility for every request. Our philosophy was well expressed by Constance Winchell, who wrote the earliest guide for us: "Thus the practice of the loaning of books by one library to another has grown from an occasional favor to a more or less organized system. This, however, should not release the borrowing library from a sense of appreciation and a realization that to request a loan is still to ask a favor" (Winchell 1930).

While sharing between libraries surely has a centuries-long history, the first U.S. Interlibrary Code was adopted by the American Library Association in 1919. It still states our purpose as follows:

> Interlibrary loan (ILL) is intended to complement local collections and is not a substitute for good library collections intended to meet the routine needs of users. ILL is based on a tradition of sharing resources between various types and sizes of libraries and rests on the belief that no library, no matter how large or well supported is self sufficient in today's world. (Boucher, 1996)

The Explanatory Supplement to the current ILL Code states that the first responsibility of both the requesting library and the supplying library is a policy, available in a written format and, when possible, posted on the library's website. All staff members in ILL should have copies of this code, and it should be reviewed thoroughly with them. It is useful for preparing your policy/guidelines.

Policy and Guidelines Examples

This section includes sample ILL guidelines from two libraries, the Albany Public Library and the State University of New York at Oswego. Each is displayed on the libraries' websites to guide users.

Albany Public Library Interlibrary Loan Guidelines

Borrowing

Interlibrary Loan (ILL) service is provided by all branches of the Albany Public Library (APL) for materials that member libraries of the Upper Hudson Library System do not own. Any customer in good standing (fines below $10.01 and no restrictive use notes) may use this service: ILL is not available to temporary card holders. The ILL Librarian reserves the right to manage the number of customer requests in light of workflow constraints.

APL will borrow/acquire:

- books

- photocopies of journal articles less than 50 pages

- microfilm

- microfiche

The ILL Librarian will have the discretion to determine if any materials are for In Library Use Only.

APL will not borrow/acquire:

- books less than 6 months old

- audiovisual materials such as audiobooks, music CDs, VHS tapes and DVDs

- textbooks

There are no renewals of ILL materials. Each customer must wait a minimum of three months from the date of return of any item before re-requesting the same ILL item.

The lending period of materials is set by the lending library, not APL, so customers will not be able to borrow material for the same loan periods as comparable Upper Hudson Library System (UHLS)–owned items. If a Reference copy of a requested item is available locally, the item will not be requested and the customer will be directed to the local owning library.

ILL is not a rush delivery service for books. The minimum wait period for materials is two weeks, and it is sometimes over a month. Customers will be notified by phone unless they request a mailed card, so it is essential that they provide a phone number that is able to receive and record messages.

Abuse of the privileges afforded by ILL service may result in the suspension and/or termination of a customer's ILL privileges at the discretion of the ILL Librarian.

Lending

Libraries outside of the UHLS may also request items through ILL.

APL will lend only:

- books older than 6 months old

- photocopies (free of charge for 50 pages or less, $.20/page in excess of 50 pages)

Assistance: Contact (name), Interlibrary Loan Librarian at (telephone number).

Public libraries serve unattached scholars, students of every age and academic level, and all persons with a variety of interests residing within their geographic area. Colleges differ. See the following example.

SUNY Oswego Interlibrary Loan Service Summary

This service is available only to faculty, faculty spouse or partner, emeriti faculty, staff, and students.

What Can Be Requested through Interlibrary Loan (ILL)?

- Books* (including those listed as Lost, Missing, or Checked out in our catalog)

- Photocopies of journal articles & book chapters (in compliance with U.S. Copyright Law)

- Media Materials: DVDs, CDs, VHS, Audiocassettes—Patrons may be restricted to 10 active ILL media requests.

- Music Scores

- Microfilm & microfiche

- Theses & dissertations

*While we do not ban requesting textbooks, this practice is NOT recommended:

- Due to cost and high demand, they are extremely hard to borrow.

- Delivery period for this type of item frequently exceeds 10–20 days.

- Loan periods for all ILL materials are at the discretion of the owning library and are NOT for the entire semester. Renewals are often not allowed on textbooks, and textbooks are frequently subject to recall by the owning library. Failure to return your ILL material in a timely manner results in blockage of service.

- Textbooks are expensive. As with all ILL materials, if an item is lost either in transit or while in your possession, or damaged (which includes but is not limited to underlining, highlighting, marginalia, water or other liquid spills, torn or chewed pages or cover, etc.) you are responsible for payment. The payment is set by the owning library via an invoice and is non-negotiable—it is whatever amount they declare.

What Cannot Be Requested through ILL?

Materials owned by Penfield Library that have a circulating capacity within or outside the library (i.e., Reference material, Course Reserve material, IMC (Instructional Media Collection)

How Is ILL Material Delivered, and How Long Does It Take?

- Articles are delivered electronically & generally average 2–3 business (M–F) days.

- Physical items are shipped to us & generally average 5–7 business (M–F) days. All physical materials obtained through the Interlibrary Loan Service must be picked up in Penfield Library at the Check-Out & Reserves Desk.

- Some materials may be restricted to in-library use only by the lending library or at the discretion of the Penfield ILL Librarian.

- Distance Learners should see the Services for Distance Learners web page regarding requesting physical ILL materials.

What's My Cost?

- Faculty, Emeriti Faculty, Staff, Graduate students, Upper Division Honors Track students and McNair Scholars are subsidized up to $200 per person per academic year (including summer) or until Penfield's ILL subsidy budget is depleted for the given fiscal year. Only those requests that are research/work related will be considered for subsidy. Personal/hobby type requests will not be subsidized.

- Undergraduate students are offered the choice of paying fees, before the material is ordered, if fees are indicated.

- Any fines, fees, charges, unusual shipping requirements, or invoice(s) incurred because of late return, loss or damage to the ILL material are the patron's responsibility & will be charged against your library account.

Due Date

- The due date is printed on the book band. Do NOT remove the book band.

- Material delivered electronically is yours to keep.

- Electronically delivered material is available from your ILLiad account and is limited to 30 days.

Renewal Requests

- Renewals can be submitted through the ILLiad system if your material:

  - Allows renewals. Check the book band.

  - Is not overdue.

  - If this is the first renewal you are requesting for this material the lending library may opt *not* to renew or to renew for a shorter period than requested. In that case you will be advised by email and need to return the material as indicated.

Responsibilities—All Patrons

- You are responsible for ensuring the material is not defaced or damaged, to return/renew the material on time, as well as for any legal consequences due to violating copyright from personal reproductions.

- ILL loan materials (physical items that need to be returned) may not be placed on Reserve.

- Recalled ILL material(s) must be returned immediately [when] the lending library has advised us they must have it returned immediately. Failure to immediately return recalled ILL material(s) will result in a block of ILL service as well as $2.00 per day fines.

- Any fines, fees, charges, or invoice(s) incurred because of late return, loss, or damage to the ILL material are the patron's responsibility & and will be charged against your library account.

- Any ILL patron who has material(s) more than two weeks overdue may be blocked from ILL service and library circulation.

- Faculty owing $50.00 or more of any ILL fines, fees, charges, or invoices will be blocked from ILL service and library circulation.

- Students and staff owing $10.00 or more of ILL fines, fees, charges, or invoices will be blocked from ILL service and library circulation.

Document Delivery

Electronic copies (scans) of articles and book chapters, as permitted by copyright and as available in paper copy in Penfield may be requested by SUNY Oswego faculty, graduate students, and Distance Learners using the Interlibrary Loan form.

This service is offered to other libraries. Requests for items are only accepted via OCLC/ILLiad, ALA forms, or via Email. Penfield Library follows the most current approved ALA Interlibrary Loan Code for the United States, as well as copyright laws and CONTU guidelines. Rush requests are accommodated as time and staffing permit.

Materials Available for ILL Lending

* All circulating materials except for those listed below.

Materials Not Available for ILL Lending

Microfilm/Microfiche: case-by-case basis, Non-circulating Media, Reference: case-by-case basis, Periodicals, Reference: case-by-case basis, Reserve, Rare materials/Archives, and Puppets.

Charges

- Loans free

- Copies free—first 50 pages, may be fewer if oversized

Loan Period and Renewal

- Monographs: 35 days, 1 renewal.

- Browsing Collection: 2 weeks, No renewals.

- Media: 2 weeks, No renewals.

Lost Items

Material that is 3 months overdue is declared lost, invoiced, and no longer eligible to be returned in lieu of payment. A $25.00 processing fee is charged in addition to the amount charged for the item. Replacement copies are not generally accepted.

Guidance Needed and Offered

Reviewing these codes will help you learn the lending and borrowing responsibilities of libraries. Library districts may create more restrictive or more generous codes. Since there is no official ALA oversight, libraries may refuse to participate in ILL with libraries that do not follow the guidelines, or they may suspend other libraries, just as libraries suspend patrons who do not follow rules.

The most recent ILL guidance is in ALA Fact Sheet 8 produced in January 2013, with an incredible list of resources and guidelines that you will want to review: http://www.ala.org/Template.cfm?Section=interlibraryloan&template=/ContentManagement/ContentDisplay.cfm&ContentID=104201.

You may also want to review the following list of basic things you should know, also from the ALA: http://www.ala.org/rusa/sections/stars/5-things-every-new-resource-sharing-librarian-should-know.

Best of all is the online LISTSERV, where everyone, everywhere, can ask questions, raise concerns, and seek help: ILL-L. To subscribe, access this URL: http://listserv.oclc.org/archives/ill-l.html.

Understanding the Legal Aspects of ILL: Copyright Law

The following legal summary, as well as the earlier policy examples, are part of the chapter titled "Don't Say No When Faced with Rules and Policies" (Nyquist 2014).

The U.S. Constitution

Article I, Section 8, Clause 8, of the Constitution of the United States, enacted in 1790, also known as the Copyright Clause, empowers the U.S. Congress "to promote the Progress of Science and useful Arts, by securing for limited Times to Authors and Inventors the exclusive Right to their respective Writings and Discoveries."

First Sale Doctrine

Copyright law has been revised several times by Congress, most recently in 1976, and tested in courts. It contains the source of what is called the First Sale

Doctrine, which allows owners of a book or other physical copy of a copyrighted work to rent it, resell it, or, as in the case of libraries, to loan it. It does not permit the making or distribution of additional copies. This "right" originated in court cases involving secondhand bookstores, but is encoded in Copyright Law, Title 17, U.S. Code, Section 109.

Fair Use

Fair use originated because we did not want the author or owner to prevent us learning from, commenting on, or even parodying copyrighted original works. The exclusive rights of authors, creators, or other copyright owners, such as employers and publishers, are encoded in Section 106, while Section 107 addresses fair use:

> Notwithstanding the provisions of section 106, the fair use of a copyrighted work, including such use by reproduction in copies or phonorecords or by any other means specified by that section, for purposes such as criticism, comment, news reporting, teaching (including multiple copies for classroom use), scholarship, or research, is not an infringement of copyright. In determining whether the use made of a work in any particular case is a fair use the factors to be considered shall include:

1. The purpose and character of your use

2. The nature of the copyrighted work

3. What amount and proportion of the whole work was taken, and

4. The effect of use upon the potential market for or value of the copyrighted work

The fourth factor is the most important. A person borrowing a book or video from a library may want to buy it after free exposure. A library borrowing an item may also want to buy it. However, efforts to correlate ILL copying with a decline in journal or magazine subscriptions (print or electronic) deserve our attention.

Photocopying Rights and Guidelines Specifically for Libraries

Section 108 of the Copyright Law, says that:

- Libraries qualify for these special copying rights if their collections or archives are open to the public or outside researchers.

- Libraries and archives are allowed to make copies for replacement, security, or preservation.

- Reproduction and distribution rights apply to a copy made at a patron's request for scholarship, study, or research. The copy then becomes the property of the patron, but a notice stating that the material may be protected by Copyright Law 17 USC must be displayed. This is also where the limit to one article from a journal is found.

- An entire work or substantial part may be copied for individual research.

- Individuals who make use of unsupervised reproductive equipment are not covered by Section 108, but libraries are protected if the equipment displays the copyright notice above.

- Isolated and unrelated reproduction of the same material is permitted providing interlibrary arrangements do not have as their purpose "aggregate quantities as to substitute for a subscription or purchase of such a work."

- Reproductions do not apply to musical works, pictures, graphics, sculptures, or movies or other audiovisual works other than an audiovisual work dealing with news.

Are CONTU Guidelines a Suggestion?

Because portions of Section 108 of the Copyright Law required clarification and guidance, a Commission on New Technological Uses of Copyrighted Works (CONTU) was appointed in 1976 by Congress. The resulting guidelines are summarized here:

1. Periodicals published within the past five years are the focus of the guidelines and have become known as the "rule of five." Periodicals older than five years are still not open to unlimited copying under Section 107.

2. During one calendar year, no more than six copies may be requested and reproduced from a single journal title. The sixth request shows the library should enter a subscription. The usual response is to pay copyright fees or purchase from a vendor.

3. The library may request an article it owns or will own, but not available, without counting it.

4. The borrowing library request form must state "CCG" to show it complies with CONTU Guidelines. Lending libraries need not keep copyright records but should look for the "CCG" on the lending request form.

5. The borrowing library must maintain records of all requests for these copies that were filled for the recent three calendar years.

The term used for these guidelines is *safe harbor*, any place or situation that offers refuge or protection. The alternative to *safe harbor* is *litigation*, an expensive and lengthy process. Number 5, above, was a compromise, few of which happen in the world of Copyright Law. According to Laura N. Gasaway (1996), librarian and law professor, "Publishers favored permitting libraries to borrow only two items within the most recent ten years of a journal, while libraries wanted to be able to borrow ten items per year from the most recent two years of the journal."

Conclusion

Unfortunately, ILL is not taught in library school; librarians learn it on the job, usually as they go along. For a solo librarian, it is initiation by fire. But help is available from the ILL cooperative community of librarians and staff members. The best example of this is LVIS (Libraries Very Interested in Sharing) established in 1993, representing the first global OCLC resource-sharing group agreement. This is the subscription address is http://www.cyberdriveillinois.com/departments/library/libraries/OCLC/lvis.html.

Bibliography

Boucher, Virginia. 1996. *Interlibrary Loan Practices Handbook.* 2nd ed. Chicago: American Library Association.

Coffman, Steve. 1999. "Building Earth's Largest Library." *Searcher* 7, no. 3 (March): 34.

Gasaway, Laura. 1996. "Copyright and Interlibrary Loan: The Uneasy Case for the Digital Future." *Colorado Libraries* 22 (3): 14–17.

Hilyer, Lee Andrew. 2006. *Interlibrary Loan and Document Delivery: Best Practices for Operating and Managing Interlibrary Loan Services in All Libraries.* Binghamton, NY: Hayworth Information Press.

Knox, Emily. 2010. *Document Delivery and Interlibrary Loan on a Shoestring.* New York: Neal-Schuman Publishers.

Nyquist, Corinne. 2014. *Resource Sharing Today: A Practical Guide to Interlibrary Loan, Consortial Circulation, and Global Cooperation.* Lanham, MD: Scarecrow Press.

Weible, Cherie L., and Karen L. Janke, eds. 2011. *Interlibrary Loan Practices Handbook.* 3rd ed. Chicago: American Library Association.

Winchell, Constance. 1930. *Locating Books for Interlibrary Loan: With a Bibliography of Printed Aids Which Show Location of Books in American Libraries.* New York: H. W. Wilson Co.

Chapter 19

How to Weed Library Materials

Sherill L. Harriger

Overview

The weeding, or deselection, of library materials from a library collection is not a new phenomenon. Library literature traces weeding, or deselection, back to 1892, when the Crane Memorial Public Library in Quincy, Massachusetts, was running out of room, giving birth to the Quincy Plan consisting of "weeding all but the most popular materials, producing finding aids for readers, and transferring research materials to locations that were most convenient for potential users" (Dilevko and Gottlieb 2003). Needless to say, ever since then, there has been controversy about the whole idea of weeding library materials.

I have been working in academic libraries for forty years. I now hold the position of library director at a small Christian university in Florida. Through my years of working in academic libraries, I have found the two main reasons to weed a collection are lack of space or unacceptable book content, by which I mean inaccuracy of information.

First Weeding Experience

When working at a university in Pennsylvania, one of my responsibilities as the circulation department library technician was to make sure the books were on the shelves ready for student use. But I wasn't told what to do when the shelves were too full and there was absolutely no room for shifting. Even though I had no formal library training, I knew this problem had to be confronted head on, so I broached the subject of weeding a particularly over-crowded LC classification with my mentor, a reference librarian, as the only alternative to the space shortage. I quickly found that the idea of weeding was not going to be readily accepted; consequently, I had to find a way to make the idea appealing to the library administration. I then offered an alternative to full-scale weeding, calling it "temporary storage weeding." I recommended that all uncirculated duplicates and books with a copyright date over ten years old that had not circulated for the last ten years be placed in storage in the building's basement. With my mentor as an advocate, the library administration agreed to this proposal. When the books were removed from the shelves and placed in storage, the book cards were pulled and placed in call number order in circulation trays at the circulation desk. If a particular book that had been placed in storage was needed by a library patron, the book would be retrieved from the basement, checked out to the patron, and then returned to the general circulating stacks.

However, at the end of an additional five-year period, we once again found there to be a space shortage, so the books that had previously been placed in basement storage were brought back upstairs and placed on sorting shelves in the circulation area. Discipline-specific faculty members were then invited to review the books by a certain date to make sure the library staff was not going to discard a title that might be vital for their discipline; unfortunately, only a few faculty members came to review the books.

At the end of the designated time frame, the books were to be removed from the collection, which then caused another problem. The disgruntled head of the cataloging department informed me that she did not have the staff to withdraw the books because of the amount of time involved in pulling the cards from the card catalog. Remember, back then the online public access catalog was nonexistent; consequently, each book in the library collection had multiple cards in each set, including author card(s), title card(s), and subject cards. Since many of the books designated for deselection were research titles, the amount of subject cards alone that needed to be pulled from the card catalog was extensive. Undaunted, I then suggested that circulation department student assistants be trained to pull all of the card catalog cards and that each set would be double-checked by a full-time circulation department employee before being taken to the cataloging department for removal. Reluctantly, the head of the cataloging department agreed to this arrangement, and we were finally able to discard unneeded items from the collection.

Florida Library

In the fall of 1989, I started working as a library technician in the library where I am currently the library director. Between 1990 and 2003, I completed my associate of arts degree, bachelor's degree, and MLIS degree and then was named the assistant library director. Upon the retirement of the former library director in 2005, I was then named library director. Shortly thereafter, even though we were in a new building, I was once again confronted with a shelving shortage. Upon reviewing the shelves, I realized that we were using only six shelves per shelving section because of having to accommodate oversized books. Consequently, my staff members pulled all books from the main general circulation collection that were between twenty-eight and thirty-two centimeters in height and recataloged them, designating them as quarto "q." These books were then placed in special shelving designed to accommodate books of that size. After the oversized books were removed from the general circulation stacks, the remaining books were then shifted into shelving with seven shelves per section, thus gaining one shelf per section and alleviating the shelving constraints.

Informal Approach for Weeding

Shortly thereafter, upon reevaluating the collection, I realized that a number of sections were going to soon become problematic, so I tried an informal approach. At each faculty meeting, I would invite faculty members to come and review the books that pertained to their specific discipline and weed all nonessential or obsolete volumes and/or pull editions that needed to be updated. The response I most often received was a quizzical look and a raised eyebrow and unfortunately very few "takers," but once in a while, a faculty member would come in and do a cursory review. However, a relatively young science professor, after reviewing his section, commented that he was very surprised by what he found—some books that he wished he had in his own personal collection and others that he had pulled from the shelves, earmarked to be discarded immediately because they contained "bad science."

Weeding Using Printed Shelf Lists

During the spring of 2007, we selected two sections of books to be reviewed. These were the Library of Congress Classifications "L" (education) and "BF" (psychology). An Excel shelf list spreadsheet was generated from the online public access catalog for each classification. The book entries were then sorted by copyright date and listed by decades, for example, 1960–1969, 1970–1979, and so on, to the most current.

The first four columns on the spreadsheet were entitled:

* Copyright Date,

* Call Number,

- Title, and

- Barcode Number.

The last three columns on the spreadsheet were entitled:

- Initial Here to Remove,

- Find Replacement Yes/No, and

- Book Sale or Discard.

We included the very last column because of the comments made by the science professor so that items deemed no longer academically viable could be immediately removed and discarded. The Excel files were printed and placed in three-ring binders and given to the heads of the education and psychology departments for review. Unfortunately, this method did not work very well because it took a long time to get feedback from the faculty. When the binders were finally returned, very few items were designated for withdrawal.

Historical Value

The academic dean of the institution was fully aware of all of the different methods being used to try to get faculty to weed the collection, but he then made a statement concerning content that had not been considered. He stated that, even though a book may be old, unattractive, and possibly not used very much, it still could have a considerable amount of "historical value." Consequently, we then created a label with a graphic and the words *Historical Value* (none could be bought commercially) to be placed above the call number of books that discipline-specific faculty deemed historical in nature. This visible designation on the book thus prevents it from inadvertently being withdrawn in the future.

Use of Book Carts

Several years later I commented to the dean of the School of Business that the business books, Library of Congress Classification HA to HJ, needed to be weeded. She stated that she did not have the time to go to the stacks and weed, but if the books were brought to her, she would review them as time permitted. Consequently, the cataloging technician pulled books from the business section that were eleven or more years old and placed them on a book truck, and the truck was then wheeled to the dean's office. Along with the books were colored slips for her to place in selected books:

- Withdraw

- Find Replacement (Most Current Edition)

- Historical Value

When the dean completed assessing the content of a truck of books, the cataloging technician would retrieve the book truck and remove the books with slips and process them accordingly. The remainder of the books that were left on the book truck was then reshelved. The cataloging technician would then fill up another truck of books and return it to the dean. This process worked very well and did not create an undue burden on either the dean or the library staff.

Conclusion

Professionally speaking, I know that the weeding of library collections should fall completely under the purview of a librarian; however, I do not wish to assume that I have the expertise to weed books from such areas as the sciences, music, or religion. That is why I campaign so strongly to get input from discipline-specific faculty. Additionally, I am fully aware that the methods outlined within this document are not standard, but they have proven to be practical and effective.

Weeding is not an easy process, but it is a necessary process in order to keep the collection vital to the mission of the institution.

Bibliography

Dilevko, Juris, and Lisa Gottlieb. 2003. "Weed to Achieve: A Fundamental Part of the Public Library Mission?" *Library Collections, Acquisitions, & Technical Services* 27 (2003): 73–96. http://moyak.com/papers/weeding-books-libraries.pdf.

Part IV

Marketing and Outreach

Chapter 20

How to Build an Army of Library Advocates

Lee Ann R. Benkert

Overview

Advocates can shoulder a crucial element of a librarian's job description—keeping the lights on. This chapter provides an understanding of why advocates are important, followed by a tiered approach to building an internal advocacy campaign to support and promote your library. Key elements include knowing your target audience, communicating your value, and arming your advocates.

The examples provided stem from my experience managing a small library[1] in a military space education and training center. I am a solo librarian with one part-time assistant, and our library's users are on-site students and faculty who are active-duty, reserve, or retired military; government civilians; or defense contractors. Considering the organization's nontraditional academic environment (course terms are three to four weeks and the faculty is small), unique service population, and specific teaching focus, our library is considered a special library[2] with an academic slant. Three years ago, my library launched an advocacy campaign targeting our internal stakeholders[3]—users, middle management, senior leaders—considering these folks have a direct line of sight to our services and control the resources and capabilities needed in order to deliver those services.

Who Are Advocates?

According to publisher ABC-CLIO's Online Dictionary for Library and Information Science, a library advocate is a "person who appreciates libraries and their role in society to the extent of speaking and acting publicly in their support." In other words, advocates are proud promoters of your library. They come from all corners of the community or organizational chart, spreading the message that your staff and services bring value to the organization and to the community at large. At meetings you are not invited to and in peer-to-peer conversations around the proverbial water cooler, they sing your praises, sharing with others your mission-critical impact. Think of them as a powerful campaign team that actively builds your user base as well as demonstrates your value.

Why Are They Important?

As a small library manager, it can be challenging to not only deliver quality services but to also promote those services across your organization. You are but one person. Even with a modest staff, it can still be difficult. But promoting your services and the impact those services have on your organization is absolutely essential to keeping your library functioning. If your library's services fail to tie to the organization's mission, there is little guarantee that your library will remain in business. Even if it is crystal clear to *you* that your services tie directly to the mission, if your organization's senior leaders cannot see that connection, your library is in danger of being downsized or even eliminated.

In a climate of fiscal uncertainty and shrinking budgets, advocates can help ensure that your doors remain open. Prompted or unprompted, they speak to the benefits the library provides, having either an acute awareness of or direct experience with your services. Their words can have more impact than yours alone—reaching decision makers, influencers, and funders who may not be aware of your services. To use a military term, advocates are "force multipliers," multiplying the efficacy of your message in a way you could not have accomplished on your own.[4]

Advocates vs. Users

Advocates may or may not be users of a library's services. Heavy users have the potential to make great advocates, but so do nonusers. In fact, several of the non- and light users at the senior level in my organization are our biggest advocates.

The distinct difference between the two is advocates speak up while users may not. Why do advocates speak up? Because they recognize your library's value and are eager to communicate that message. (It's the same reason you advocate for your own library.) While advocates may or may not use, support, and market your products and services, they are actively engaged in spreading the message that your services are not only valuable but also valued by the organization.

Types of Advocates

Silent Advocates

These are usually folks who use your services but don't speak up about their experiences. However, when asked, they are happy to provide their thoughts—to you, to other users, or to senior leaders. The key is someone has to ask them.

Vocal Advocates

These are your word-of-mouth marketers and are great folks to have on your side. They sing your praises to others across all levels of the organization, often without prompt. I have found the best vocal advocates have evolved from silent advocates. They just needed to know that their feedback was valued. Vocal advocates may or may not use your services, but they definitely see value in what you are offering and are willing to communicate that message.

Power Advocates

These are the folks who have influence over others or the organization at large. Within the organization, these folks are often, but not always, in leadership positions. However, they may exist outside the organization, too (e.g., well-known members of the community). Their direct or indirect influence and advocacy can have great impact on the health and future of your library.

How to Build Advocates

Building advocates is not an overnight process; it's a long-term project that requires energy and patience—and, most important, a strategy. The following tiered approach gives you a clear picture of who you are targeting, what message you are sending, and how to spread that message with the intent of developing a team of advocates.

Know Your Audience

Anyone has the potential to be an advocate. But targeting everyone in (or outside) your organization is neither a good use of resources nor generally feasible. Begin with a focus on target groups in order to streamline your efforts and ensure your time is well spent.

Target Groups

Ask yourself: Who uses my services? Who doesn't but could? Who are those people's bosses? Who approves our budget? Who signs my paycheck? Who

are those people's bosses? Who are the key decision makers in the organization? Who are the key influencers? If you are new to the organization, pose
these quotes to your boss or colleagues; most often, they will be impressed by
your interest and eagerness.

Next, group those folks into broad categories you could target. For example,
when my coworker and I drafted our advocacy campaign plan, our segmented
groups resulted in: students, faculty, senior leadership, and the greater military
community. I decided that our target groups would be faculty and senior leadership (the latter category comprising project managers and military officers).
They each comprise fewer people than the other two groups, and my coworker
and I have more face-to-face contact with both of them. Thus, we could target
them with far less effort.

What's on Their Minds?

Now, identify the needs and wants of your target populations. This may involve
casual observation or a more systematic approach, such as a formal needs assessment (also referred to as a community need analysis). Needs assessments
can be viewed as reference interviews on a larger scale—you are probing the
individuals in your target group for more information in order to assist them
with an unmet need. In their book *Assessing Information Needs: Managing
Transformative Library Services*, Grover, Greer, and Agada provide a step-by-step
methodology for conducting formal needs assessments, which can help you
successfully identify your targets' needs.

Even if you choose not to conduct a formal assessment, at minimum, put
yourself in your target groups' shoes. Successful business researcher and
entrepreneur Mary Ellen Bates often encourages information professionals to
think about what keeps your target groups up at night.[5] Do they worry about
their next big presentation? Are they struggling with how to manage their
e-mail inbox? Do they long for a promotion? Some of these questions you
can obtain by talking to your target populations and asking probing questions.
Others you can glean from observing the organizational culture and from
hallway chatter.

As an example, here is a sampling of the concerns I collected from my target
populations:

- Faculty: Receiving stronger critiques from students

- Faculty: Performing well in order to stay gainfully employed

- Senior leaders: Getting promoted

- Both: Looking good to the boss

Now ask yourself probing questions about these concerns. For example, why would "receiving stronger critiques" be a concern to our faculty? Within our organization, student critiques are viewed as a metric of individual and organizational success. As such, they are read by everyone in the chain of command, from faculty to middle management to senior leadership. This data is also routinely used in annual performance evaluations. Thus, good critiques allow faculty to address their other concerns ("performing well" and "looking good to the boss").

Solve Their Concerns

Each of the concerns you identify is an opportunity to learn more about the needs and wants of your target audience. The next step is to find ways to solve their concerns, thereby demonstrating that the library—and library staff—is crucial to their success as well as to the success of the organization. Ask yourself: How can you make their job easier? How can you get them closer to ["looking good to the boss"]? Do any of your existing services address their needs? Do you simply need to tweak your marketing so they become aware of your existing products?

Perhaps repurposing a current service is the answer, as was the case for my library. After collecting and analyzing our target population's need, my coworker and I developed a strategy of delivering customized services to match each faculty member's interests. We started with the lowest-hanging fruit: hand-delivering and e-mailing news articles, reports, and videos. It didn't increase our workload significantly, as we were finding and cataloging these items anyway. We just decided to be proactive about getting the information in front of them. We also repurposed an existing news-alert service to provide added value via searchable, desktop access to their areas of interest.

These services have been a hit, as our instructors appreciate receiving timely information that is relevant to their lessons. Many have commented that this service not only saves time spent doing their own research but also allows them an easier way to conduct in-class discussions on hot topics. Facilitating student learning using current events and information is of great importance to our faculty, not only because it helps students master their learning objectives, but also because it plays into the composite student-learning experience. As you might expect, this experience inevitably makes its way into the student critiques—thus, addressing several of the faculty's need and wants.

What Does All This Have to Do with Advocacy?

Delivering great products and services tied to your target groups' needs is at the heart of developing advocates. If you choose to ignore the needs and wants of your target groups, you are missing an opportunity to allow your library to support the organization and truly shine. That shine (in essence, your success) gives the voices of your advocates weight and influence, which can directly or indirectly influence how long your doors remain open.

Be an Advocate

Delivering great service is one component to demonstrating your library's value. Now you've got to spread the message of your success. Put another way, you've got to *be* an advocate to gain advocates.

What's Your Message?

Tip: First, identify what your library does well and how it supports your organization's bottom line. Then translate that evidence into terms that will resonate with the folks in your organization. Start by identifying your value proposition: What unique, demonstrable impact do your services have on the organization? Craft that answer, and then you're ready to start sharing it with others.

Earlier, I provided examples of how my coworker and I identified faculty needs and then delivered services to successfully meet those needs. Examining that success, we asked ourselves, What effect did our efforts have on the organization? What could we prove? Then, we brainstormed a list of metrics that mattered to our target populations. Mapping *our* impact to *their* metrics helped us craft a custom message that would resonate with each target group.

For example, project managers like statistics. They can easily translate hard data into labor hours and money saved and can report this information to their bosses. Therefore, in our case, my coworker and I feed our success stories to our project managers in the form of numbers that meant something to them: research hours saved. However, our military officers received a slightly different message tailored to their area of focus: student learning. We highlighted the library staff's role in helping faculty be more knowledgeable and prepared, thus directly improving their individual performance in the classroom and indirectly impacting student learning. By customizing messages, our senior leaders had greater awareness of the good work we were doing, could easily link the library to the success of the organization, and could easily translate this information to their bosses—thus meeting *their* needs.

Finding your target groups' measure of success and relating your successes to it helps you convey a crystal-clear message to your advocates. Your target groups' metrics may not be immediately identifiable and may even change over time, but don't let that deter you. Experiment and find what works. Focusing on the impact, not the service offered, helps. Our news-alert service is our *vehicle* to success; its *impact* is the success. Your list of products and services might be impressive, but your impact is what will truly get their attention.[6]

That's Not My Thing

Tip: If you find yourself uncomfortable with spreading the message of your library's success, try looking at it as education—you are educating those around you on the benefits that your library and your staff provide. This helps give your advocates the tools they need to not only understand your value but to also share it with others.

Arm Your Advocates

Communicating a clear message is crucial to the success of your advocacy campaign. Your advocates need to have at their disposal not only an awareness of what your library offers but also ways to speak about your services and success. Your job is to arm them with an arsenal of useful information to support their advocacy efforts.

Give Them What They Need

At my organization, it is standard practice for senior leaders to bring distinguished visitors to the library for impromptu tours. Often, our senior leaders do the talking, hitting on key points of interest to their guests. Early on, I witnessed our leadership only highlight the products they could see (e.g., books, magazines, computers) or services they used (e.g., interlibrary loan). Recognizing an opportunity, I drafted "talking points"—brief highlights of what the library brings to the organization—that they could use when executing tours:

The library and staff:

- track down hard-to-find answers,

- supply faculty with current events to support student learning,

- track emerging trends in the space defense field,

- partner with local libraries to deepen our pool of accessible resources, and

- provide a quiet environment supportive of student learning and faculty meetings.

The commander of our unit is now fond of introducing my coworker and me as his "two friendly, human search engines," which often gets a chuckle from his guests. Supplying him with this phrase (and other useful information) helps him look good while also accentuating the value that the library—particularly the staff—brings to the organization.

Use Their Language, Not Yours

Tip: Be sure your message reflects the priorities of your advocates. Kate Arnold, president-elect of the Special Libraries Association, puts it best: "Use language that resonates with whoever [*sic*] you are talking to."[7] Unfortunately, this lesson is often learned the hard way. For example, our library has a lending agreement with a local university that allows us to tap into their unified catalog and obtain books from libraries across the state. We consistently referred to this service as our *lending agreement*, but after dozens of blank stares, I realized that phrase wasn't intuitive to nonlibrarians. So we swapped it for *academic partnership*, which was met with success. Once again, we had made both our organization and our library look good.

Similarly, for months, I supplied my chain of command with impressive statistics highlighting one of our news-alert services, which I called *proactive distribution of articles of interest*. One day, I got a call from my supervisor, who essentially called the phrase senseless. I ended up swapping in the phrase *situational awareness*, which is immediately intuitive to military personnel and better communicated the value of this service. Moral of the story: Use language that resonates in their world, not yours.

Success

It's a great feeling to hear the message you've been promoting come out of your advocates' mouths. It means they've internalized what they've heard and adopted it as their own. It's even better when they use it to go to bat for you.

Recently, when layoffs were pending, our senior leaders gathered behind closed doors to make tough decisions. I was told that, during deliberations, our commander declared, "The librarians are off the table. We need them. They make the faculty smarter. As far as I'm concerned, as long as we have instructors at this school, we will have librarians, too." It cannot be a coincidence that many of our power advocates were invited to that meeting. My direct supervisor also came to me afterward and said, "You and I both know that, when you started,

I didn't know what a librarian did; now we can't live without you." These comments are clear signs of a successful advocacy campaign. They are testaments to the aggressive efforts my coworker and I made in initiating and nurturing strategic relationships throughout the organization in order to build an army of advocates—an army that defended us in our time of need. It wasn't easy, but the time and energy invested paid off. Now, as new folks enter the organization, it is easier to demonstrate the value of the library as our advocates assist in our efforts.

Conclusion

The Online Dictionary for Library and Information Science indicates that the "most effective advocacy campaigns are often based on an action plan." Ensure that your action plan involves listening to your target audience and delivering what they need. But don't stop there. You must demonstrate a clear connection between the services you deliver and your organization's bottom line. Communicate this message in a way your advocates can easily digest and repeat—and you'll be well on your way to amassing an army of library advocates.

Useful Resource

Grover, Robert J., Roger C. Greer, and John Agada. *Assessing Information Needs: Managing Transformative Library Services*. Santa Barbara, CA: Libraries Unlimited, 2010.

This book offers both the philosophy and methodology behind conducting needs assessments. The authors include academic, public, school, and special library environments and offer a good model for translating user needs into useful services.

The conclusions and opinions expressed in this document are those of the author. They do not reflect the official position of the U.S. government, Department of Defense, the U.S. Air Force, or Air University.

Notes

1. For simplicity, I use the term *library* synonymously with *information center* and *resource/research centers*. Similarly, I use the term *user* for *patron* or *customer*.

2. Special libraries are libraries that fall outside the following categories: academic, school, or public. Jill Hurst-Wahl and Ruth Kneale define this career field in R. David Lankes's *The Atlas of New Librarianship* (Cambridge, MA:

The MIT Press, 2011), companion website accessed November 16, 2013, http://www.newlibrarianship.org/wordpress/?page_id=1204.

3. Versus external stakeholders (legislators, government officials, voters).

4. "Force multiplier," *Joint Publication 1-02: Department of Defense Dictionary of Military and Associated Terms*, November 8, 2010 (as amended through October 15, 2013), 100, accessed November 16, 2013, http://www.dtic.mil/doctrine/new_pubs/jp1_02.pdf.

5. Mary Ellen Bates delivers great presentations on a wide variety of topics of use to information professionals. A sampling of her presentations is accessible via webinar, *MEB's 123s*, http://batesinfo.com/meb123.

6. In one of her presentations, Mary Ellen Bates describes library "features" versus "benefits." Very useful distinction when communicating your value. See note 5.

7. "The Evolving Value of Information Management: And Five Essential Attributes of the Modern Information Professional," Financial Times, special report prepared in conjunction with the Special Libraries Association, 2013, 17, http://ftcorporate.ft.com/sla.

Chapter 21

How to Grow a Library with Databases and Subscription Journals

Robin Henshaw and Valerie Enriquez

Overview

A growing small library often needs more "stuff," such as databases and journal subscriptions, to serve an expanding user base of new departments and functions. When you get more stuff, you need to let people know that you have the stuff and how and when they may use the stuff because it is overwhelming. We implemented a multifaceted approach: We developed a social space on the library's intranet site, conducted outreach through department meetings, led training sessions, and offered follow-up support. In addition to more stuff, we provide more services (literature and patent searching, copyright compliance, pharmacovigilance monitoring) and work with vendors and other external partners.

Growing Your Library

Reevaluating the Library Function

The goal of any library is to have the right stuff at the right time for a reasonable cost. And while most in an organization would say they are quite interested in stuff, it is the librarian who combines skills and knowledge with the ability to use, deliver, and interpret stuff, not only to the advantage of the individual, but also to the advantage of the entire company (Ard 2012).

However, before adding more stuff, it is often helpful to step back and consider:

- What groups in the organization will be supported by the library function, and who are the stakeholders? Has this changed since the library was first established? Librarians who develop strategic relationships with different groups throughout an organization benefit by knowing their users and the needs of their departments.

- Does the library currently have the backing of senior management? Libraries supported by upper management get things done. Find advocates within the organization, nurture and develop those relationships, and collaborate whenever possible. Look for people who matter and whose business and budget requests are heard.

- Where does the library function live within the organization? Does this still make sense, or is restructuring needed to stay in step with changing needs? Users should see the library as a central point that disseminates information throughout the company, regardless of reporting structure.

- How is the budget managed? Is it centralized under the library function or decentralized, with departments charged individually for library services? Centralization streamlines cost administration but may create the perception of disproportionately large expenses. Decentralizing the library's budget spreads the costs but also requires more time spent tracking and billing back individual allocations. Database, journal publishers, and document-delivery providers often provide tools to help track costs in support of a decentralized model.

- How are current resources working, or are they not? Conduct needs assessment of users through focus groups, brown-bag lunches, or an online survey. Where are there gaps or pain points?

- What resources currently exist? What is needed now and in the coming year? Will these resources be temporary, for short-term projects, or longer term, reflecting current and new directions for the company? Are there free resources that can help fill these gaps?

- Will there be IT backing to support and implement new stuff?

- How will a successful library function be measured?

Tip: Taking time to work through these questions will enable small library managers to more accurately predict what stuff will be needed, when it will be needed, and ensure there is support within the organization.

Dr. Michael Stephens, who writes about trends and library technologies, describes "The Hyperlinked Library." His model is one of

> an open, participatory institution that welcomes user input and creativity. It is built on human connections and conversations. The organizational chart is flatter and team-based. The collections grow and thrive via user involvement. Librarians are tapped in to user spaces and places online to interact, have presence, and point the way. The hyperlinked library is human. Communication, externally and internally, is in a human voice. The librarians speak to users via open, transparent conversation. (Stephens 2011)

Small libraries, often more nimble than those of larger organizations, can benefit by embracing the interconnectedness of their function with the rest of the company, putting a human face to the place, and using it to build support for growing the library.

Identifying Your Perfect Stuff

Whether physical or electronic, the small library must consider what resources will fill the gap between what is available and what is needed. Collection development requires a comprehensive understanding of company goals. Can resources be eliminated by shifting priorities? Can money be saved by centralizing resources, perhaps purchasing an institutional journal or leveraging an existing database subscription? Interconnected libraries are aware of various departments' stuff and consolidate, negotiating cost savings and providing institutional access.

The hyperlinked library put its stuff everywhere, even outside the walls of the library (Stephens 2011). A library's collection of resources is as individual as the organization itself. Some need more resources for searching literature, others need news or government information, and yet others need information on patents and competitive intelligence.

Corporate libraries may also manage special collections specific to departments or programs. Examples include competitive intelligence, marketing, and drug pipeline databases. Often librarians both manage such resources and act as in-house experts in their use. Specialized resources require additional evaluation. For example, if two databases offer competitive intelligence information, can the same information be found in both databases, or are they complementary? One may offer pipeline or product pricing information, while the other offers information on company financials. If two databases offer the same information, do the results of a search done in each match, and if not, why? Perhaps they have access to different sources, making both valuable. A case can often be made for purchasing licenses to two databases for this countercheck.

Tip: Freely available sources for literature searching include Google Scholar, PubMed (for scientific and biomedical searching), and ERIC (for education).

Tip: Patent searching can be done at no cost through FreePatentsOnline.com (FPO).

Tip: Government websites provide census, clinical trials, and medical information.

The question for many small libraries is when to invest in databases that aren't free; how many licenses to get for a database; and which users, beyond the library staff, should have access.

Once an article of interest is located, the question becomes how to get access to it in full text. Small libraries without the budget to build in-house journal collections can employ document-delivery providers who deliver individual articles for a fee. This fee is comprised of two parts—a document-delivery charge and a copyright fee. The document-delivery provider controls the cost charged to organizations to deliver the full-text article, while publishers set the fee for copyright. This can be minimal or cost more than $100 per article. Most document-delivery providers alert requestors when their article cost exceeds a set amount.

Consider who will request the full-text articles. For small libraries with lower volume, it may be more cost effective for the librarian to manage requests and fulfillment. Other organizations may prefer not to have a gatekeeper and allow end users to manage and fill their own requests. For these, training sessions that focus on copyright costs and how to check for open-access articles are good ways to mitigate expense without stopping the research process.

Another way of adding new stuff at no, or low, cost is through an article rental service. DeepDyve offers free accounts with access to many full-text articles for five minutes a day. If the article is worth pursuing, it is possible to rent the article for longer, and if worth keeping, the article can be purchased. DeepDyve currently has agreements with thousands of publishers, but users of the service should not expect to find every article they are looking for (Weinstein 2013).

Vendor Management

In conjunction with collection development, managers of small libraries may negotiate contracts with vendors for stuff. Good vendor relationships allow negotiators to improve contract terms by obtaining lower pricing, removing overly restrictive contract language, expanding user access and content, and ensuring your organization has postcancellation access to product content. Even in organizations that prefer to keep vendors at arm's length, successful library managers tend to form partnerships with their suppliers rather than treat them as "just vendors." New skills are also necessary as the librarian's eyes are often the first to see contracts, even before legal does a more formal review.

Ensuring Compliance When Using Stuff

With the library connected to the organization through great relationships, users surveyed for needs, and contracts negotiated, the next step ensures that databases, journal subscriptions, and individual articles are used in a legally compliant way.

Tip: Recruiting a liaison in the legal group for copyright support is critical. This person can help develop and implement a copyright policy for the whole organization.

But even with a strong legal partnership, library leaders must have a basic understanding of copyright. Organizations, such as the Copyright Clearance Center, offer fundamental certification classes and organizational licenses, but it should be noted that each journal has its own set of permissions as to what sharing is allowed. Moreover, copyright compliance reaches beyond printing, sharing, and electronically storing articles in full text to include company use of music and video.

For example, if the organization uses music for callers on hold, inserts songs into training materials, or plays recorded music at on-site functions, a music license should be obtained, as these are considered "public performances." The American Society of Composers, Authors, and Publishers (ASCAP) and Broadcast Music, Incorporated (BMI), hold the rights to much of the music played in the United States. A business license with one or both will safeguard compliance in this area.

Want to liven up a training session by inserting a clip from *Office Space* or share a brilliant TED talk you found on YouTube? Is the company showing a movie during "Take Your Kid to Work Day"? If so, a motion picture license from Copyright Clearance Center or the Motion Picture Licensing Corporation helps protect an organization from copyright infringement. Any public performance of a legally purchased DVD, YouTube clip, or online streaming is protected by copyright. Interconnected library managers will often be asked to make calls on copyright. Purchasing licenses such as those noted here helps with compliance and allows small library managers to sleep soundly at night.

Everybody's Talking, so Listen, Don't Shush

Once we have all this stuff, how do we inform others of its existence and utility? A quick Google Scholar search for the phrase *information overload* with *library science* in late 2013 produced 2,250 articles. Compounding the problem, in 2013 the average number of e-mails a person sent and received each day was projected at 115, increasing annually (Hoang 2011). With the growing number of journals and databases available to researchers, another form of information overload itself, how can a librarian raise awareness without spamming?

The learning styles and needs of a library's users are as diverse as its stuff. Some may prefer focused individual training. Others are comfortable in a group setting, with discussion and questions. However, many researchers do not have the time to fit a training session into their already-full schedules and would prefer to look over a quick reference guide.

When a new employee is hired, it is a good practice to do a brief introductory session of no longer than half an hour. This introductory session does two things: It puts names to faces and introduces the resources and services of the library. Prior to meeting with the person, learn about his or her department and assigned projects. Afterward, send a follow-up e-mail message with the librarian's contact information and links to resources. This helps reinforce the information provided in the new-user training session and emphasizes that the librarian is available to provide assistance if needed.

One-on-one training can help cut down on the "noise" users experience and reduce the amount of irrelevant stuff that the user has to process. However, if the user population is a couple hundred people or more, an individual training approach is not always feasible. This is particularly true in cases where everyone in the organization must learn information, such as with copyright policies.

Tip: If users do not have time for a large training session, a mass online asynchronous training session should be used. This could be as simple as offering a brief online presentation followed by a short quiz or requirement for users to sign an agreement stating that they understand what is expected of them in compliance with a new policy.

When information applies only to select groups or departments, tailoring training materials to meet specific needs can help. Many proprietary databases offer multifaceted ways to search for articles or data. A tutorial on chemical-structure searching or patent-prior art searching might be useful to one group, whereas another group may need to know how to search for clinical trials and experimental pharmacology information. Long presentations covering every function of the database may leave users completely overwhelmed with information that may be useful to others but not them.

How Can We Be of Assistance?

Librarians who provide access to useful research databases and journal subscriptions must also emphasize other important services. In an editorial, clients who used health science libraries said they valued the expertise of librarians over the library or its collections (Martin 2013). The traditional walk-up or e-mailed reference request is merely the tip of the information needs iceberg. Librarians must understand their users in order to assess how to best serve them. They must unearth the questions their users don't know how to ask.

In order to give information, librarians must get information. Take a seat at the table. Find out when working groups meet, and join them. Take notes, as it is a great way to become familiar with the vocabulary of that user population or project. If you hear the words "I don't know," jot that as a literature search or conduct the search in real time if you have a laptop with you. Follow up later with a more robust search if additional information is needed. Embedded librarians are becoming more prevalent and hold new titles, such as "liaison librarian" or "informationist" (Crum 2013). At-the-ready researchers can help save an organization time and money. For example, the NIH (National Institutes of Health) grew a program of informationists embedded within a clinical care team. Thirteen researchers were interviewed as part of an evaluation process for the program, and it was unanimous that the informationists' work saved them time and that the searches were more thorough and comprehensive than what they could do on their own (Whitmore 2008).

Tip: In addition to conducting searches, the librarian can set up e-mail alerts or RSS feeds that automatically send the user any new information on the topic. Setting up e-mail alerts and RSS feeds are good additions to training sessions for searching a particular database.

Enterprise Social Software

When it comes to promoting a library's resources and services, e-mail only works to a limited extent. New strategies are emerging. In fact, 64 percent (n = 525) of hospital, health, and academic librarians surveyed claimed new roles supporting social media (Crum 2013). This doesn't just mean tweeting or instagramming collections or training sessions. Some organizations have their own internal social networks.

Jive by Microsoft is an enterprise social software. Departments can use it to build web spaces for storing and sharing documents, as well as starting discussions, making announcements, and writing blog entries. A library web space is also a good place to post lists of links to journals and databases available through the institution. Layout can be standardized, and adding content usually requires only a downloadable plug-in to easily upload or save a document.

For a small library, this is a useful repository for training materials and documentation from vendors. Each document can be assigned tags to aid in searching, and comments are enabled in case readers have follow-up questions. Project working groups can also request private web places to share articles, drafts, meeting minutes, and other documents. The librarian can supplement these private web places with RSS feeds for relevant literature searches. Researchers can view abstracts and contact the librarian for the full article if it is not already in the institutions holdings. Having a one-stop shop online saves research time and builds a sense of community, especially if there is no dedicated physical space for a library in an organization.

Publicizing the library's social-networking space can be challenging. People stick to the familiar: e-mail, links to folders on a department drive, or SharePoint (another content management system from Microsoft). Enterprise social software potentially adds to the noise of information overload. It is yet another thing to check on top of e-mail, phone calls, texts, instant messages, or any other method of communication an organization can use. The library web space must be positioned as a time saver. Rather than wait for an answered e-mail or phone call, users access documentation that may answer their questions immediately. Regular use by the librarians will send a clear signal to the user population, encouraging them to access the internal social-networking site. Otherwise, even the sharpest tool is useless if it is hidden away where no one knows how to find it.

Tip: Use the library website to communicate with users, and encourage them to access the library's social-networking sites.

Transcontinental Collaboration

What happens when library staff is separated by geographic distance? Interlibrary loan existed long before the Internet, but today's level of distance collaboration was unthinkable in the days of the card catalog. Conventional phone calls and e-mails are a good, quick way to keep each other posted on goings-on and current projects. However, sometimes a more visual medium is needed.

Web-conferencing tools with screencasting capabilities, such as WebEx or GoToMeeting, provide a virtual way to show users how to use library resources.

Vendors can also demonstrate their products to librarians or other interested partners without having to travel on site. For small organizations with fewer IT resources, Google Hangouts offers another way to have online face-to-face time and exchange information through screen share.

Jive, mentioned previously, also provides a way to create groups and share documents. Privacy settings ensure that only members may view and post within the group. This is an effective way to collaborate without flooding e-mail inboxes. The document uploader controls versioning to prevent confusion during collaboration and make it clear which document is the most up to date or final version. It also frees up hard drive or network drive space.

Managing multiple job duties and collaborating across multiple time zones can be daunting. However, adept communication skills and the help of a few technological tools can cut the noise of information overload.

Conclusion

While the physical space of many small libraries appears to shrink, the number of electronic resources continues to expand after the big bang of the Internet. Yet with all this neat new stuff out there, it is important to keep the fundamentals of reference and outreach in mind. After all, we must honor the past and create the future (Crawford and Gorman 1995) by providing the same thorough level of service as in the days of print material while at the same time taking on additional roles and skills in handling electronic media.

Bibliography

Ard, Constance. 2012. *Adding Value in Corporate Libraries and Information Services*. Peoria, IL: Ark Group.

Crawford, Walt, and Michael Gorman. 1995. *Future Libraries: Dreams, Madness and Reality*. American Library Association. http://www.ala.org/offices/publishing/editions/samplers/futurelibraries#Head5.

Crum, Janet A. 2013. "Emerging Roles for Biomedical Librarians: A Survey of Current Practice, Challenges and Changes." *Journal of the Medical Library Association* 101: 278–86.

Hoang, Quoc. 2011. "Email Statistics Report, 2011–2015—The Radicati Group, Inc." The Radicati Group, Inc. Edited by Sara Radicati. http://www.radicati.com/wp/wp-content/uploads/2011/05/Email-Statistics-Report-2011-2015-Executive-Summary.pdf.

Martin, Elaine R. 2013. "Shaping Opportunities for the New Health Sciences Librarian." *Journal of the Medical Library Association* 101: 252–53.

Stephens, Michael. 2011. "The Hyperlinked Library." http://dl.dropbox.com/u/239835/StephensHyperlinkedLibrary2011.pdf.

Stephens, Michael, and Maria Collins. 2007. "Web 2.0, Library 2.0, and the Hyperlinked Library." *Serials Review* 33, no. 4 (December): 253–56.

Weinstein, Deborah. 2013. "DeepDyve Gives Its Users Five Minutes of Free Access." *Medical Marketing and Media.* http://www.mmm-online.com/deepdyve-gives-its-users-five-minutes-of-free-access/article/304088.

Whitmore, Susan C. 2008. "Informationist Programme in Support of Biomedical Research: A Programme Description and Preliminary Findings of an Evaluation." *Health Information & Libraries Journal* 25: 135–41.

Chapter 22

How to Provide Quality Service to Internal and External Patrons

Joyce Abbott

Overview

On day one of my MLIS program, the very first discussion we had concerned what to call people who utilize the services of a library. Thirty-plus students argued passionately for an hour about the important distinctions between *patrons*, *customers*, *users*, and *clients*. Apparently what we call the people we serve is a direct reflection of our profession and the quality of service we provide.

But what you call the people you serve really does not matter in the slightest. Libraries serve members of a community. It is more important to recognize how to serve different types of needs than to argue about different classes of customers. I use the term *customer* because I find it to be the most honest and familiar term to describe what librarians spend so much of their time doing: customer service.

Two Types of Customers

When your library is part of or attached to a larger organization, the most important distinction to recognize is between internal and external customers. External customers are typically the primary consumers of your service. They are in the library to receive information or instruction related to your organization's mission. Internal customers are employees of the organization: your managers and coworkers who rely on you to provide them the most relevant information and helpful service in order that they may do their job to the best of their abilities. It is important to understand the distinction between the needs of the two, how your interactions with each group affect you, and how these interactions can impact the reputation of your library and of small specialized libraries as a concept.

Servicing External Customers

External customers are the members of the community to which your services are geared. They are any person who is seeking your services within the context of the larger organization that houses your library.

This means that, on top of being a champion for intellectual freedom and information literacy, you also will be expected to become something of a subject-matter expert, at least when it comes to collection development and subscription to databases and periodicals. Whatever your organization does, if you weren't well versed before, you must become so in order to give your external customers the best and most germane interaction possible.

Oftentimes, external customers will request information that appears to be wholly unrelated to the mission and scope of your library. Keep track of these requests, and discuss with the customers how they are related to their reason for being there. Remember, it is the customer's need that ultimately drives what services are made available both in a library and in any service organization. An increase in otherwise unrelated information needs might turn out to be related after all.

For those requests that most definitely do not mesh with your library's mission, be prepared to refer customers to the best local and online resource for their needs. For those topics that are outside the scope of your organization yet still come up regularly, it is in everyone's best interest for you to create a selection of subject guides for each frequent topic. For a good example of a subject guide, you may wish to browse through the guides publicly available through the Library of Congress at http://www.loc.gov/index.html.

The Mission of the Organization vs. the Mission of the Library

Libraries are not always stand-alone entities but a part of a larger organization and interacts with, supports, and depends upon the parent organization for customers, funding, and staffing. In this case, an information professional will have the standards and practices of the organization to take into account when developing services, resources, and even a style of customer interaction.

There are libraries attached to or located inside of:

- hospitals

- community centers

- social service centers

- schools

- prisons, and

- museums

As the information economy becomes recognized as a reality by more institutions, we can expect to see more libraries, e-learning centers, computer labs, and other information hubs popping up within public and private entities. Gone are the days when the librarian worked autonomously to further the mission of the library as its own being. Information professionals in these smaller hubs must gear their services, their collections, and their approach to customers toward the demographic they are working with and within the context of the organization as a whole.

For example, your library is located inside an at-risk youth center. In the course of your duties, you notice that many customers are in need of research and reading-development skills. As a part of your governance over your small library, you may take it upon yourself to create more reference materials teaching customers good research skills and make more of an effort to engage customers who are doing research on their own. However, because the issue of literacy is such a large undertaking and likely falls within the larger mission of the organization, you would be remiss if you didn't bring this need to the attention of management. With the resources and manpower that a larger organization can offer, you as a librarian may be able to work with the rest of the staff to recognize customers in need of more service and develop a specialized program to meet this need. In turn, as one of the few or possibly only information professionals in an organization, you must advocate for your customers by using your library to add value and resources to programs already offered elsewhere in the larger catalog of services.

Alternatively, as a means of information support, you are responsible for providing continuity between message and service. Perhaps you are the librarian in a social services center. The center begins offering support groups for victims of domestic violence. In order to provide resources to complement and enhance this program, your library should include relevant materials in the collection. You might go a step further and create a resource sheet for participants detailing the books, periodicals, and websites recommended by staff to complement the work being done in the group. As a librarian, it is not your place to discuss the goings-on of the group or the concepts being shared. But as the resident information guide, it is your place to ensure that the information you are providing is approved by management and appropriate to offer to customers. This will involve engaging your internal customers. Discuss the texts they use in their research and the professionals on the forefront of the work at hand. In order to ensure you have appropriate materials ready, you must know what your internal customers will consider appropriate. While it may be the librarian's first instinct to provide information on all approaches to the therapeutic process, it is more appropriate to primarily provide and highlight the therapeutic approach being used and endorsed by your organization at all levels. To do otherwise will send mixed messages to external customers.

Providing Relevant Programming

There will be times when you as a librarian see a need for service that you are qualified to fill within the context of your duties. However, management may see it as either conflicting with the organization's mission or otherwise going in a direction that does not mesh with the organization as a whole. Here are several real-world examples:

- In a small hospital library, you see a need for a program to highlight books about worry and grief for small children. Management states that, because the customers in the library are in the hospital for very short periods of time, they would not be able to benefit from a longer program and suggests isolated story times instead.

- In a library attached to a women's center, you see the opportunity to bring in a program that teaches women how to introduce literacy to their children in age-appropriate ways. Management states that the program would focus on the children, thus taking resources away from their mothers, who are the primary customers. You could instead create a resource guide to provide to customers who may be interested in a similar program elsewhere.

- In a museum library, you have the opportunity to partner with local artists to host hands-on classes and demonstrations to get people involved in making art as well as appreciating it. Management states that, at this time, the museum is focusing their outreach on the academic community and would prefer a series of talks from more well-known artists and authors.

In each of these examples, the program proposed would have been potentially beneficial to the existing customers, as well as drawn a new customer base to the entire organization. These are legitimate and appropriate ideas. Equally legitimate are management's reasons for declining them. These are frustrating times to be sure, but do not get disappointed. Your library is one car on a train. You may not control the direction in which it is traveling, but you do control the quality of service that you provide in that direction.

The task you are dealt here is determining where the line is between your purview, the library, and the overarching mission of the organization that houses that library. While having to constantly check in with and tailor your programs and offerings to a narrower, more specific mission may feel restricting, it can also mean more freedom to really dig deep and look into ways that those specific information needs have not been approached before. Librarians tend to think macro and large scale. It can be just as satisfying and challenging to think in more specific, micro terms.

Servicing Internal Customers

This ties into how you serve your coworkers and management, otherwise known as internal customers. You must serve your internal customers with no less alacrity than you would show for your primary, external customers. As an information professional, you are as much there to support their needs as those of the primary customers. As a rule, for each new program or initiative your organization takes on, you as the librarian should be able to provide valuable resources and staff to support their work. Each new initiative may not require your input, but it will need your support and expertise.

One of the best actions you can take to engage internal customers is to develop a staff-only collection. This will contain reference materials that are written for professionals in the field rather than consumers of service. When choosing these materials, you will want to do reference interviews with staff members who are considered subject-matter experts. You should walk away from these interviews with a grasp of the subject that will allow you to seek out and monitor the major trends and developments in a field. If you keep abreast of these trends, you can begin to bring new recommendations to the table and practice a brand of reader's advisory to your professional colleagues.

Service like this will show your coworkers the value in having an on-site librarian, as your skills will enrich their output and lighten their load when researching and evaluating information. This close working relationship also serves to maintain the lines of communication. It is all too easy to see the library or information center as an extra and an add-on that can be easily cut when budgets get tight. If you are able to fulfill the needs of your internal customers as well as your external ones, then your library will be a hub of activity and considered as invaluable to the organization as the most primary of services. A healthy library that is doing its job will be a standard checkpoint in the creation and implementation of all programs and initiatives of your organization.

The "Roaming Librarian"

Many libraries are taking on the trend of moving librarians out from behind the desks and into the stacks, to roam and give a more accessible impression to customers. The theory is that if you meet a customer where he is, he is more likely to ask for help rather than stand in line for your services behind an imposing counter. Let's look at this approach on a larger scale. Think of your career as one of a roaming librarian. You are out in the world, out of the library, and in a position to engage customers in a variety of new settings. Narrowing your scope to working within another service model doesn't compromise the principles of librarianship as much as it allows librarianship to be adapted to a wider range of needs. Using this new model of service will only cement the profession as one that is vital and adaptable to any type of need. When you are in a small or specialized library within another entity, you are a roaming librarian, meeting needs in unconventional ways.

Tip: Create subject guides for frequently requested topics even if they are outside the mission of your library. For ideas, see Library of Congress subject guides at www.loc.gov/index.html.

Tip: Provide programming that is relevant to your users.

Tip: Reach more users by being adaptive.

Conclusion

When a library is not an autonomous entity, it must have as its primary function to support and complement the services and philosophy of the parent organization. That may go against the inherent desire for full intellectual freedom and full access to all possible information. However, I believe that taking that approach will only illustrate how important it is to include information professionals and information centers into every kind of public space. The need for information access and information literacy is no longer tethered to the public or academic library. And as such, we should all be roaming librarians, meeting the needs where we see them.

Chapter 23

How to Build and Leverage Key Relationships in Your Organization

Lana Brand and Raleigh McGarity

Overview

Once assumed valuable and essential places, libraries as both conceptual constructs and physical entities are now being scrutinized for their quantifiable worth by administrators. The current economic and social structure no longer supports the library as a sacred, indispensable resource but rather places pressure on librarians to prove the worth and necessity of their resources and services. For these reasons, building relationships through outreach, promotion, and marketing is imperative for the survival of all libraries, especially those that are small and nonacademic.

Although marketing and outreach have emerged as integral functions in the operation of modern libraries, many librarians have not been trained in these areas and are overloaded with more traditional library work, unbeknownst to their user populations. Many larger libraries have created entirely dedicated librarian positions to meet this need. A specialized position is preferable though unrealistic for small libraries that are lucky to be staffed by even a single full-time librarian. However, just because a library is small does not mean that it serves a small user population or that is has a low demand for service. This demand and the resulting benefits must be brought to the attention of key members of the larger organization to ensure sustained library funding and to encourage potential growth.

This chapter elaborates on the purpose and place of building internal relationships in the management of a small library, the best way to go about this work as a solo librarian, and the practical lessons learned in a nonprofit health system setting. Additionally, how-to checklists and other relevant resources are provided.

The Purpose of Building Relationships in the Operation of the Library

Library resources and services are only worthwhile if people use them. Therefore, meeting needs and increasing usage among customer stakeholders is a large part of a comprehensive outreach strategy. This involves identifying exactly who your customer stakeholders are, assessing their needs, responding to those needs with appropriate resource and service development, and subsequently promoting those resources and services to the appropriate stakeholders.[1] This list of tasks is daunting to a librarian who already has a full-time workload, which is why the best way to go about this work involves initiating and leveraging internal relationships to streamline implementation.

In order to meet the needs of customer stakeholders, your financial stakeholders must recognize the benefit of doing so. In the estimation of most organization administrators, worth is determined by a cost-benefit ratio known as return on investment (ROI). ROI answers, How great is the benefit compared to the cost of providing said benefit? This level of evaluation and presentation of data is a relatively new addition to solo-librarian work, and thus its efficient completion is addressed in this chapter.

Building Relationships with Key Members of the Organization

Identifying Key Members and Assessing Their Needs

Customer Stakeholders

Outreach should be targeted. Customer stakeholders may seem synonymous with people who use library resources and services; however, to accurately identify customer stakeholders you must examine your organization's mission statement, vision, and values along with corresponding goals and objectives.[2] Groups that will directly contribute to these organizational endeavors are actually your customer stakeholders.

For example, health care organizations like ours broadly seek to improve the health of the community it serves. Of course, this means that all of our community members are customer stakeholders, but this chapter focuses on stakeholders who provide the community with health care, our employees. Reaching out to thousands of employees as a solo librarian is no easy feat, and leveraging relationships with key members of the organization to do so is imperative. Within these employee stakeholders, there are subsets that have unique needs. These smaller groups will need special resources and tailored services and will require slightly different promotional approaches. Assessing these needs can be exceedingly difficult for a solo librarian. Creating needs-assessment surveys may provide meaningful data to inform your purchases and justify your time. Then there is the matter of eliciting an adequate number of responses and analyzing the data. While free online tools like SurveyMonkey can make creation and distribution easier, using library and information science research or adapting assessment tools developed at similar institutions can streamline the process. These existing resources combined with feedback and facilitation from your key organizational members can provide an efficient method of needs assessment.

In our organization, physicians, advanced practitioners (APs), nurses, and allied health providers carry out different health care functions and consequently require different resources and services. Their schedules and interactions with patients also vary drastically, requiring customization and flexibility with promotional efforts. This diversity requires a solo librarian to align with knowledgeable representatives and leaders within these groups, heretofore referred to as *champions*, and to elicit their formal and informal feedback in creating and executing an effective outreach plan.

Financial Stakeholders

The identity and needs of your financial stakeholders are more obvious. Simply put, they are the groups who donate or allocate funds to the library budget. Their job is to ensure that goals and objectives are accomplished in order to realize organizational mission, vision, and values. Thus, if you are contributing to this attainment, documenting your contribution, and presenting this documentation succinctly, you are meeting the needs of your financial stakeholders.

Nonprofit organizations like ours are often governed by a board of community members who are invested in the organization's mission. While forming relationships with board members is desirable but unlikely, their needs as stakeholders are made clear through senior leadership; however, the board members direct the vision of the organization and work with senior leadership to define goals and objectives for realizing the vision. These senior leaders can often be identified by simply looking at an organizational chart. Any senior administrator who knows you exist and realizes your value is a buoy to your existence and success. For example, support and input from a chief nursing officer, chief medical officer, or a chief information officer would clearly be ideal but, depending on the size of your organization, may be hard to garner on your own.

If you report directly to a senior leadership member, you will have a direct line of communication. Alternatively, you may report to a midlevel leader who can funnel your messages to senior leadership when appropriate.

Helpful Tips

Consider the organization's mission, vision, goals, and objectives.

Target outreach—determine who affects the organization's success the most.

Listen to key members in both formal and informal situations to assess needs.

Do not forget less-visible but essential customer stakeholders.

Attracting and Establishing Relationships with Key Members

Once you have identified your allies and heard their needs, the next step is to connect them with corresponding resources and services, which may already exist or may need to be developed. As mentioned previously, each outreach group identified will require tailored strategies to attract attention and establish relationships.

Physicians and Advanced Practitioners

Physicians and other APs are at the root of all medical decisions made in the hospital and thus have a great need for the latest evidence at their fingertips. They also have the most influence over senior leadership's budget decisions, making their information needs the driving force behind the library budget. This group of customer stakeholders, while smaller than the others, has the most influence over large purchases like expensive online point-of-care tools or databases. A librarian's ability to seamlessly integrate these resources into their work flow and to provide services that enhance evidence-based practice are especially important to improving patient outcomes; however, proving this importance through practical application is vital to establishing a presence within this culture.

Recruiting champions from this group may be challenging but rewarding. Physician and AP leaders who are responsible for performance improvement, patient safety, or informatics at the hospital can benefit from aligning with the library but may not know it yet. These people are not always obvious by their titles, and those who are will sometimes be inaccessible. First approaching administrative and support staff surrounding these leaders is often the best initial access point. For example, working with a physician practice to achieve the goals they have for their practice can prove that the library is a valuable asset. Reaching these administrators is only possible if you can offer them and the health care providers they manage a value-added service; if your proposition creates more work for them without serving their own purposes, they likely will not respond or participate.

At best, you will have willing "power users" of the library who are aware of resources and services, already use them regularly, and are willing to promote them to their colleagues. This peer-to-peer persuasion is especially effective within this customer group; messages are much better received from one another. Their culture is a rigorous one, and they do not have time to waste on anything that is not clearly beneficial to their practice (i.e., time/cost savings, streamlined work flow, improved care). If a peer vouches for a tool or service, they will trust it is truly valuable. Additionally, many resources have industry-wide reputations that elicit widespread appeal.

Once they are invested in learning about what the library or librarian has to offer, you will need to provide instruction on how to access and use the tool or service. With such demanding schedules and weighty decisions, their attention is finite and their time is limited. Outreach efforts, whether to individuals or groups, must be succinct and efficient, or else your audience will lose interest. Minutes matter, and conforming to busy schedules, in spite of your own, is necessary in establishing new relationships. This means attending meetings before or after typical work hours, traveling to off-site offices, and providing the highest levels of customer service (e.g., registering online user accounts, downloading apps to mobile devices, troubleshooting technical problems). While this type of flexibility is taxing on the librarian, it is an up-front investment that will lessen once you have built solid relationships and your value is apparent.

Nurses

Nurses provide essential support to the physicians and APs. They currently form the largest sector of health care providers and spend the greatest amount of time in delivering patient care as a profession, so they directly impact the quality and safety of care.[3] To meet the increasing demand for and complexity of health care, nurses' scope of practice and leadership engagement will likely expand in the coming years, making this customer stakeholder group's clinical-decision-support needs increasingly important.

Nurse leaders are usually aware of this shift and are looking for ways to engage their fellow nurses in evidence-based practice. While nurse managers are obvious leaders, they are often consumed with staffing and scheduling issues. Alternative, and perhaps more appropriate, connections are clinical educators, who are charged with making staff aware of new guidelines, organizational requirements, or products. Because they are the trusted providers of necessary skills and information, their endorsement gives traction to your messages. Of all nurses, they will be the most likely "power users" and will know how your resources and services can best be utilized. Other "power users" and valuable allies will be nurses responsible for developing and maintaining organizational policies. These nurses are usually the bridge between the patient care nurses and senior leadership and the disseminators of updates to professional practice. They are responsible for integrating the most current evidence into nursing practice, which means librarians and library resources will be essential to their work. Both groups of nurses typically gather regularly, and establishing a library presence, preferably a permanent one, at both meetings will allow you to demonstrate your general value and allow them to envision other ways library resources and services can be applied more broadly.

Once you have aligned with nurse leaders, opportunities for outreach to the patient care nurses will become evident. Because nurses are a previously underserved population, they appreciate the novel support. Still, they are an extremely busy group who are usually overloaded due to nursing shortages and new demands for electronic charting and documentation. Like physicians and APs, time is a valuable commodity that must be deliberately allocated. Because of varying shifts, making hands-on instruction available to all nurses can be tricky. While unit in-services are possibilities, attempting to form relationships during educational events already required for orientation, certification, or licensure can be a more effective and convenient approach for librarians.

Allied Health Care Providers

Building relationships with smaller groups of health care professionals within your organization can also make an impact. Areas like pharmacy, rehabilitation services, and materials management may not be as visible, but all contribute to the goals and objectives of the hospital. Investing in resources and services that cater to these narrower groups can greatly increase library utilization. Even with budget cuts, highlighting cost-free information sources or existing services can be the foundation of a lasting relationship with that customer stakeholder group. They often become satisfied, repeat customers and potential champions of the library.

Support Services

Partnering with an active employee in another support service area with similar goals can lead to a symbiotic and highly productive relationship. Search an organizational directory for other teams or departments devoted to learning, like "continuing education" or "educational services." Explore their online presence or print materials to learn more about their functions and to identify opportunities for collaboration. Employees in these types of roles will likely know the potential champions for the library in customer stakeholder groups because they will be their champions as well. Once you determine the best person to contact, make sure you first propose a way in which library resources or services might assist them before requesting assistance. For example, librarians can support continuing medical education by researching identified practice gaps or providing grant support. They can also augment employee recruitment efforts by human resources through giving library tours and highlighting resources and services for potential employees. Champions can also be found by joining committees relevant to library functions, such as those concerned with policy development, patient education, or clinical decision support. Not only does committee involvement build professional presence and relationships, but it also provides opportunities for informal assessment of information needs. Although the meetings may take you away from the library a few hours a month, the visibility and connections are priceless.

Helpful Tips

Recruit respected "champions" to spread messages; word of mouth goes a long way.

Align library resources and services with existing goals.

Leverage the efforts of others to streamline work for yourself.

Avoid limiting the scope of your services at the expense of relationships.

Tailor outreach and instruction to each customer stakeholder group.

Be visible outside of the library.

Be flexible, accessible, and succinct when providing instruction.

Evaluate Impact and Gain Administrative Support

Quantifying your impact and presenting your measured value to your financial stakeholders is crucial in gaining administrative support, and gaining administrative support is the only way to combat staff and resource cuts. In order to do this, librarians must collect and track daily statistics on the usage of the library collection and services, as well as the attached costs. Then, the benefit to the organization of that expenditure and resulting usage must be determined. While determining the tangible benefit of library usage is difficult, customer surveys that collect estimates of value and narratives of impact combined with documentation of usage and expenditures can help put a dollar amount on time and costs saved through library usage. Again, this feedback can only be collected when you have cultivated meaningful relationships with your customer stakeholders.

Once the contributions of library and information services are evaluated and summarized, the librarian must find a way to communicate this assessment to financial stakeholders. This can be done formally by presenting these results to your manager or director, who will then be entrusted to report them to senior leadership at the appropriate time. Senior leadership can also be reached informally by disseminating the results to your champion customer stakeholders and generating a buzz about the library's assets.

Helpful Tips

Do not assume your value is obvious.

Track library resource and service usage statistics and outreach efforts.

Quantify value to customer stakeholders (e.g., time saved, cost saved).

Present data as related to organizational goals and objectives.

Conclusion

Demonstrated, concrete value combined with strong, widespread organizational ties secures a proven and enduring place for the library and its staff. When customer and financial stakeholders are acutely aware of the implications of the library's existence, they will fight for its survival. These elements of library work cannot be overlooked if small libraries are to thrive in the future.

Notes

1. National Network of Libraries of Medicine, *Measuring Your Impact: Using Evaluation for Library Advocacy*, continuing-education workshop, 2011.

2. Eileen G. Abels, Keith W. Cogdill, and Lisl Zach, "Identifying and Communicating the Contributions of Library and Information Services in Hospitals and Academic Health Sciences Centers," *Journal of the Medical Library Association* 92, no. 1 (2004): 46–55.

3. Institute of Medicine, *The Future of Nursing: Leading Change, Advancing Health* (Washington, DC: The National Academies Press, 2011).

Chapter 24

How to Advocate for the Small Library within the Organization

Lindsay Harmon

Overview

The small library's manager is often its sole representative within a larger organization, such as a college, corporation, or nonprofit. To be an effective advocate, the librarian must translate library language into terms administrators understand, clearly demonstrate the alignment between library and institutional goals, and constantly communicate the library message throughout the organization.

This chapter describes a step-by-step process for clearly and effectively communicating library goals and action plans to administrators and other nonlibrarian audiences. While this process was developed for a small college library, it can be easily adapted to fit the needs of any librarian managing a small library that is part of a larger organization.

Promoting the Library, Step by Step

When you're the manager of a small library, almost everything is your job. This is particularly true if you are a solo librarian. Cataloging, circulation, reference, and instruction may be all in a day's work for you—and that's on the days when the copier isn't jammed or the Internet isn't down. With all of the day-to-day activities that have to be accomplished in the library, having time to represent the library outside of its walls can seem nearly impossible.

However, when you're the manager of a small library, promotion and advocacy are particularly crucial because, in many organizations, you are the library's face and voice. Incorporating these activities into your daily duties is possible with careful planning, clearly identified priorities, and a good understanding of your target audience.

At the small proprietary college where I work, I *am* the library to about four hundred students, thirty instructors, and thirty staff members. I am the only person on campus who has a background in library science or, with the exception of a handful of student aides, any idea what a librarian does. This has allowed me to create my own job description in many ways, but it was an intimidating role to assume seven years ago when I was hired after graduating from library school.

As luck would have it, one of the first duties I was assigned was writing a report that summarized the library's goals and my plans for implementing them. This document was being created in preparation for an upcoming regional accreditation visit, but it would also serve as the basis for internal planning and budgeting decisions for the next academic year. Although it was a daunting task to start with, it ended up being such a valuable tool that I've repeated it on an annual basis ever since.

Following is a description of the steps I follow to prepare this document. While the process was developed in an academic library, it could be easily adapted to any type of library. Although it might seem time consuming, in reality the process from start to finish requires perhaps ten hours of work over the course of a month-long period that I usually schedule for the early summer, when there are fewer students on campus. This investment of time and effort has proven to be well worth it during the busy academic year when I have a clear plan in place for what needs to be done and what steps must be taken to achieve these goals.

Step 1: Gather Data

At my institution, budgeting decisions tend to take place in late June and early July; therefore, my yearly planning process begins in the late spring, just prior to the conclusion of the academic year, with user surveys distributed to the college's students and faculty. These surveys are distributed electronically to students and faculty, and participation is rewarded through drawings for prizes, such as Amazon or art supply store gift cards (our curriculum is focused on studio art). The student and faculty surveys follow the same format on most questions, allowing for side-by-side comparison of information about library usage patterns; they also include questions targeted to the specific user groups.

For example, the spring 2012 surveys asked both students and faculty to rate their level of agreement (often, sometimes, rarely, or never) to the statement "I have to wait to use the library copier/printer." The question was included after a perceived increase in the number of students reporting that the library's sole copier/printer was often occupied by faculty who were using it for large print or copy jobs, such as course syllabi and handouts. Relocating faculty copying outside the library to a dedicated machine in another area of the college seemed like an obvious solution to this problem; however, justifying the purchase of an expensive piece of hardware required more than just anecdotal evidence. In response to the survey, 75 percent of students and 70 percent of faculty reported waiting sometimes or often to use the printer/copier. This was particularly significant because printing and copying was the most frequent reason for visiting the library that was cited by both groups. In addition, a survey question about the times of day in which these two groups used the library indicated overlapping periods of peak library use.

Step 2: Identify Library Priorities

The data that I gather via the annual surveys, in conjunction with current library activities and initiatives, allow me to determine my priorities for the upcoming academic year. As described earlier, as a solo librarian I am responsible for completing any projects that I propose while also carrying out the regular daily activities of the library. I have found that limiting the number of goals that I set to four or five per year allows me to devote sufficient time to carrying out the tasks necessary to achieve each one.

Before I spend too much time on detailed plans for how I will achieve these goals, however, I've learned that this step must also involve feedback from my administration. Rather than surprise them with a list of potentially expensive or complicated proposals, I schedule a meeting with my immediate supervisor, the academic dean, to discuss the survey results and my initial recommendations. The first few times I undertook this process, I provided him with a multipage document that included graphs of all of the survey data and a detailed written summary of the findings; however, I soon discovered that I'd end up being called upon to condense this information to a list of bullet points. Now, I come to this meeting with a document of no more than one page that includes the most important findings and my suggested actions. This allows me to give my boss a heads-up about what I intend to focus on for the upcoming year; in turn, he provides feedback and information from his perspective (e.g., institutional budget priorities, upcoming initiatives) that allows me to refine my list and propose actions that are more likely to be seriously considered.

My list of priorities for the 2012–2013 academic year included decreasing the percentage of students having to wait to print or copy, as reported in the annual library survey. Because the problem seemed to be stemming from heavy faculty use of the shared copier/printer, I suggested focusing on ways to minimize or eliminate this, and my boss agreed. He also alerted me to the fact that institutional priorities for the upcoming year included reallocating classroom and office space and upgrading existing hardware. Based on this information, I decided to propose the purchase of a dedicated faculty copier to be located outside of the library, perhaps in an office near the faculty lounge. Because large-volume faculty copy jobs, rather than printing, seemed to be the main cause of the long waits, I suggested that a standard copier without networked printing capabilities would be sufficient; faculty could still print in the library as needed.

Step 3: Map Library Priorities to Institutional Mission and Goals

Once I have my short list of goals for the upcoming year, I can begin gathering the evidence to build the case for my administration. To do this, I look for ways to demonstrate the alignment of the library's goals with those of the institution. Core institutional documents, such as the mission, vision, and values; the strategic plan; and periodic reports such as those submitted to our regional and national accrediting bodies, are excellent sources of this type of information, and I keep copies of all of these documents in the library for easy reference. Because I am appealing to administrators who are concerned with the whole institutional picture rather than just the library portion, clearly demonstrating the connections between the library's goals and institution-wide priorities allows them to more easily see the benefits of the proposed action for students and faculty and the potential return on investment for the institution. For example, how does the initiative add value to the college? How could it contribute to achieving key benchmarks, such as student retention and completion?

To help ensure that my faculty copier proposal would be seriously considered, I linked the suggested purchase to the library's mission of supporting student learning by emphasizing the necessity of student access to technology in order to complete required course assignments (at our small commuter college, the library is the only place on campus where students can print and make photocopies). In addition, having reviewed the criteria for another upcoming regional accreditation visit, I was able to cite the requirement that the institution provide "to students and instructors the infrastructure and resources necessary to support effective teaching and learning" ("Criteria for Accreditation and Core Components" 2013).

Step 4: Know Your Audience, and Target the Message Appropriately

Once all of this information has been gathered, the next step is to communicate it to the necessary parties in the most effective way possible. Understanding your audience is key. At the college where I work, budgeting and purchasing decisions are made by an executive team consisting of the college's owner/president, the vice president, and the academic dean, none of whom have a library background. Handing them a proposal full of library jargon is almost certain to ensure that it will be returned with a request for clarification or, worse, disregarded entirely. Similarly, submitting a proposal that is narrowly focused on benefits for the library rather than the institution is in danger of being flagged as nonessential at the outset.

Because of this, I've learned to keep my message simple, clear, and institution focused. A simple six-column table allows me to clearly demonstrate the connections between library goals and institutional priorities. As shown in table 24.1, library goals are grouped into several main categories.

The link between each goal and a specific part of the institution's mission, strategic plan, or other governing documents is broken out in a separate column, as is supporting data from sources, such as the annual library surveys. Each goal is subdivided into specific activities that must be accomplished in order for it to be achieved, and each of these activities includes a timeline and/or status report. The document is updated each spring, and new goals or activities are added based on the data gathered from that year's surveys and other sources.

In the example shown in table 24.1, the row dedicated to the issue of student wait times for the printer/copier includes relevant passages from the institution's core documents, data from the student and faculty surveys, the recommended action for addressing this issue (purchasing an additional copier for faculty use), and a detailed timeline of activities that will be required to carry it out. This information was provided along with the rest of the library's 2012 goals and action plans to the academic dean, who presented it to the executive team at a closed meeting. Because the proposal was being made by someone not affiliated with the library, it was especially important for me to clearly state the justification for the recommended action to ensure that it was accurately communicated.

Step 5: Follow Up, and Report on Results

The goals and implementation plan document not only serves as a guide for the year's activities, but it also provides a starting point for "closing the loop" by assessing the results. In addition to gathering other relevant data during the year, I solicit feedback on the success of the previous year's initiatives through the annual library surveys, either by repeating the relevant question or questions from last year's survey or by adding a new question specifically addressing the action being assessed. These results are added to the document so that a clear

Table 24.1 Example Row from 2012 Irving Shapiro Library Goals and Implementation Plan

Library Technology

Issue	Link to Core Documents	Data	Recommended Action	Completion	Timeline/Status
Reduce student waits for library copier/printer.	Library mission: "The mission of the Irving Shapiro Library is to provide support for all aspects of teaching and learning at the American Academy of Art." NCAHLC Criteria for Accreditation Core Component 3.D.4: "The institution provides to students and instructors the infrastructure and resources necessary to support effective teaching and learning (technological infrastructure, scientific laboratories, libraries, performance spaces, clinical practice sites, museum collections, as appropriate to the institution's offerings)."	According to the 2012 Library Survey: 75 percent of student and 70 percent of faculty respondents indicated that they waited sometimes or often to use the printer/copier. 85 percent of students and 88 percent of faculty reported visiting the library to print or make copies. The most common periods of library usage are between 2nd and 3rd sessions (45% of students, 47% of faculty), before 1st session (36% of students, 35% of faculty), and between 1st and 2nd sessions (36% of students and 29% of faculty)	Add a designated faculty-only copier in a location outside the library.	Summer 2012	June 2012: Submit proposal to executive team. July 2012: Select copier model and arrange for purchase in conjunction with facilities and IT. Have student workers clear space in designated office for installation. August 2012: Install copier. Include information about new copier in faculty mailing with fall semester contracts. September 2012: Classes begin. Remind faculty to use designated copier during fall faculty meeting presentation and include reminder in library's faculty news email. Fall 2012 semester: Track usage statistics on both faculty and library copiers. Redirect faculty making copies in library to new machine as needed. Spring 2013: Repeat question about copier wait times in annual library survey.

picture of the process from idea to completion is available for later uses, such as in annual reports.

In the case of the faculty copier, the proposal was approved, and a new copier was installed in a faculty-only area of the school prior to the fall 2012 semester. During the following academic year, I observed much less competition for the copier/printer, especially during peak times, such as the first day of classes and midterm and finals weeks. However, to quantify this, the spring 2013 surveys included the same question about having to wait for the printer/copier. This time, 42 percent of students and 40 percent of faculty reported having to wait, an improvement of 33 percent and 30 percent, respectively. This data was then included in my spring 2013 planning document as evidence of return on the investment in the additional copier.

Helpful Tips

Serving as the library's primary advocate in an organization of nonlibrarians can be a daunting task. In addition to the process described earlier, here are a few more things to keep in mind as you craft your message.

Know the Mission

Become intimately familiar with your organization's mission, vision, and values, as well as the main priorities detailed in its strategic plan, and get in the habit of referring to them. Not only will this help guide your big-picture planning, but you will also be able to highlight connections to library activities even in informal conversations with administrators.

Be Aware of Upcoming Events and Institutional Initiatives

Is a visit from your accrediting body in the near future? Is your institution launching a new program or piloting a new course? Events and initiatives such as these may offer excellent opportunities for collection development or updating library technology. Know what's coming, and learn as much as you can about it. For example, visit your accrediting body's website, and research what is required of accredited institutions' libraries, or review lists of recommended books, journals, and databases for new areas of study.

Keep Abreast of Events and Trends Relevant to the Institution

Know what's happening in your sector or industry, and understand how it relates to your institution and the possible implications for the library. As a librarian at a proprietary visual arts college, I read such publications as the *Chronicle of Higher Education* to keep up to date on trends in higher education in general and the issues surrounding for-profit colleges in particular. I also subscribe to LISTSERVs, such as that of the Art Libraries Society of North America, to find out what's going on in other art-focused libraries.

Cut the Jargon

As the only librarian in the organization, you're probably the only one who knows the meanings of terms like *collection development* or *integrated library system*. To be an effective advocate for the library, you'll need to translate your message into language that your target audience can understand. Have a nonlibrarian colleague, friend, or family member read what you've written and highlight any terms they don't understand. Chances are your boss won't either.

Present Arguments in an Easy-to-Understand Format

Tables, bulleted lists, and other highly visual formats get your message across without requiring the recipient to read and interpret a lot of text. Ideally, your core message should be evident at a glance or quick scan.

Conclusion

While employees of larger libraries are surrounded by colleagues who share their backgrounds, interests, and priorities, the solo librarian or manager of a small library often is the only representative of the profession within the parent organization. Because of this, having a process in place for clearly communicating the library's goals and the ways in which they fit into the larger institutional picture is essential for incorporating effective library advocacy into the day-to-day duties of a small library manager. With careful planning, clearly identified priorities, and a good understanding of the target audience, even the busiest library manager can find time in his or her day to be a library advocate.

Further Reading

Dando, Priscille. 2014. *Say It with Data*. Chicago: ALA Editions.

> In her preface, Dando asserts that "to be successful, all librarians should be invested in an ongoing plan of positive communication with stakeholders and decision makers in order to wield positive influence" (vii). She demonstrates this through a four-part strategy for evidence-based advocacy that can be applied to libraries of any size or type.

Smallwood, Carol, and Melissa J. Clapp, eds. 2012. *How to Thrive as a Solo Librarian*. Lanham, MD: Scarecrow Press.

This practical guide focuses on the nuts and bolts of essential tasks for the manager of a one-person library. In particular, chapter 17, "From Solo Librarian to Super Librarian," discusses formal and informal strategic planning; the book also includes a section on public relations and marketing.

Bibliography

"The Criteria for Accreditation and Core Components." 2013. Higher Learning Commission of the North Central Association of Colleges and Schools. http://www.ncahlc.org/Information-for-Institutions/criteria-and-core-components.html.

Chapter 25

How to Provide Quality Reference Service

Mara H. Sansolo

Overview

Library school prepares you to be *a* librarian in *a* library, not *the* librarian in *your* library. The course offerings likely included broad overviews of topics, such as reference, cataloging, and administration. There may have even been courses that focused on specific types of libraries, such as public or academic; even these are a very broad overview. You can have an academic library that serves 50 or 50,000. Library school simply does not have the time or money to train students for every possible library situation they may find themselves in after graduation.

The Pasco-Hernando State College (PHSC) East Campus is located in rural Dade City, Florida, within the Tampa/St. Petersburg metropolitan area (four other campuses are located throughout Pasco and Hernando Counties). PHSC serves students in career, technical, and two-year associate-level programs. Students in the associate's program can either receive an AS in a specialized field for entrance into the workforce or an AA, which will guarantee them admission to one of Florida's state universities at the junior level. [As of fall 2014, two upper-level degrees will be offered: a bachelor of science in nursing (BSN) and a bachelor of applied science in supervision and management.]

Aligning with most of the nation, Florida has encouraged that remedial education classes be taught at the community-college level rather than at a public four-year institution (ECS 2002). The end goal is for students to transfer into one of the state's public universities with an AA in hand, thus eliminating many lower-level and remedial courses from the schedule.

PHSC's East Campus (EC) consists of four buildings, housing the library, the Public Service Academy (police, fire, and EMT training), and many classrooms and meeting spaces. The building on the far west side of campus houses the library and the Teaching Learning Center (TLC). The TLC offers tutoring and testing services for students. EC had a fall 2013 headcount of just over 1,700 (as a comparison, the nearest state university has over 40,000 students enrolled for the same semester). This includes all non-degree-seeking, career services, and Public Service Academy students. While the student population is very diverse, surveys conducted by state and national organizations consistently show that the majority of students are under the age of twenty-five.

The PHSC library system has over 60,000 print volumes, with approximately 18,000 housed at the EC library. In addition, PHSC owns over 100,000 eBooks. There are also sixteen open-use computers and four study rooms available on a first-come, first-served basis. Computers are usually in full use, as Dade City is in a rural area and high-speed Internet is not always readily available. For a number of students, the library and other computer labs on campus are their only access to the web. Staffing levels are proportionate to student population, and thus the EC library has four employees, an associate director and reference librarian (both with a master's degree) and two office assistants. There is one service point in the library, the circulation desk, which also acts as the reference desk and the ID card center for the campus.

As the reference librarian, my duties include reference assistance and bibliographic instruction. However, since EC is so small and staffing is proportional, there are times when I am the only employee in sight or the only staff member in the library. When this occurs, I am charged with handling all other aspects of operating the library, such as circulation, book processing, technical support, interlibrary loan, and opening or closing the building. In addition, libraries in community colleges (such as PHSC) are unique in that, rather than just providing normal library services to the campus, many of them also house the audiovisual department, providing the technology that instructors require for classroom use (Rusk 2006).

Keys to Being a Successful Reference Librarian

Introduce Yourself

The first thing that you will want to do in your new position is to establish good relationships with campus faculty and staff; this should begin on your first day. In the beginning, this will take up moderate amounts of your time, but once you have built the core relationships, it will be more of a maintenance thing. To put it simply, if they do not know that you are now in the library and they do not normally frequent the library, then how will they know you are there to help?

There are a couple of ways to go about introducing yourself to instructors, the first of which is to go door to door at faculty/staff offices and introduce yourself. On a smaller campus, this will take minimal time. In addition, your campus will most likely have some sort of campus-wide (or departmental) meeting for faculty and staff. Make sure you always attend these functions, and if given the opportunity, speak up and give some information about the library and its services. Finally, and probably the easiest, is to always wear your nametag. Not only will this make it easier for faculty and staff to put a face with the name, but also they may outright come up to you with inquires. The same goes for students approaching you.

Promote Library Services

When you introduce yourself and the library, you want to promote services and programs offered, so you will need to take on the task of marketing and providing quality reference services and programs. In general, there are two types of reference services, in person and remote (any time the patron is not in the physical building).

Know Your Community of Users

As a rule, you should understand the level of community college students. In general, whether the student is eighteen or sixty, they have, at most, a high school diploma. As we all know, high school research requirements are completely different than those of a college, and that first semester can be quite a shock to students. It may have even been decades since they were enrolled in school. Remember to always be patient with them. You have studied this for years, and they may have little to no research experience.

Ditch Your Desk

In-person reference services have evolved throughout the years, thus many academic libraries are eliminating the traditional reference desk. You do not need a reference desk in order to provide reference services. Single service points are now popular among many academic library types, and when you are pressed for space, as you often are in a community college, the fewer desks, the better. It also makes it less confusing for the students. They wish to be assisted at the first point of contact.

The three most common types of remote reference are by phone, e-mail, and virtual chat. A number of states and regions offer a virtual reference program where patrons can chat remotely with a librarian. In the case of Florida's "Ask a Librarian" program, a librarian is available to chat every day until midnight.

Libraries and librarians often take turns staffing the reference desk, and as an academic librarian on a statewide shift, you may be assisting public library patrons and schoolchildren working on their homework.

In my experience, most students prefer reference at the point of contact or by e-mail. They are not likely to phone a librarian. Additionally, for distance learners who cannot physically come into the library for help and who are likely to have jobs, e-mail may be the easiest way for them to get in touch with you.

Reference service over the phone seems to be a dying art, but that does not mean that the phone will not ring. Students still need help logging into the library's resources, and again, having a phone number conveniently located on the library's website will encourage them to call you and ask you for their patron number or PIN.

Market Your Services

The services you provide are only great if people know about them. Marketing your services and programs is the key to making them successful. An obvious way to advertise is all of those bulletin boards on campus. Of course, if you want the library to stand out, it needs to be eye catching. Catchy slogans and graphics will draw in people who otherwise may just gloss over the board of campus advertisements. For example, a library at which I was previously employed dubbed reference help "Research Rescue" and had a picture of a life preserver on all documents. (Bulletin boards are generally centrally located for maximum exposure.)

Most faculty and staff check their physical campus mailboxes on a regular basis, and by creating flyers to put in them, you know that you will catch their attention rather than sending a buried e-mail. (*Tip:* Use brightly colored paper to grab their attention!) There is often a way for faculty and staff to communicate to the employees of the campus as a whole, and you should take full advantage of this. Not only can you advertise general library events, but you can also showcase programs and sessions that are geared toward teaching faculty and staff.

In general, colleges have a learning management system (LMS; such as Blackboard or Canvas), and there are often means of communication within it. With such programs as Canvas, administrators can set up a "class" that consists of all employees and allows for open communication and posting of announcements.

Establishing a good bibliographic instruction program is a key to getting students and faculty to use the library to its full extent. The first step is to develop instructional materials, and there are a few ways to go about doing this. If your institution has multiple campuses, get in touch with the other librarians. It would also be a good idea to shadow one of them for a day while they are doing instruction sessions. Follow LISTSERVs for library instruction, as there are many ideas passed back and forth on a daily basis. Don't be afraid to Google! Many conference presenters and other professionals post their developmental materials online for others to work from. Additionally, reputable publishers, such as the American Library Association, have multiple publications on developing an effective program, many with specific examples.

Again, you will need to market this program; this is where those relationships that you built come in handy! Two quick ideas are to use staff mailboxes and e-mail lists to advertise and to advertise prior the beginning of the semester (e.g., for spring orientations, advertise in November, when faculty members are working on syllabi).

Next, you must implement the program, basically working out all of the logistics of how it will be run. You will want to determine location, if you want to go to the normal meeting room for the class, or if you want them to meet in a computer lab so that they can follow along with what you are showing them. This is also integral if you have them do a worksheet to test their new skills.

Tailor materials to the class and/or assignment; much of what you show to a nursing class will not be applicable to a general English-composition class. It is key to get in touch with instructors for copies of assignments and syllabi.

Grow and Develop Professionally

Professional development and networking not only look good on your CV, but they also benefit you greatly in the day-to-day running of your library. Professional development includes conferences, webinars, and college-wide training activities.

The Disney World for librarians is the American Library Association (ALA) annual conference, held in a different city every summer. Walking into their exhibit hall can be sensory overload, but the ideas and relationships made can take your librarianship to a new level. Smaller institutions often mean smaller budgets, so you may not get to make the cross-country trip to the ALA annual conference each year. (It never hurts to ask!) However, many states have their own library associations, as well as regional organizations within the state. It will be easier to get funding for a one-day conference in the next town over than for that trip to ALA. No matter how small the event, they always look good on a résumé or CV.

The great thing about library webinars is that a number of them are prerecorded, so you can stop and start at your leisure, which allows you to progress in your professional development while still being able to perform all the functions and duties of your job. Webinars address a variety of topics, from how to operate your library's LMS to how to create a Pinterest account for your library. Oftentimes, these webinars are free of charge, so take full advantage of them. Supervisors want to see evidence of such development initiatives taken by you; this will also benefit you greatly in performance and other reviews. Many institutions have some sort of college-wide staff development activities and meetings. These will help you keep abreast of the goings-on at your college.

Another way to be successful in librarianship is networking, and this can be done on multiple levels. The largest library association in the United States is the American Library Association, which is a gateway to many other national associations, such as the Association of College and Research Libraries (ACRL). These associations and their related divisions often have publications, conferences, and e-mail LISTSERVs of their own.

State and local library associations help you to network with colleagues in the same region, which can be very helpful. Most states have a library association, with divisions, such as a state ACRL chapter, within them. You can communicate with academic librarians in your state to keep up with trends and legislation. Even more specific, there may be regional associations within your state. If you are a solo librarian, this is the best way to keep in touch with local librarians. Within these organizations you will come into contact with a number of public librarians as well. Regardless, you will want to network with everyone, as you never know when you may need their expertise.

LISTSERVs (e-mail discussion lists) are an excellent way to keep current with library trends and standards, as well as to scout out ideas to implement on your campus. The ALA makes available to library professionals a number of e-mail discussion lists on everything from dance librarianship to intellectual freedom (lists.ala.org). Your state library association may also have a LISTSERV dedicated to issues and topics that are specific to your situation, such as state funding and legislature. In addition, many libraries are part of a network or consortium in which resources are shared, usually on the basis of location. These organizations will focus on topics related to local conditions and allow for collaboration between colleges and campuses.

Use Social Media

Twenty years ago the term *social media* was not even on our radar. Today, it is a way of life. In fact, it can be considered essential to many professions, and librarianship is one of them. You do not have to know everything about every social media site on the web, but as a librarian, your duty is to keep up with the latest trends, and this is what is happening right now.

LinkedIn is an excellent tool for networking. Always stay connected to people you have worked with or attended school with. They may be charged with recruiting authors, presenters, and even employee candidates. Endorsements are relatively new to LinkedIn; connections of yours can endorse you for skills, such as library instruction. When someone looks at your profile, they will see how many people have endorsed you for each skill. Always be sure that your information is current. If you have applied for any sort of award, grant, or fellowship, the person who makes the final decisions will most likely scope out your social media sites to see what you are up to, and by keeping your LinkedIn profile up to date, they have access to information that may be more current than your résumé or CV.

Some of you may be saying "No Facebook at work!" But in reality, social media in the workplace can benefit you greatly. Now, playing games all day will not advance your library skills, but seeing statuses from former colleagues and library school students on their current library activity can be very beneficial. This also opens up a door for collaboration between libraries and librarians. After you graduate, don't leave your school's group! General university alumni associations are only so helpful, but your library school may have its own association with a group on Facebook, and these often offer opportunities for professional development for graduates.

Check with your marketing or other department to see if you can create a Facebook page for your library if one does not yet exist. This is an excellent way to draw in patrons by advertising services and programs, and again, by "liking" other similar libraries, you can see what the latest trends and activities are.

Twitter is good for short, up-to-the-minute updates on library events and conferences taking place. Since Twitter limits posts to 140 characters, you have to be very concise in your postings, so only the most beneficial information is put forth. It is also helpful to follow other similar libraries and their librarians to see what programs are being offered. In addition, if you cannot attend one of those big library conferences, Twitter is an excellent way to keep up with the conference as it is happening. Associations, such as ALA, often create a hashtag for events; this allows you to track tweets of people who are at the conference and who are talking about it. (For example, the ALA 2013 annual conference used the tag of #ALA13.)

Helpful Tips

Dos

1. Do get to know the regulars. Chances are that since your campus is so small, you will have a core group of people who use the library on a consistent basis. If someone is going to be in your library every night until closing time, you should get to know them so that you can anticipate their needs and provide the best possible service. Small campuses often focus on customer service, and the library should be no exception.

2. Do take advantage of any modules or other training that is made available for incoming students; this is a simple way to learn the intricacies of your library and its resources.

3. Do go out of your way to help patrons. You will come in contact with students from all walks of life, and you want them to have a positive view of the library.

4. Do ask to attend professional development events. As budgets decline and travel/registration costs increase, it may be harder to keep up with the latest trends (Kendrick 2013), but it never hurts to ask! The worse thing they could say is no! If you want to attend that ALA conference that is on the opposite side of the country, you will need to make your case as to the invaluable information you'll bring back to benefit yourself, your colleagues, and the institution. Sometimes it is handy to show exactly what sessions you will attend and how they relate to improving your librarianship. ALA in particular has a page on their conference website devoted to helping you make your case to attend.

Don'ts

1. Don't limit yourself to only handling reference inquiries. There may be times when you are the only staff member in the library, so you will need to take on every duty that is needed. These include circulation, interlibrary loan, audiovisual support, ID card creation, technical/printer support, cataloging, and so on.

2. Don't think that there is a "one size fits all" model to managing a library. Even branches within a single institution can operate in different manners. Again, library school only provides a general overview, not necessarily how to deal with a college population with dual enrollment students as young as fourteen and adults well into their sixties. Location also plays a role. In a rural community college library such as the place I work, the library is

often the only high-speed Internet access that students and the community have.

3. Don't hide in your office and wait for students and staff to seek you out. Be proactive in marketing the library and its services. Make yourself well known on campus.

Conclusion

While reference is a service traditionally performed at a fixed location, it is crucial to bear in mind that providing high-quality, effective reference service requires the librarian to be proactive and creative, employing social media and sometimes even soliciting queries from library users.

Additional Reading

Burkhardt, Joanna M., Mary C. MacDonald, and Andrée J. Rathemacher. 2010. *Teaching Information Literacy: 50 Standards-Based Exercises for College Students*. Chicago: American Library Association.

Whether you have the opportunity to embed in an online class or just provide a one-shot instruction session, this book has fifty examples of activities that students can do, along with background information.

Kendrick, Kaetrena D., Echo Leaver, and Deborah Tritt. 2013. "Link Up the Sticks: Access and Barriers to Professional Development for Small and Rural Academic Librarians." *Codex* 2 (3): 38–77.

This article outlines the obstacles rural academic librarians tend to encounter when looking for professional development opportunities. It also outlines strategies for working with your institution's polices, including emphasizing programs that are virtual and promoting use of LISTSERVs.

McCabe, Gerard B., and David R. Dowell. 2006. *It's All about Student Learning: Managing Community and Other College Libraries in the 21st Century*. Westport, CT: Libraries Unlimited.

This book is essential reading for community- and other small-college librarians. It truly covers every topic, from budgeting to staffing, marketing to virtual reference, and everything in between. The eighteen chapters have all been written by professionals in the field, and this is one of the most current books on the market that is targeting this type of library.

Bibliography

Education Commission of the States (ECS). 2002. *State Policies on Community College Remedial Education: Findings from a National Survey.* Denver: Center for Community College Policy.

Kendrick, Kaetrena Davis, Echo Leaver, and Deborah Tritt. 2013. "Line Up the Sticks: Access and Barriers to Professional Development for Small and Rural Academic Librarians." *Codex* 2 (3): 38–77.

Rusk, Michael. 2006. "Organizational Structure of Library/Learning Resource Centers." In David R. Dowell and Gerard B. McCabe, *It's All About Student Learning: Managing Community and Other College Libraries in the 21st Century.* Westport, CT: Libraries Unlimited.

Part V

Using Technology

Chapter 26

How to Conduct Virtual Reference

Creating and Using Knowledge Products

Amelia Costigan

Overview

Catalyst is a nonprofit organization dedicated to creating more inclusive workplaces and expanding opportunities for diverse populations. The core of Catalyst's work is its original research focusing on workers across job levels, functions, and geographies in order to learn about issues related to women's advancement in business. Through this rigorous research, tools for HR professionals, consulting services for members, convening events, and the annual Catalyst Award, Catalyst continues to raise awareness of how diversity benefits both women and business as well as provides guidance on how to enact real-world change.

The Information Center (IC) is a virtual library within the organization and works to support the organization's mission. Although the IC is part of the research department, the work performed by the librarians supports all of the work of Catalyst organization-wide. The basic work performed by the IC staff [one vice president (VP) and chief knowledge officer (CKO), five librarians, one fact-checker, and one data visualization specialist] include reference service, creation of information products, and knowledge management.

Each day, the IC staff engages directly with some of the almost seven hundred organizational members, as well Catalyst staff, the media, scholars, researchers, nonmember organizations, and the general public, on a variety of issues related to women and work through reference requests. The IC staff is also responsible for maintaining copyright standards organization-wide, as well as fact-checking all external-facing resources (research reports, speeches, blog posts, slide decks). Other tasks of the IC librarians include maintaining the catalog of mostly digital resources with abstracts, citations, and links to complete texts on issues related to women and work (the IC is moving toward a fully digital collection); writing the *Daily News* (curating relevant news stories on women and work and writing commentary to distribute to staff and social media); updating and maintaining the IC's webpages; participating in cross-organizational committees (such as the Catalyst Awards Committee, the Catalyst Canada Honours Committee, an issues specialty team, or the social media team); creating procedural guides for the organization, such as the internal "Meeting Guide" (to facilitate successful virtual meetings), the "Citation Guide," the "CMS Users Guide," or the recent "Fact-Checking Guide."

This chapter, though, focuses on the role that information products play in the efficient management of a small special library. Information products support both the goal of providing outstanding service to the IC's members and users as well as supporting and furthering the mission of the organization as a whole. Information products also streamline the workload of the staff. They not only help the staff to work more efficiently, but they also provide higher-quality service, as each product is worked on collaboratively and is fact–checked, and all the sources used are available in endnotes for transparency. When search terms such as *sexual discrimination* or *women work India* are Googled, a Catalyst freely available knowledge product comes up in the top ten search results. These publicly available products allow the IC to reach a much larger and diverse audience than only through membership and are an overall value-add for the Information Center.

Role of the Information Center

The IC's role within the organization is to support members on their diversity journey by providing reliable and accurate information that can be through reference requests, product creation, or fact-checking. Organizationally, Catalyst believes providing credible data can lead to real-world change. Member organizations, the media, and staff rely on the IC to find current and trustworthy information and analyze and distill that information, as well as add insight, when possible. The IC's role is also to support the organization-wide mission.

Knowledge Products

Special library users are often looking for particular insight or exact data points and not how to best find information for themselves. The IC classifies the requests it receives on a continuum, based on complexity. The complex, "unknown unknowns" are those such as "Do you have any articles on how companies manage inclusion around the world, particularly in the Middle East and Asia, where some Muslim men will not shake hands with women colleagues? How do organizations tackle this?" The "known unknowns" can be ones with no clear answer, such as "Who coined the term *glass ceiling*?" The "known knowns" are straightforward requests, such as "What is the current percentage of women CEOs in the Fortune 500?"

The IC answers over 850 reference questions yearly. More than half of them are in-depth researched responses on "known unknown" topics, which we can take anywhere from one to three hours to answer. Over 10 percent of the IC requests are questions where there may not be an answer available—the "unknown unknowns"—and researching or creating an alternative meaningful response may take anywhere from three to twenty hours. The rest are the ready-response type, which usually takes less than fifteen minutes to answer (or less when an appropriate knowledge product is available).

Since becoming the IC in the late 1980s, the number of knowledge products created has increased as the measureable success, and demand indicated this was an efficient means for the IC to provide. From 1987 to 2003, the IC produced no public knowledge products. By 2005, as the number of daily requests increased, the IC was creating 36 public products a year [in the form of statistical Quick Takes (QT)] and today now has 87 statistical products (lists, Quick Takes, and pyramids), 10 tools, 9 infographics, 235 charts (some dynamic, using Highcharts software), and 2 products in process (PIPs, or products that are for public consumption but are not available on our website), for a total of 343 knowledge products. As easily accessible ready-reference responses, products can cut down on the number of daily requests by providing a self-help option for users or a ready-reference response for librarians to send. And because the IC products often come up in general Google searches, the products help to lead to better understanding on the subject of women and work to a wider audience. Library staff include these knowledge products when creating a customized reference response that may then also include insight and additional outside resources.

To paraphrase Peter Drucker, the IC's general philosophy about information is to transform data into information, information into knowledge, and knowledge into insights. The IC's knowledge products fall into that spectrum but can be loosely categorized into data products and insight products with some overlap on this continuum. Examples of some of our knowledge products follow.

Industry Pyramids

Industry Pyramids are snapshots of U.S. and Canadian industry data as well as four country-specific pyramids that are updated at least two times per year as well as when there is a woman CEO change for a particular industry. The pyramid shape is used to illustrate the drop-off of participation of women, starting with total industry labor force to executive officers up to CEOs. The Industry Pyramids are quoted in news articles as well as various reports, including the White House National Economic Council's *Jobs and Economic Security for America's Women.*

Quick Takes

These are statistically based global "fact sheets" that were first started in 2004 by the IC's director and VP and chief knowledge officer as a way to answer some of the most commonly asked questions and provide some self-service for the public and members. The goal was to create only ten, but today there are over fifty Quick Takes on a variety of subjects, such as "The Statistical Overview of Women in the Workplace," "Women in High Tech Globally," and "Women in the Labor Force in Brazil." It is important that Quick Takes provide credible and accurate data, and therefore all data points are fact-checked and sourced in the endnotes. In addition, as data is released yearly by the Bureau of Labor Statistics, the EEOC, World Economic Forum's *Gender Gap Report*, and other sources, each QT is updated and again fact-checked to provide the most recent information to users. Today, Quick Takes are among the most widely accessed knowledge products on the Catalyst website and receive well over 200,000 views per year. They are quoted regularly in the media, such as the *Wall Street Journal, New York Times,* and *Forbes,* and reports, such as the White House Project's *Benchmarking Women's Leadership.*

Current Lists of Women CEOs in the Fortune 1,000 (U.S.) and Financial Post (Canada)

The Information Center maintains an accurate count of women CEOs in the largest companies in the United States and Canada and identifies and updates leadership changes throughout the year as they happen. The media are heavy users of this list product, and therefore it is essential that the IC has the most up-to-date information available.

Historical List of Women CEOs in the Fortune List

This resource is a tool for researchers looking to source information on the history of women in CEO roles. The list is not available on the website but is given freely to any interested user who requests access. The IC informally tracks how this information is used.

Insight Products

First Steps

First Steps provides more insight and overview on popular diversity and inclusion topics, such as diversity councils, gender identity in the workplace, and engaging men as diversity champions. This is a new line of products created to address more complex issues and provide more insight for our users than is available through statistically based products. In addition to an overview of the topic, First Steps includes common vocabulary as well as some examples of best industry practices. Originally created by the Information Center, other departments within Catalyst are now also creating First Steps products.

Country Overviews and Legal Landscapes

A subset of First Steps, Country Overviews and Legal Landscapes supports Catalyst's strategic plan for global expansion. The Information Center is charged with creating a line of knowledge products for each market that Catalyst moves into. The country background white papers provide a snapshot overview of the legislative, societal, and work culture differences in specific emerging markets. The reports provide a general understanding of how each country's people and cultures operate through the lens of women's roles in the economy, family, education, and workforce. The Legal Landscapes provide a general understanding of the laws related to gender diversity in the workplace in specific countries.

Trend Pieces

These researched pieces are written and fact-checked in a timely manner in response to current topics in the news. "Do Women Outearn Men?" is an example of one created to counter the false claims in the media that women's salary currently outpaces men.

Products in Process (PIPs)

PIPs are formalized request responses that have been cleaned up, organized, and fact-checked for some of the most frequently asked questions. The final PIP is a PDF that is not publicly available on the website. Instead, this is something the IC staff has available to quickly answer common, more complex reference questions from members. Like other IC products, all information is cited in the endnotes.

Visualizations

To further expand Catalyst's research, the IC hired a visualization specialist to create information graphics and data visualizations, making complex research and content more accessible as well as user friendly for social media. This is a new effort to engage more individuals with the organization's work.

Measuring Return on Investment with Google Analytics

Overall, knowledge products are a value-add for a special library. Since the IC is part of a nonprofit entity, the return on investment (ROI) can be difficult to quantify and measure. One way is through measurable outcomes via usage through page views or PDF downloads. Because the information products can be accessed by individuals through the website, the metrics can be captured through Google Analytics. Last year the top ten unique web views to the Catalyst-wide website were all products created by the Information Center. The media citations of information products are tracked by the public affairs office. Last year, the IC's products were cited in the media over 110 times. Additionally, the IC uses an electronic reference tracking system that tracks all information products sent when providing reference services. These measurements indicate that these products are continuing to be accessed and used.

Information products support service, which is a value of a special library (although one that is more difficult to measure and quantify). Access to the research skills of the Information Center's librarians is a key membership benefit. User satisfaction with this service is qualitatively tracked through comments from members or membership managers who use Ask Catalyst, the online reference request form. But outcomes obtained from usage of the material are difficult to track. Some outcomes from usage can be identified: user has material available for a successful presentation to leadership or enough information to start an employee resource group. This is an area that the IC is endeavoring to measure in more meaningful ways. The IC's outstanding service was validated through the winning of SLA's Business and Finance Division's 2011 Centers of Excellence Award. While it is not as easy to measure credible data's impact on better understanding, that is part of the ultimate goal—better understanding leading to concerted efforts, which result in more inclusive workplaces and societies.

How to Determine What Becomes a Knowledge Product

All reference requests come asynchronously through a web-based information request management system that has customized forms that the requester or the librarians fill out. These forms allow the IC to track requests and spikes in trends when running a report or exporting data sets. When a trend is detected, a decision needs to be made whether it deserves the time and staff needed to create an information product and whether a statistical-based product or insight product would best serve user needs. A statistical product will need not only the initial time to create and fact-check, but also time must be set aside to update and fact-check periodically throughout the year with new data. A First Step is a more time-consuming process upfront, as insight is added to collected knowledge. But this product does not require the maintenance and updating, such as that needed by a strictly data-driven product. If it is decided that a product is needed, the IC must next decide whether to simply transform data into information, information into knowledge, or knowledge into insights. To help with that decision, the following questions are asked:

Will creating an information product on this topic:

- benefit the organization?

- benefit the Information Center?

- benefit the work flow?

- benefit the users? And which users?

An information product must support the mission of the organization and benefit the Information Center either through reducing work flow or increasing the ROI. The decision made is based on benefits and need as well as the cost of staffing time to create, fact-check, edit, and design the product.

Once it is decided to move forward with a product and the product category is selected, one librarian leads this initial phase of research, framing and writing the draft. If it is a topic that a Catalyst staffer outside the IC has expert knowledge of, they will be asked to review. Upon completion, the draft is reviewed within the IC by the VP and chief knowledge officer as well as the staff of librarians. Content reframing may be suggested, as well as inclusion of additional source materials. If it is an insight product about a new geography or topic in which Catalyst does not have an internal expert, it will be sent for external review. This might be to a contact working in a Catalyst member company, a Catalyst board of advisors member, or a recognized expert in the field. An updated draft is then created from this feedback and again reviewed by the VP and CKO. At this point, the draft goes to the fact-checker to ensure accuracy and reliability as well as review consistency of citations style. After all changes are input, the selection goes to editorial for copyedits and then design for layout into one of the information product templates. Only after all these steps are completed does a product upload onto the Catalyst website for public use.

A product in process is created when the IC wants to respond to a spike in requests on a certain topic or a news trend. This type of product is also reviewed and fact-checked but avoids the step of editorial and design, as this type of product is not frozen and may evolve as it is used and therefore is more dynamic than the products posted to the website. The IC creates a PDF that is then available to Catalyst staff and members through the Information Center librarians. The resources for these products are often found by searching the archives of the information request management system. These reference requests (PIPs) are cleaned up and organized, and insight may be added. As users provide feedback on the PIP, the IC librarians add or revise the content. These could eventually be turned into a First Step or other publicly available product if the metrics show that more insight and depth is required.

Tips for Product Development

Just Because You Can Create Something, Doesn't Mean You Should

It is useful to have a strategic plan in place before embarking on a product development plan. A pitfall is a lack of understanding of the role of the product to the user or the role of the product to the organization. This can result in having too many products or products with muddled content. It is also essential to understand the staffing needed to create an accurate product using credible sources. At one point, the IC had too many Quick Take products, which became a staffing management issue, as many of the data points needed full updates at least one or more times per year. In addition, there was not a clear definition of what constituted a QT, which resulted in a product that was a hybrid of statistical information and qualitative research material. A strategic plan as well as usage metrics from Google Analytics helped to weed the collection down to a more manageable fifty-three from seventy.

If You Are Going to Do It, Do It Well

If you want end users to consider your products as credible and worth sharing, make sure you create them with that in mind. Accuracy is essential for credibility, so part of the process needs to include fact-checking, transparency of all calculations (for ease of checking), and clear citations. Editing, design, and proofing should also be part of your process. Credibility is eroded if there are spelling errors or if a product looks unprofessional. Make sure the products represent your organization and your work in a positive way.

Create and Track a Measure of Success

Make sure to match your metrics with the purpose of the product, and after the product is launched, continue to monitor how it is used. If breadth is important, measure the number of page views or downloads (or number of times it is requested). If depth is important, track requests for additional related data or insights. If a product was created to satisfy a specific user group, survey them to discover whether it achieved this end goal.

Evolve Your Offerings

As you measure your successes, learn from them. Discover what works for your audience, and build on that. Do your users have an insatiable need for more charts and graphics? If so, make that a focus of development. But also learn from what isn't working. If users request more or different types of data in your products, then consider revising them to include it. If shorter text-based reports are more likely to be shared among senior staff, then update some of your current products to reflect that need.

Don't Be Afraid to Discontinue a Product

Understand when you cannot maintain or keep a product. If it is too labor intensive to update or if the product is not satisfying the needs of the user or is rarely used, that might be a sign it no longer serves its purpose. Remove it from the website, and archive it. Don't think of it as a failure; consider it a learning experience.

By building on the research and expertise of librarians, a focused line of knowledge products not only reduces the workload of a special library but also increases its value within the larger organization. Although the initial time used to create a knowledge product must be factored, time is saved by the staff in not answering repeat reference questions and having ready reference available to users on the website. By creating products that support the overall organization's mission, the special library's value also increases. Finally, media citations of knowledge products serve as a tool to market the value of the library's contribution to the overall mission of the parent organization.

Acknowledgments

Specifically, thanks goes to Jan Combopiano, vice president and chief knowledge officer, for providing invaluable feedback and insight on drafts of this chapter.

Useful Resources

Librarian of Fortune blog, http://www.librarianoffortune.com.

Nicole Wallace, "Visualizing Data Helps Charities Get Attention: Graphics Give Nonprofits an Advantage in Reaching the Public and in Improving Their Work," Chronicle of Philanthropy, March 4, 2012, http://philanthropy.com/article/Visualizing-Data-Helps/130990.

The Proverbial Lone Wolf Librarian's Weblog, http://lonewolflibrarian.word press.com.

Chapter 27

How to Manage Technology in a Small Library

Zach English

Overview

Although I am not a technology whiz, working in small academic libraries has allowed me to work with a number of emerging and traditional technologies.

I began working as a professional librarian right after graduating with my MLIS degree in 2010. I was hired to be the campus librarian at the Orlando campus of Everglades University (EU). EU is a small institution located in Florida, with three campuses around the state. Prior to being hired, I had worked for a year as a paraprofessional in an academic library, and I had interned for a semester at a community college, so I did have some relevant experience to draw upon for this position.

However, being a solo librarian posed wholly new challenges because, although I knew how to do some of the required tasks, the biggest challenge was to figure out how to fit them all into my day. I was responsible for every aspect of services at my library: reference, instruction, circulation, collection development, cataloging, and so on. I provided services to approximately 150 students, 30 faculty members, and 10 staff members. The director of library services, based at the main campus in Boca Raton, was my library manager, providing policies, training, and continual assistance so that I had some "ground control" to guide my solo flying. The Orlando campus's vice president and academic dean were my on-campus managers. After I had been there four months, a part-time library assistant was hired to work twenty hours per week (most of his hours occurred when I was not in the library). I worked at the Orlando campus for about a year and then transferred to the Boca Raton campus, where I was promoted to the position of director of library services after serving as the campus librarian for another year.

Our collections at EU are small—we have about 20,000 print and audiovisual titles across our three campus libraries. Ten to fifteen computers and a printer/photocopier are reserved for patron use at each campus library. A classroom at EU will have a computer or laptop as well as an LCD projector and speakers reserved for faculty use, and the campuses also have wireless networks. The library website is an AGent VERSO integrated library system (ILS), provided by Auto-Graphics. On our site we offer access to over twenty-four academic research databases provided by vendors, such as ProQuest, EBSCO, and Gale.

One nice thing about working in small libraries is that you can work with technology even if you don't start out with any IT or web-development experience. While a large academic library might have an electronic resources librarian, a systems librarian, and a technical services department, as a solo librarian you get at least a modicum of experience in each of these areas, although you don't specialize very much in any one area.

Small libraries can be petri dishes for experimenting with new technologies. In this chapter I describe various areas of library technology and recommend some best practices that I have drawn from these experiences.

ILS

As previously mentioned, our ILS is called AGent VERSO. When users log in to the library site, they see two general areas: our online catalog and our collection of databases and electronic resources.

We share a union catalog with several other universities, most notably Keiser University. Our patrons can search for over 120,000 items statewide within this union catalog, and if items they want are located at other campuses, they can order them through interlibrary loan (ILL). Among our collection of databases and electronic resources, we have included links to video tutorials, PowerPoint guides, and our library blog.

Each EU librarian must learn how to use the online catalog, the automated circulation system (including ILL), the article and e-book databases, and the cataloging functions. Each campus library has a barcode scanner that connects to our computer towers with a USB cord. Each of our databases has a unique interface, subject matter, and functionality that the librarians must become familiar with. They must also know how to guide patrons in person and over phone, chat, and e-mail to find information in the databases, as well as how to help patrons access e-books and articles on their mobile devices. Troubleshooting technical difficulties related to the databases is handled by the director of library services, who is the point of contact between the EU library system and the database vendors.

Most new acquisitions are cataloged and bound remotely by the university's vendor. However, we purchase outside of our vendor for occasional individual purchases, and when these items arrive, the librarians must catalog them into our collections.

EU Library Blog

Our library blog was created with WordPress. WordPress is easy to manage even if you have no experience with web design because the editing interface will seem familiar if you've ever used Microsoft Word. One thing I learned about was how to use Google to look up directions that appear on the WordPress community forums. For example, I do not have in-depth HTML knowledge, but on our blog posts I wanted to be able to set up anchored links on a table of contents–type list of subject headings. After a few minutes of Googling, I found the directions for how to quickly accomplish this.

We host screencasting videos on a site called Screencast.com (more details about that later). We downloaded MP4 files of these videos and created a YouTube account, with which we uploaded the MP4s to YouTube. We experimented with embedding the YouTube videos in some of our blog posts. However, we found that doing this reduced the quality of the embedded videos. YouTube provides a cog wheel that you can click on if you want to improve a video's quality, but this is a step that some users may overlook. Thus, we stopped using YouTube to host the videos, and instead of embedding them in the blog, we provided links on the blog that open into new windows, on which the higher-quality Screencast.com versions of the videos can be viewed.

Ask a Librarian

Ask a Librarian (AAL) provides chat reference service to library patrons throughout Florida. Librarians across the state volunteer their time to staff either the collaborative desk (where questions come from every type of library patron), the academic desk (used only for academic library questions), or the texting desk (for text message questions from every type of library patron).

Librarians can also staff the local desks, where they only take questions from patrons who are using their own library system. For example, a library may locate their AAL icon next to their online catalog and databases. When patrons click on this icon, they are taken to the local desk. If a librarian is not available, the question will be sent to the collaborative or academic desks, thus allowing librarians outside the patron's system to assist. Such assistance is possible through use of the Knowledge Base, a collection of information and tips that directs nonstaff members in how to guide patrons through searching the catalog, logging in, renewing books, and so on. Some libraries also provide log-in credentials on their Knowledge Base page, which allows nonstaff librarians to enter their sites and use their proprietary databases (such use is only allowable when helping patrons who are members of these libraries).

Although the EU librarians have regularly contributed several volunteer hours each week on the collaborative and academic desks, I experimented in 2012 with also staffing EU's local desk. This allowed me to assist a modest number of our own patrons online. However, I eventually found that confusion was being caused due to a limitation of our ILS. When EU patrons would open a database link on our ILS, this would kick them off the chat session. The only way to work around this problem was for the patron to open a new browser tab and log in *again* to the library site, which would then allow them to navigate to a database within the new browser window without getting kicked off the original window's chat session.

For a while I tried to direct patrons to do this. However, I found that jargon, such as *tab, window,* and *database,* are not as commonly understood by college students as librarians might assume. These directions appeared to be counterintuitive to our patrons. Many college students—even those who are taking classes online—are far from being computer savvy, and I eventually determined that this limitation of our ILS was something it would be better for us to avoid. As a result, we still provide AAL services to our patrons, but we had to take the link off of our library site, and therefore we no longer staff the local desk—our patrons' questions are sent to the academic desk instead. This is still worthwhile since the nonstaff librarians who take these questions are guided by our Knowledge Base page.

We also experimented with setting up a phone number that our patrons could use to send us questions via text message. AAL's texting service works by showing the patron's question in the texting desk on the librarian's computer screen; this desk is reserved solely for text message questions. When librarians see a text message, they can type a response on their computer keyboard with a length limit of 140 characters. We were excited by this initially until we discovered that, due to the nature of AAL's texting service, we were unable to send more than one text message in response to a patron's original question. If we wanted to text the patron again to provide more information than we were able to fit into 140 characters, we could not do so unless the patron had texted us back first. Thus, we again felt that the limitations of the technology were causing more confusion than it was worth, so we reluctantly decided to stop providing the texting number to our patrons. I am still interested in possibly using a texting service that will provide the ability to send more than one text in response to a reference question.

Ask a Librarian has nevertheless been a very valuable service for Everglades University and the state of Florida. The librarians have gained experience in how to assist patrons through chat reference, which is a crucial part of any librarian's reference skill set.

Screencasting Videos

I have created twenty screencasting tutorial videos while working at Everglades. The software I use for these videos—Jing, Snagit, and Camtasia—are products made by a company called TechSmith. With Jing and Snagit, I record my computer screen and provide voiceover narration with a microphone. I write a script before the video is recorded, and when recording, I read the script while navigating to the respective areas on my computer.

Camtasia is an editing program that lets you refine the raw footage of Jing and Snagit videos. I have used Camtasia several times to provide additional video features, such as music, zooming in and out, pop-up arrows and circles, and others. Recently, in collaboration with other staff, I recorded a Camtasia video that orients new online students to Blackboard, the learning management system (LMS) used for our online campus.

As mentioned previously, we host our videos on a site called Screencast.com. An annual subscription provides us with plenty of bandwidth, and the number of video views can be tracked each month. Videos can also be downloaded as MP4 files. We provide links to fourteen of our videos on our library website.

Additional Hardware and Software

We order physical library materials and hardware from Office Depot and the Library Store. We use motion-sensor door-counters. At the Boca Raton campus, the glass door to the library is regular size, so the counter is placed at the top to record how many times the door is opened. At the Orlando campus, the setup is slightly different. Since double doors lead into the library and the campus prefers to keep them propped open, I bought a door counter that has two plastic sections—one for each side of the double-door frame. The motion-sensor beam goes from one plastic section to the other, so that anyone who walks through will be counted.

The computers in the library are maintained by the university's IT department. Each campus has an IT support tech who roams to multiple campuses throughout the week. If something goes wrong at a campus, the librarian submits a work order through an online help desk site. This work order then remains in the IT tech's queue until he is able to visit the campus and resolve the problem. For printer and photocopier issues, we work with another company whom we can call and ask to come to campus as soon as possible to service the machines.

With regard to computers and printers, the librarians are involved in any troubleshooting that can possibly be taken care of on the spot. Such problems may include issues with: server connections; printer technology and print network connections; the classrooms' LCD projectors, which sometimes have old bulbs that need to be replaced; and faculty/staff programs, such as Microsoft Office and Adobe Acrobat. The librarians also sometimes assist students, staff, and faculty with accessing and troubleshooting issues that may be occurring with their university e-mail accounts and their accounts on CampusVue (the university's electronic student information system).

IT must authorize the installation of any software on a campus computer. The librarians have assisted with the installation of computer software, including: construction management software such as PlanSwift, SureTrak, ConsensusDocs, and Microsoft Project; Adobe Acrobat; the screencasting programs Jing, Snagit, and Camtasia; and the testing software Wonderlic (the librarians often proctor the university's entrance evaluations).

The librarians have also been at the forefront of implementing the use of two emerging academic technologies at EU: Smarthinking and Turnitin. Smarthinking is an online tutoring site that the university subscribes to. The librarians conduct workshops about Smarthinking and help students get their accounts set up. In 2011, the university subscribed to Turnitin, an online plagiarism detection site. I was the chair of a university committee that came up with usage guidelines and trained faculty in how to use the site. Committee members assisted the faculty with interpreting score reports, retrieving log-in information, and uploading papers.

Embedded Online Library Services

During 2012, I served as the campus librarian for the Boca Raton campus and for our online division, and I continue to provide these services today as the director. Our online division currently includes approximately seven hundred students and several dozen faculty members.

The librarian who provides services to these online students and faculty is an "embedded librarian." Being an embedded librarian means that I promote my accessibility and my instructional services within each online course by uploading self-paced PowerPoint guides and by providing an orientation PowerPoint, a quick guide, and the main library link in all online courses. In 2013, our online students asked me an average of forty-four reference questions per month (through phone, e-mail, and chat). I make sure to prominently display my hours and contact information in the online classes so that students know they can reach out to me with questions they may have.

Tips for Technological Best Practices

In reviewing the aforementioned activities, I have drawn the following "technological best practices" for librarians working in small libraries.

Assess the Effectiveness of Your Technologies

Keep an eye on usage statistics for all technologies. If something is not being used much, ask yourself what the reason might be. Could the situation be improved by conducting more outreach and marketing or by providing better instruction and library guides? Could an aspect of the technology be tweaked to allow for better usability—for example, perhaps a "Full Text Only" box should be checked as a default search setting? Or perhaps there is something about the technology that does not mesh well with the needs of your student and faculty population. Online surveys through SurveyMonkey or Zoomerang can assist with finding the answers to these questions, and in small libraries one also has more opportunity to see firsthand what problems may be occurring.

If an Idea Doesn't Work, You Can Change Course

Sometimes experiments fail—and as a librarian who works on a small scale, you won't have invested so much time, money, and energy on the experiment that you are unable to change course. If the goal the technology was intended to achieve is still an important one, consider the other products out there that might work better for you.

Google Is Your Friend!

Whether you want to look up HTML directions in the WordPress forums, find out what the highest-rated apps are, troubleshoot a problem with a Microsoft

Office product, or answer a wide variety of other questions—Google can be an invaluable aide.

Focus on Making Technology Intuitive for Your Users

If the way to complete a task is not obvious, many library users will not complete it. For example, the cog wheel in a YouTube video allows you to improve the video's quality, but many users don't know about this option because the cog wheel is small and it's not immediately obvious what its function is. When designing or considering new technology, it is crucial to ensure that the steps are as intuitive as possible so that users won't miss them. Failure to check up on these small details could undermine the rollout of a new technology.

Effective Time Management Is Essential

Working in small libraries, especially as a solo librarian, challenges you to manage your schedule realistically. With every project, you'll need to start by asking, "Is this something I can truly hope to achieve, given that I have duties in many other areas of our library services?" If the answer is no, you may then need to consider whether the project is so important that it necessitates the hiring of an assistant or student worker so that you will have more time to spend on it.

Use Self-Paced Guides to Save Time

The EU librarians collaborate to make step-by-step handouts and PowerPoints, showing our users where to click, what to download, and how to search. A technology will often require a complex series of steps that cannot be memorized by users during the first run-through. Visually engaging documents that re-create these steps can facilitate better student learning outcomes and will save you time.

Maintain a Good Working Relationship with Your IT Department

Sometimes your IT rep will take longer than you would prefer to fix something. Although this can be stressful, it is in your interest to stay professional and respect the fact that he or she probably has many other work orders to get through. Keep this relationship positive, and handle any disagreements or other issues through the appropriate professional channels.

Engage Your Stakeholders

Our academic deans, vice presidents, online trainer, department chairs, and faculty members have been crucial stakeholders who have contributed ideas about how to implement technologies, such as Turnitin, Smarthinking, Blackboard, and screencasting videos. Strive to incorporate their perspectives. If you can set effective guidelines, this campus-wide buy-in will give legitimacy to what you are trying to achieve.

Conclusion

Working in a small library is an exciting, challenging, and humbling experience. Although the inherent limitations of a small environment mean that you may not get to work with some of the services and resources that large academic libraries provide, there are also some benefits to having things reduced in scale, including: more firsthand knowledge of patron needs, more ability to interact with faculty members, and the ability to experiment with new ideas more quickly. It is my hope that this chapter has provided some useful insights for anyone who is embarking on the wonderful world of small academic librarianship.

Chapter 28

How to Create an Effective Library Website

Jill Goldstein

Overview

I am the lone librarian and library director of a for-profit college of health sciences that offers associate's degrees and certificate programs. Our urban campus has two library locations that are staffed by student workers, making me the only professional librarian on staff. There are many challenges to being a solo librarian; in particular you miss out on the camaraderie of other library professionals. But it also affords you the freedom to be innovative.

Most educational institutions function as not-for-profits and do not measure success solely on their bottom-line performance. This is not the case in my institution or in any profit-centric business. Ideally, running a school like a business should streamline operations and increase productivity, but this is not always the case. Many of the traditional goals of an educational institution do not drive profit. As a librarian working in this kind of environment, you may frequently find yourself at odds with the overall mission of the school. Presently, there are very few articles about librarians working in for-profit institutions, and there are no organizations that cater specifically to this type of profession. With the large increase in the population of adult learners returning to school, many are choosing to attend for-profit colleges. With the increase in this student population, it seems likely that more literature will follow. Another challenge is that other library professionals may not always act so welcoming to a librarian from a for-profit institution. They may feel that your work does not have the cache of being an academic or law librarian. But working in a for-profit educational institution has its own specific set of challenges and rewards.

You are frequently working with less-advantaged, older, and minority students. These students are less likely to have proficient language or technical skills. Many have no computer at home.

As a librarian and a manager, you may feel conflicted toward the overall mission of your institution. However, you may take advantage of the fact that you are likely the only librarian on staff and exercise many of the skills you acquired in library school. Personally, I have had the chance to sharpen my collection development, teaching, management, and cataloging skills. In addition, I have had the opportunity to be on academic and management committees and play a small role in how the school is run.

Nontraditional Student Population

The school I work in has five program areas of study: massage therapy, personal training, nursing, surgical technology, and medical assisting. Most of the students enrolled in these programs are over twenty-five years of age and are classified as adult learners. This population poses its own challenges, which are very different from the challenges facing the traditionally aged college student.

The stress of having to manage family and a job along with their student responsibilities is a common challenge for adult students. One of the key elements in educating these students is in teaching them how to access information quickly and accurately. This can help them keep up with the classwork and avoid the stress of falling behind.

Most of the students I work with have been out of school for some time and are not comfortable using technology. Many have not been provided with the opportunity to work with newer innovations and are playing a game of catch-up. Offering these students easy access to library information and resources is essential to their academic and career success. Even the few who have computers at home will frequently be assigned research papers that require them to rely on resources beyond Google and Wikipedia. Students need to know where to look for reliable resources especially when confronted with the many distractions from the Internet.

Creating an Information Portal

Websites are great platforms for marketing, and it is likely that the administration in a for-profit institution will view their website solely as a sales tool. This was very much the case in my institution. Creating an information portal within a sales and marketing framework was not simple. One of my biggest challenges was making the students aware of existing library resources, which had been buried deep within our website and were nearly impossible to navigate to. Initially, I intended to work collaboratively with the IT department to simplify the navigation. However, the staff was only able to give me a limited amount of support. With no dedicated web designer on staff, making any kind of progress was painstaking. Our website had one single page devoted to the library, which was not prominently featured on the front page. It was by no means an ideal situation.

My school does not have the IT staff or resources of a large university, and so expanding the existing website to include the necessary resources for current students was not a top priority. Thankfully, the days of having to know HTML coding or the complexities of web-design programs were no longer necessary for creating an effective website. I found many resources available to the novice web designer. This included open-source and commercial products, as well as software packages that are specific to the needs of libraries. I choose to use LibGuides by Springshare for its ease of use and customizability, and the number of libraries using it impressed me. Of course, you may find something that works better for your specific needs.

I did not have a great deal of coding experience or the manpower of larger institutions. LibGuides allowed me to create a simple and effective website without any additional help. Once I got a trial version of the program, I found everything to be quite intuitive. In a for-profit institution, academic programming is often based on the job market, and changes in the curriculum are quite common, so I needed a product that provided a lot of flexibility. It is quite likely that I would have to add or remove an existing guide sooner rather than later. Before beginning, I needed to identify our specific needs. In this case, I was dealing with a large population of adults who lacked basic literacy and technical skills. This made usability my top concern. I knew that students needed to be provided with an easy-to-use website. The adult student population in my school is typically juggling many life responsibilities. Between family and work; schoolwork may not always be top priority. Therefore, simplifying access to library resources was essential.

Our school's library collection includes books, periodicals, and videos, as well as digital subscriptions to several databases and journals, all of which are related to the health sciences field. Presently, there are two physical library locations. The first one serves our massage therapy program and houses program-specific materials, including many pertaining to anatomy and physiology, kinesiology, and Chinese medicine. About a block away, our second library location contains materials relating to the fields of nursing, medical assisting, personal training, and surgical technology. Both library locations have computer workstations, copy machines, and printers. Since many of these subjects share common resources, I had to come up with the best method of cross-referencing information from individual programs. For example, our subscription to a nursing and allied health database contains information applicable to all programs, and I wanted students to be able to easily access the information they needed, regardless of their field of study.

Subject Guides

Since my institution has five subject areas of study, I created five subject-specific guides. These subject guides are all linked and easily accessed through the library homepage.

This homepage serves as a portal to all available library resources. From the homepage, one can search the library catalog, the collection of electronic books, and the ProQuest nursing and allied health database. Library information, such as location, hours, and contacts, are also posted here. This information can easily be updated to let students know of any schedule changes, special events, or emergency closings.

At my institution, students frequently check their school e-mail through a student portal site. I have put an access point to library resources on this

Welcome to the Swedish Institute Libraries

Research assistance, subject guides, and useful resources compiled by your friendly librarians. Know what we know - find it in LibGuides!

Browse All Guides | Search: [   ] [All Guides ▼] [Search]

Guides

Show: Popular | Recent | All

⭐ All published guides

1. **Massage Therapy**
   by Jill Goldstein - Last Updated Oct 25, 2013

2. **Medical Assisting**
   by Jill Goldstein - Last Updated Aug 9, 2013

3. **Nursing**
   by Jill Goldstein - Last Updated Feb 11, 2013

4. **Personal Training**
   by Jill Goldstein - Last Updated Sep 24, 2013

5. **Surgical Technology**
   by Jill Goldstein - Last Updated Apr 30, 2013

Using the Library

The library holdings include books, CDs, DVDs, periodicals, and databases that support the school's curricula.

Searching the Catalog

The Swedish Institue Library Catalog is called **Cybertools**. You can search by Keyword, Title, Author, and/or material type.

Swedish Institute Libraries

Search for [   ] (Search Now)
☐ Exact Words (Clear Search)
Search by [Keywords   ▼] (Go to Power Search)
Material Type [All   ▼] (Properties...)

Library Hours

Lillian Phillips Library
226 West 26th Street, Sixth Floor
M-F 8:00 a.m. to 8:30 p.m.
Sat 8:30 a.m. to 2:00 p.m.

Health Sciences Library
151 West 26th Street, Fourth Floor
M-Thurs. 8:30 a.m. to 6:30 p.m.
Fri. 8:30 a.m. to 5 p.m.

Featured Librarian

Jill Goldstein

Tags

Show: Popular | All

No results were found

Ebrary

Ebrary is an online digital library of full texts of over 70,000 scholarly e-books. It provides a set of online database collections that combine scholarly books

student portal as well as the original website. I have also created shortcuts to the homepage on all the shared library computers and made it the default homepage for all web browsers. This means that every time a student goes to check their e-mail or Facebook, they are more than likely to stumble on the library homepage.

Acupuncture Advanced Person
Assistant Nursing Student Jour

Student Resources

- TopSchool
- My Email
- My Documents
- My Calendar
- Moodle
- LibGuides
- Syllabi
- Shared Files
- SI News

Blog Archive

▼ 2014 (3)

   ▼ January (3)

      New sign-in page
        for Google
        Apps services

      Weather Update

      Weather Notice

General Website

Library

There are two library facilities, one at each building. The library located at 226 West 26th Street on the 6th floor serves the Massage Therapy program and includes resources in the biosciences, nutrition and complementary and alternative medicine, including acupuncture and Oriental medicine.

The second Swedish Institute library is located at the 151 West 26th Street building on the 4th floor and includes specialty resources for the Nursing, Clinical and Administrative Medical Assistant, Surgical Technologist, Advanced Personal Training, and Medical Billing and Coding programs. Libraries are equipped with computer terminals, study table, printers and copiers.

All students and instructors have access to a 75,000+ volume online collection through ebrary. The collection supports all programs and includes standard library collections in general education including social sciences, humanities, English, mathematics and sciences. Students can access full-text items through a virtual bookshelf and use study/research tools including web links, highlighters and bibliography and footnote formatting templates.

The college also subscribes to online nursing and allied health periodicals and a multimedia database through ProQuest. Students and faculty can access journal, magazine and newsletter articles through the ProQuest portal.

Swedish Institute is a member of the METRO consortium of New York metropolitan area public, medical, and university libraries. Through METRO, students can access collections on-site at other METRO member libraries with several libraries offering borrowing privileges. METRO includes a number of nearby medical library collections.

A library cooperation agreement also exists with our sister school, nearby Pacific College of Oriental Medicine.

PUBLICATIONS

LibGuides provides access to all of Swedish Institute's publications plus oher resources
Cybertools for Libraries
Ebrary
Proquest
Natural Standard
Medline Plus
PubMed
Science Direct
USDA Nutrient Database

As the site may compete for attention with the many distractions on the Internet, I highly recommend making your homepage as eye catching as possible. While you may not choose to put a picture of yourself up, including an image of anything the students can recognize and identify with can help ease some of the technical anxiety they have. It may be as simple as your school logo or a photo of the library itself.

Use the School's Logo on Your Homepage

Ease of Use

In order to successfully serve the needs of our school, I strived to understand what worked best for the student body. It quickly became quite clear to me that a large portion of my student body had little experience using library resources. Many did not know how to even use or access the library catalog, let alone find peer-reviewed journal articles. This required creating the most straightforward and easy-to-use website possible. Students who lack computer skills are often technophobic and easily frustrated, as many of these same students do not have a computer or Internet service in their homes.

When All Else Fails, Embed

I discovered it was best to keep the website simple and embed as many links as I could provide students with one-click access. This was the strategy I used when I created the online resources for the students at my institution. The LibGuide software facilitated this process by using customizable boxes where one can embed videos, pictures, texts, and hyperlinks. An important lesson I learned while creating the subject guides was to be consistent. This helped make the design look better, and more important, it made access much easier. Once students became comfortable with the consistent layout, they might feel less anxious using library resources.

Keeping Navigation Consistent in Subject Guides

Less Is Always More

I did my best not to put too much text on a webpage. It turned out to be more effective to communicate with our audience via logos, pictures, and video links. This interactivity seemed to be easier to use and more compelling to experience.

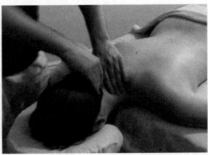

Welcome to Massage Therapy

About the Program
Founded in 1916, Swedish Institute has the oldest Massage Therapy Program in the country. Its dynamic curriculum develops strong skills in both Western and Eastern styles of massage, a solid knowledge base in the biosciences, and an emphasis on integration of these components into practical applications in classes and clinics. Business and ethics courses are also an important part of professional development. The program can be taken on either a full-time or part-time basis, with classes available during morning, afternoon, or evening/weekend hours.

The website I created with LibGuides has received positive feedback from both students and educators. It has successfully helped students with computer and literacy challenges begin to develop the essential skills necessary for employment and has been cited as exceptional by our accrediting agency.

Tip: You'll find many resources available to novice web designers—open-sourced, commercial, and software packages.

Tip: Make your homepage appealing and interesting, using photos of the library and the school logo.

Tip: Keep it simple. Embed links for easy access.

Conclusion

Every library needs a website. Even if you have never created one before, you can create a simple library website that can be easily accessible to users who lack computer confidence. I used LibGuides by Springshare, but there are many others available, including WIX and WordPress.

Index

About the Contributors

Joyce Abbott holds a BA in anthropology and an MLIS. She has worked in public service, nonprofits, and enterprise content management. She believes in the flexible nature of the information profession and is always looking for new ways to connect people with the information they need.

Joy M. Banks has more than ten years of experience working with special, academic, and public library collections, specializing in cataloging and digitization projects. An MSLS graduate of Clarion University of Pennsylvania, she is currently the librarian and archivist at Bok Tower Gardens, a national historic landmark in central Florida.

Lee Ann R. Benkert is a librarian for the National Security Space Institute, a U.S. military school for space personnel. She manages a small library with help from a skilled part-time assistant, allowing her to focus on internal marketing and advocacy. She received her MLS from Emporia State University in 2010.

Lana Brand earned her master's degree in library and information science at the University of South Florida's School of Information. She is a health sciences librarian at Northeast Georgia Health System's Library and Resource Center and is a member of the southern chapter of the Medical Library Association's Hospital Libraries Committee, the Georgia Health Sciences Library Association's Consumer Health Committee, and the Medical Library Association's Academy of Health Professionals.

Ashley Krenelka Chase is a library administrator at the Dolly and Homer Hand Law Library at Stetson University College of Law in Gulfport, Florida. Ashley has a BA in English from Bradley University, a JD from the University of Dayton School of Law, and an MLIS from the University of South Florida.

Sheila A. Cork received her MLIS is from the University of Southern Mississippi in 2002. Cork is the librarian at the New Orleans Museum of Art (NOMA). For two years following Hurricane Katrina, Cork became the grant writer/librarian for NOMA and wrote successful funding requests to local and federal government agencies as well as to private foundations.

Amelia Costigan works as a special librarian in the Catalyst Information Center (IC). In addition to answering reference questions from members, the media, academics, and the public, Costigan also creates numerous IC products. Costigan holds an MFA in painting and previously worked as an art director in New York, with a focus on strategic editorial design for nonprofits as well as book and magazine design.

Jezmynne Dene is the director of the Portneuf District Library in Chubbuck, Idaho. Her BA in southwestern history is from the University of New Mexico and her MLIS is from the University of Illinois, Urbana–Champaign. A patient and enthusiastic librarian, Jezmynne enjoys enabling her staff to succeed and moving her library into the future while staying relevant and important to her library's community of users.

Beth Dwoskin retired from twenty-five years of cataloging at ProQuest. A writer and a consultant for a small synagogue library in Ann Arbor, Michigan, she is the author of *Guide to the Jewish Sheet Music Collection from the National Library of Russia, St. Petersburg*, published by ProQuest, and "Poets and Audiences: The Evolution of Poetry in America."

Zach English is the director of library services at Everglades University in Boca Raton, Florida. He earned his MLIS degree from the University of South Florida. He is a member of the Florida Library Association and the Southeast Florida Library Information Network (SEFLIN).

Valerie Enriquez is the assistant librarian at Ironwood Pharmaceuticals in Boston. She received her MLIS with a concentration in archives management from Simmons College in 2011. Prior experience includes the former Center for Advanced Visual Studies (now the Center for Arts, Culture and Society) at MIT, Countway Library at Harvard Medical School, University of Arizona at Tuscon Archives and Special Collections, and DataONE. She has a particular interest in technology and information-sharing behavior.

Miguel Figueroa-Pagán is a librarian with thirteen years of experience in small academic libraries. Living and working in Puerto Rico means serving a Spanish-speaking population. His main interests are open-educational resources and the student's use of the Internet for information search.

Paul Glassman is director of library services and associate professor at Felician College. During summer sessions he teaches art librarianship and library design at Rutgers. He launched the architecture minor at Yeshiva University. An alumnus of Bowdoin College, he holds, in addition to a library degree, M.Arch. and MBA degrees.

Jill Goldstein is the library director of the Swedish Institute College of Health Sciences. She holds an MLS from Pratt SILS, where she graduated with distinction. Jill is a certified archivist and a member of the Beta Phi Mu Honor Society.

Jeff Guerrier has held the position of librarian in the Department of Drawings and Prints of the Metropolitan Museum of Art, the Jewish Museum in New York City, and the Montclair Art Museum in New Jersey and created a private art library in Greenwich, Connecticut. Now an independent librarian, he currently resides in New York City.

Lindsay Harmon has been the librarian at the American Academy of Art in Chicago since 2007. As a solo librarian, she is responsible for everything from collection development to copier repair. She has an MLIS from Dominican University and a BA in English and journalism from the University of Iowa.

Sherill L. Harriger has worked in academic libraries for forty years. Her MLIS is from the University of South Florida. Since 2005 she has been library director of the Pontious Learning Resource Center. She can be contacted at sherill.harriger@warner.edu.

Wanda Headley manages the Natural Hazards Library at the Institute of Behavioral Science, University of Colorado, Boulder. An MLS graduate of Texas Woman's University, she has over ten years of experience as a solo librarian.

Robin Henshaw was most recently the librarian at Ironwood Pharmaceutical. She has over twenty years of experience in information management as a librarian, researcher, and consultant, along with extensive database experience in a variety of industries. She is the former metadata editor for First Monday, one of the first openly accessible, peer-reviewed journals on the Internet.

Charles Ed Hill received his MLS in 2012 and began working at the Natural Hazards Center at the University of Colorado, Boulder, in October of that year. He leads a team of work-study students in cataloging and metadata operations for the library, as well as web development for the center.

Elizabeth Martin is currently the head of professional programs at Grand Valley State University. Elizabeth has management experience in small academic and school/public combination libraries. She was the director of the Sulo and Aileen Maki Library at Finlandia University. Prior to that she was a solo librarian for the Lake Linden-Hubbell School/Public Library. She has vast experience with wearing many hats while managing libraries.

Raleigh McGarity, MLIS, AHIP, received her master of library and information sciences degree from Valdosta State University. She is a health sciences librarian at

Northeast Georgia Health System's Library and Resource Center. Raleigh serves as the chair of the Georgia Interactive Network of Libraries Advisory Committee and is a member of the southern chapter of the Medical Library Association Public Relations Committee.

Corinne Nyquist oversees interlibrary loan and research on library namesake Sojourner Truth at SUNY New Paltz. She is active in ALA RUSA STARS and the Rethinking Resource Sharing group and was a member of the ALA committee that revised the Interlibrary Loan Code for the United States in 2008.

Mara H. Sansolo is the reference librarian at Pasco-Hernando State College in Dade City, Florida. She received her MLIS from the University of South Florida in 2012 and also holds a BA in women's studies.

James Anthony Schnur is a lifelong resident of Pinellas County, Florida. He serves as special collections librarian at the University of South Florida, St. Petersburg, and has taught courses in history at Eckerd College since 1996. He has worked in public, academic, and special library settings.

Robin Shader is the director of the Northwest Regional Library System, serving Bay, Gulf, and Liberty Counties, Florida. She is a New Jersey native and received her MLS from Rutgers University. Robin has worked in public libraries in New Jersey, Georgia, and Florida for the past sixteen years.

Lynn Sheehan is currently the head of liberal arts programs for university libraries at Grand Valley State University, where library faculty and assistants number over sixty. Prior to moving to GVSU, Lynn worked in both small special and academic libraries in West Virginia, holding positions in both small law and academic libraries.

Erica Shott is the creative reference librarian at American Greetings. She received her MLIS from Kent State University in 2007, focusing on archival management. The Creative Reference Library serves primarily artists, designers, and editors but also a smaller group of business personnel. She also manages the historic card/archival collection and oversees a small library of globally sourced attachments used by the designers during the design and development process.

Deirdre D. Spencer has served as head of the Fine Arts Library at the University of Michigan for twenty-six years. She holds an AB in art history and an MLS from Indiana University and an MA in art history from the University of Chicago and is ABD in art history from the University of Michigan.

Arwen Spinosa is the original cataloger at the Ringling Art Library in Sarasota. She has a background in special collections, book history, and studio art.

About the Editor

Alice Graves has worked as a solo librarian in academic and museum libraries. She has also taught college English and worked as a research analyst and writer for various publications as well as a content writer for several websites, including LegalZoom, the Textbook Affordability Project at the University of South Florida (tap.usf.edu), and AbleVillage. Her personal essays can be found in the *Tampa Bay Times*, Ducts.org, and Weston Magazines. She was a contributor to *Library Services for Multicultural Patrons*, edited by Carol Smallwood and Kim Becnel (Scarecrow Press, 2013). In addition to her MLIS, Alice holds an MFA in creative writing, an M.Ed., and a JD, and she is a member of the Beta Phi Mu Honor Society. She lives in Woodstock, New York, with her husband and cat.